The Heart's Essential Landscape

American University Studies

Series XXIV
American Literature

Vol. 3

PETER LANG
New York • Bern • Frankfurt am Main • Paris

Kathleen G. Ochshorn

The Heart's Essential Landscape

Bernard Malamud's Hero

PETER LANG
New York • Bern • Frankfurt am Main • Paris

Library of Congress Cataloging-in-Publication Data

Ochshorn, Kathleen G.
    The heart's essential landscape : Bernard Malamud's
hero / Kathleen G. Ochshorn.
        p. cm. — (American university studies. Series
XXIV, American literature ; 3)
    Includes bibliographical references.
     1. Malamud, Bernard—Characters—Heroes.
2. Heroes in literature. I. Title. II. Series.
PS3563.A4Z82   1990   813'.54—dc20   90-35147
ISBN 0-8204-1269-4   CIP
ISSN 0895-0512

© Peter Lang Publishing, Inc., New York 1990

Printed in the United States of America.

To my husband Mike
and our daughter Brigid
with love

I am greatly indebted to Jack B. Moore for his guidance and editorial assistance in this project and to Karen Fain for her patient help in preparing the manuscript.

Special thanks to Ann Malamud and Farrar, Straus and Giroux, Inc. for allowing me to quote from the following works:

Excerpts from *The People and Uncollected Stories* by Bernard Malamud. Copyright © 1989 by Ann Malamud.

Excerpts from *The Assistant* by Bernard Malamud. Copyright © 1957 and renewal copyright © 1985 by Bernard Malamud.

Excerpts from *Dubin's Lives* by Bernard Malamud. Copyright © 1979 by Bernard Malamud.

Excerpts from *The Fixer* by Bernard Malamud. Copyright © 1966 by Bernard Malamud.

Excerpts from *God's Grace* by Bernard Malamud. Copyright © 1982 by Bernard Malamud.

Excerpts from *Idiots First* by Bernard Malamud. Copyright © 1963 by Bernard Malamud.

Excerpts from *The Magic Barrel* by Bernard Malamud. Copyright © 1958 and renewal copyright © 1986 by Bernard Malamud.

Excerpts from *The Natural* by Bernard Malamud. Copyright © 1952 and renewal copyright © 1980 by Bernard Malamud.

Excerpts from *A New Life* by Bernard Malamud. Copyright © 1961 by Bernard Malamud.

Excerpts from *Pictures of Fidelman* by Bernard Malamud. Copyright © 1969 by Bernard Malamud.

Excerpts from *Rembrandt's Hat* by Bernard Malamud. Copyright © 1973 by Bernard Malamud.

Excerpts from *The Stories of Bernard Malamud*. Copyright © 1983 by Bernard Malamud.

Excerpts from *The Tenants* by Bernard Malamud. Copyright © 1971 by Bernard Malamud.

Excerpts from *Reading Myself and Others* by Philip Roth. Copyright © 1975 by Philip Roth.

CONTENTS

The Heart's Essential Landscape

INTRODUCTION

Bernard Malamud published eight novels and three collections of short stories in thirty-four years. Since his death *The People and Uncollected Stories* (1989) has been added to this impressive body of work. The world Malamud presents throughout this fiction is often a stark one of poverty and struggle, frustrated ambitions and loves. Yet through the sufferings, Malamud paints with tireless optimism and simple, often comical beauty, the essential landscape of the human heart.

Malamud's preoccupation with the possibility of men to change and to find fulfillment in love for others can be seen throughout his work. As early as 1959, after Malamud's first three books had been published, Alfred Kazin noted that Malamud's work represents good fiction which "can elicit and prove the world we share," and "can display the unforeseen possibilities of the human -- even when everything seems dead set against it" ("The Alone Generation" 26). And in a like vein Philip Roth said of Malamud: "What it is to be human, to be humane, is his subject; connection, indebtedness, responsibility, these are his moral concerns" ("Writing American Fiction" 151).

Malamud outlined what he believed was his task as a writer in his acceptance speech for the 1959 National Book Award for his collection of short stories *The Magic Barrel*. Here, as in subsequent comments, his emphasis was on what it means to be human, what the human possibilities are:

> It seems to me that the writer's most important task, no
> matter what the current theory of man, or his prevailing

mood, is to recapture his image as a human being as each of us in his secret heart knows it to be, and as history and literature have from the beginning revealed it. At the same time the writer must imagine a better world for men while he gives us, in all its ugliness and beauty, the possibilities of this. In recreating the humanity of man, in reality his greatness, he will, among other things, hold up a mirror to the mystery of him, in which poetry and possibility live, though he has endlessly betrayed them. In a sense, a writer in his art, without directly stating it -- though he may preach, his work must not -- must remind man that he has, in his human striving, invented nothing less than human freedom; and if he will devoutly remember this, he will understand the best way to preserve it, and his own highest value.

I've had something such as this in mind, as I wrote, however imperfectly, my sad and comic tales ("Address from the Fiction Winner" 173).

In 1974, during an interview for *The Paris Review*, Malamud was asked if art is moral. He replied:

It tends toward morality. It values life. Even when it doesn't it tends to . . . Morality begins with an awareness of the sanctity of one's life, hence the lives of others -- even Hitler's to begin with -- the sheer privilege of being in this miraculous cosmos, and try to figure out why. Art, in essence, celebrates life and gives us our measure (Stern 51).

Malamud's moral concerns were to "recreate the humanity of man," to rediscover human freedom, human possibilities. These concerns are best seen in Malamud's handling of his major characters. While his characters have often been described as "luckless *schlemiels*" and "sad and bitter clowns," these terms are reductive. Malamud himself objected to the *schlemiel* treatment of fictional characters, saying "it reduces to stereotypes people of complex motivations and fates -- not to mention possibilities. The literary critic who wants to measure the quality and depth of a fictional character has better terms to use" (Field and Field 10).

A term that better suits what Malamud's characters strive toward is the Yiddish term _mensch_, which comes from the German word _mensch_, or man. Irving Howe offers a clear definition of the term in his document of European Jews in America _World of Our Fathers_: "_mensch_: man, used as a term of approbation for someone possessing qualities of humaneness and responsibility" ("A Glossary of Yiddish Terms" 683-84). Howe also offers a definition of the code of _menschlichkeit_, the quality of behaving like a _mensch_:

> A readiness to live for ideals beyond the clamor for self, a sense of plebian fraternity, an ability to forge a community of social order even while remaining subject to a society of social disorder, and a persuasion that human existence is a deeply serious matter for which all of us are fully accountable ("A Glossary of Yiddish Terms" 645).

The terms _mensch_ and _menschlichkeit_ are closely related; they suggest the same values, commitments, responsibilities. _Menschlichkeit_ emphasizes community; whereas _mensch_ emphasizes the individual. Since Malamud was rarely interested in community as such, but tended to create lone heroes involved with a handful of people, the term _mensch_ is most useful as a description of some of the qualities the Malamud heroes come to embody.

The Malamud hero seldom starts out as a _mensch_. He becomes more of a _mensch_ as he moves toward a life of value and commitment, often after much suffering and frustration. At the outset of the works, particularly the novels, the hero is characterized by intense feelings, expectations, sensitivities he himself cannot fully express or understand. He has high hopes, often for a change in the circumstances of his life. Gradually the hero experiences a deepening of his emotional life. He becomes more sensitive to others. This growth is often related to the hero's involvement with a woman. The hero comes closest to the *mensch* when he gives himself freely to someone else. Sometimes, as in Sy Levin's departure with Pauline Gilley and her children at the end of the novel *A New Life*, the hero makes a conscious effort to think of more than self even though he still has doubts and fears.

There is a Malamud hero in the same sense there is a Hemingway hero, a Conrad hero, a Joyce hero, a Heller anti-hero. And the Malamud hero has several distinguishable characteristics.

He is first and foremost someone who suffers. He is caught up in his suffering; it molds him and contributes to his moral well-being. Some heroes, like Roy Hobbs of *The Natural*, who accepts a bribe to fix a baseball game, and Frank Alpine of *The Assistant*, who spies on the girl he loves from an elevator shaft, aggravate their suffering. Some, like the wrongly imprisoned Yakov Bok of *The Fixer*, suffer largely because the world is rotten, fate is unfair. Many suffer in failing stores, eased out by shiny, new, self-service competition; or in the long struggle for an unachieved goal or love; or in general, from poverty, illness, old age, loneliness. They learn to suffer for each other, to share the burden of their grief. As Morris Bober, the struggling grocer of the novel *The Assistant*, tells Frank Alpine, "I suffer for you . . . I mean you suffer for me" (*Assistant* 325). Yet, as Philip Rahv has pointed out, Malamud does not idealize suffering: "suffering is not what you are looking for but what you are likely to get" ("Introduction" in *A Malamud Reader* x).

A second distinguishable characteristic of the Malamud hero is his displaced nature. In some ways he is a displaced person, out of his element. His homelessness contributes to his alienation and makes him ready for big changes. Often he is in a strange environment because he is escaping an unpleasant or even shameful past. Sy Levin, the Jewish New Yorker in rural

Cascadia in the novel *A New Life*, is a reformed alcoholic. Frank Alpine, the "Italyner" among Jewish storekeepers in *The Assistant*, is an orphan, turned drifter, turned would-be criminal. Yakov Bok, the Jew living in a non-Jewish sector in the novel *The Fixer*, is a runaway from a life of economic hardship and a childless, failed marriage.

The hero often finds himself in some sort of prison, a tiny room, a store, an office. And while he may not be locked in, when the door opens he does not escape: like Schwartz, the talking, winged tutor of the short story "The Jew Bird," when he arrives, he's there to stay. In fact, the Malamud hero is the most determined of creatures, with a penchant for operating businesses that lose money, for remaining in rented rooms after he has been evicted, and for continuing to work for people who keep dismissing him. This prison motif is crucial because it identifies for the hero the trap which he suffers from and must learn to overcome: it provides the hero with the opportunity to create his freedom. Malamud said his prison metaphor represents:

> The personal entrapment in past experience, guilt, obsession
> -- the somewhat blind or blinded self, in other words. A
> man has to construct, invent his freedom. Imagination
> helps. A truly great man or woman extends it for others in
> the process of creating his/her own (Stern 54).

In spite of the alienation and imprisonment the Malamud hero endures, most of Malamud's fiction has a comic element and the hero is often the butt of the joke. But Malamud does not demean his characters with humor; he humanizes them. Malamud acknowledged the influence Charlie Chaplin had on him. As with Chaplin's tramp, Malamud's comic characters arouse sympathy and retain their dignity. The Chaplin tramp stews a shoe in *The Gold Rush*, and the Bobers live on the sale of three cent rolls to the "Polisheh" in *The Assistant*. Neither the shoe nor the sale of the roll can provide adequate sustenance. Yet Bober anxiously awaits his early morning sale of a single roll, just as Chaplin's tramp picks the nails of his shoe clean, as though they were meaty ribs. The comic element serves to bring the character closer to the natural human person; Malamud is seldom wryly or ironically superior to his characters.

Throughout Malamud's fiction the transformation of the hero is toward a life of commitment and human relationships. The hero often starts out seeking success in a rather conventional way: he wants to be a great baseball player, a fine writer. But success is not what he is likely to get, at least not in the terms he originally imagined it. He suffers; he fails. Yet throughout, the Malamud hero is identified by his capacity to feel deeply and then to act on those feelings even when the odds are against him. The hero is tested and Malamud has great faith in the hero's capacities: "I don't believe in the untested spirit, untested is unrevealed. *The Assistant, The Fixer* -- it's ridiculous to claim these are pessimistic books" (Kegan 131).

In the evolution of each work the hero comes more and more to stand for something, to have character. He becomes equal to the task he has chosen or fate has chosen for him. Yakov Bok in *The Fixer* stands up to the tzar and all of Russia and demands a retraction of the unjust charges leveled against him. Frank Alpine in *The Assistant* manages to support the Bobers on a few dollars a day in the grocery and his night job as a counterman; toward the end of the novel he appears even to be winning back Helen's respect and love. Fidelman in *Pictures of Fidelman* adjusts to all his disappointments as critic, painter, forger, and lover, and by the end of the novel has learned much about love.

Malamud's concern for what it means to be a decent human being is a moral concern of the highest order. Yet his is not the formal morality of religious orthodoxy. In fact, the most pristine, proper, religious characters in

Malamud's fiction are seen as limited by their very orthodoxy, like Leo Finkle, the Yeshiva University student in the short story "The Magic Barrel," who comes to realize he knows little about God and less about love. The more appealing religious characters are like Rabbi Lifshitz of the story "The Silver Crown" and the Harlem angel-in-waiting in "Angel Levine" who are unorthodox, if not downright shady, but still seem to possess magical healing powers.

For Malamud it is human communion that is the center of a life of value. In the opening paragraph of the novel *Dubin's Lives*, Dubin and Greenfield meet on a path in the woods. Dubin says: "This has to be the center of the universe . . . This road as we meet" (*Dubin* 3). Malamud believed all lives should be moving toward this human communion.

The Malamud hero suffers from what humankind has suffered from for thousands of years. His problems are seldom peculiar to modern man. In fact, Malamud had little concern for what occupies the work of many contemporary writers like Pynchon, Barth, Vonnegut, Calvino and others -- a notion that modern life is somehow more absurd, unstructured or meaningless than it has ever been, and that man, like Stencil in Thomas Pynchon's book *V.*, is on an endless search for structure, imposing a structure that does not exist. Nor does the Malamud hero seek intellectual solutions in the way many of Saul Bellow's characters do. Instead, he moves toward time-worn, ancient commitments, toward love for some particular person as a rule. In the story "The First Seven Years" Sobel, the assistant shoemaker to Feld, must labor for seven years for the privilege of asking Feld's daughter to marry him. The story is an old one, a reworking of the Jacob and Rachel story of the Bible. And the spirit of one is the spirit of the other.

Much of the criticism dealing with the Malamud hero has characterized him as a *schlemiel, schlemazel, schnook*, notably work by Ben Siegel, Sanford Pinsker, and Ruth R. Wisse. This view tends to see the heroes as victims and the conclusions of the works as ironic or despairing. Some other critics have suggested the hero starts out as a *schlemiel* but is transformed as he learns from his suffering and accepts responsibility for others. This view is best expressed by Tony Tanner in his essay "Bernard Malamud and the New Life" (151-68). Tanner makes some sharp observations; however, even at the outset of the works the heroes possess sensitivities and capacities that set them apart from *schlemiels* and make their eventual transformations possible.

At the same that time many critics have been emphasizing the hero as *schlemiel*, there has been a steady body of criticism stressing the possibilities the Malamud hero represents. In 1961 Ihab Hassan noted that Malamud was sensitive to what "transforms a man into a *mensch*" ("The Qualified Encounter" 199). And more recently Josephine Zadovsky Knopp has examined the uses of the code of *menschlichkeit* in the stories "The Mourners," "Idiot's First," and "Angel Levine" and in the novels *The Assistant* and *The Fixer* ("The Ways of Mentshlekhkayt" 67-84). Knopp emphasizes in what ways these works reflect Jewish values and how they might contribute to a description of the Jewish American novel. Joseph C. Landis also noted of Malamud's heroes:

> They are lonely men in a lonely world, morally plain men who are buffeted by life; but instead of yielding to degradation, they discover, a struggle at a time, the values of *mentshlekhkayt* as a pattern of human decency (146).

Others, while not dwelling on the term *mensch*, have written about the values the Malamud hero comes to represent. These critics include Philip Rahv, Alfred Kazin, Sandy Cohen, and Philip Roth. In general they see in the

Malamud hero, as Philip Rahv has said of Frank Alpine, "the ultimate recognition . . . of the humanity that he had long suppressed within himself" (Introduction xi). So this book, in fact, draws from a number of critics who present a complementary view of the Malamud hero.

Malamud's fiction can be defined and the works evaluated largely in terms of the truth and depth, or the falseness, of the portrayals of these heroes and the human world they live in. As Malamud's work unfolds, these heroes become less heroic, more fallible, more emotional, more believable, closer and closer to the natural human person.

THE NATURAL AND ROY HOBBS:
AN EARLY PATTERN FOR THE MALAMUD HERO

The Natural, published in 1952, was a curious beginning for Malamud. The novel is set in the world of big league baseball, though Malamud's subsequent fiction was unconcerned with sports. The novel is devoid of Jews, though all Malamud's other novels have major characters who are Jewish. And the novel is heavily mythic, more so than the later works.

In a 1974 interview with *The Paris Review* Malamud said as a kid he read dime store novels for entertainment and "Maybe *The Natural* derives from Frank Merriwell as well as the adventures of the Dodgers in Ebbets Field" (Stern 43).

Many of the events in the novel are borrowed from the legends of baseball. Roy Hobbs, the hero, has much in common with Babe Ruth. Ruth spent much of his childhood in the prisonlike St. Mary's Industrial School for Orphans, Delinquent, Incorrigible, and Wayward Boys. Like Hobbs, the Babe was an incredibly talented pitcher and hitter, was said to have hit a homerun for a dying boy, had an insatiable appetite (he even gobbled hotdogs during the game), and went on food binges that landed him in the hospital. In terms of his almost magical athletic ability, Ruth himself was in large part the inspiration for the equally talented Frank and Dick Merriwell and Lefty Locke of the dime store novels. Other historical events are the bases for events in

The Natural: Wilbert Robinson's attempt to catch a grapefruit dropped from a plane, the Eddie Waikus shooting (a girl shot him in her Chicago hotel room), and the "Shoeless" Joe Jackson White Sox scandal of 1919.

To the popular lore of baseball Malamud added the myths of literature. When asked why he combined myth and baseball, Malamud replied:

> Baseball flat is baseball flat. I had to do something to enrich the subject. I love metaphor. It provides two loaves where there seems to be one. Sometimes it throws in a load of fish. The mythological analogy is a system of metaphor. It enriches the vision without resorting to montage. This guy gets up with his baseball bat and all at once he is, through the ages, a knight -- somewhat battered -- with a lance; not to mention a guy with a blackjack, or someone attempting murder with a flower. You relate to the past and predict the future. I'm not talented as a conceptual thinker but I am in the uses of metaphor. The mythological and symbolic excite my imagination (Stern 52).

Implicit in Malamud's own comments is the suggestion that his use of myth in *The Natural* may be an artificial leavening, inflating a subject that does not stand on its own. The weakness of the novel is that it seems artificial at times. The heavy-handed use of myth detracts from the story, and the Grail and baseball do not always mix smoothly. It is not until *The Assistant* and the stories of *The Magic Barrel* that Malamud finds his stride, his voice, and material that needs no bolstering.

However, the wealth of criticism on the use of myth in *The Natural* attests to the incredible assortment of myths Malamud managed to work into the novel. The sheer number of allusions is impressive, if distracting. Earl Wasserman has detailed the Arthurian and Jungian patterns in the book (45-65); Robert Ducharme, the Homeric and Arthurian patterns (9-13); James Mellard, the pastoral pattern of vegetation myths (67-83); and Frederick W. Turner, the myths of the hero and the Horatio Alger story (109-19).

The critical interest in Malamud's use of myth has tended to color the view of Roy Hobbs. He has been seen largely in terms of how he measures up to the various mythic heroes. Now, with seven other novels, three collections of short stories, and a posthumous collection by Malamud published, Roy needs to be measured against the other Malamud heroes, and his successes and failures examined closely in more human terms.

In spite of the fact that Roy can bust the cover off a baseball and, more amazingly, aim foul balls at Otto Zipp, dwarf-heckler, as though he were teeing off with a golf club, he is also depicted in smaller terms. And while he may not be as rounded a character as the later heroes, he is readily identifiable as one of their family.

Hobbs establishes the pattern for later heroes: he starts out with intense feelings and high hopes for a new life, he is displaced, he is escaping from a frustrating past, he has setbacks in his new life, and he becomes entangled with women who in large part determine his fate.

In the opening paragraph of *The Natural* Malamud makes it clear that he is dealing with more than just myth; he is going to illuminate the character of Roy Hobbs the man. Roy lights a match and holds it over his head as he looks out the dark train window, and soon he sees, "the bright sight of himself holding a yellow light over his head, peering back in" (*Natural* 9). It will take the rest of the novel, fifteen years of Roy's life, before he will come to see himself clearly. And it is on the maturing, developing of Roy Hobbs that the more serious side of the baseball tale hinges.

At the outset of the novel Roy, like other Malamud heroes, is characterized by intense feelings and expectations. Some of this intensity is generated by the self-consciousness of an adolescent on his first train ride to the big city, awed by girls with "heartbreaking legs" (*Natural* 15), porters, and dining cars. In terror, he flees the dining car, not knowing how to order, leaving his solitary four bit piece as a tip.

But the intensity early in the novel also comes from a sensitivity, even *gentilesse*, that Roy exhibits, especially in relationship to Sam Simpson, the aging, alcoholic scout who has discovered Roy and is taking him to the Chicago Cubs. Roy begs Sam to take the berth and let him ride coach, but Sam declines. When Max Mercy, the sports columnist, tells Sam, "Well, hang onto the water wagon, Bub" (*Natural* 21), Roy shoots Mercy a dirty look. And later when the columnist calls Sam "rednose" (*Natural* 28), Roy tells him to watch his talk. When Sam dies, perhaps as a result of Roy's pitch that caught him in the chest, Roy's tear splashes Sam's nose. The warmth and closeness between Roy and Sam is surprising considering the fact that they have known each other a very short time. Perhaps Sam is a surrogate father figure for Roy, a lonely young man without family. This pattern of heroes with surrogate fathers appears repeatedly in Malamud's work, the most striking example being the relationship of Frank Alpine to Morris Bober.

Like many other Malamud heroes, Roy starts out with a hole in his gut that reaches down to his toes. He feels compelled to fill up the vacancy in his life. He latches on to Harriet Bird whose "black fluttering of wings" (*Natural* 21) seems reminiscent of a vampire bat. When she welcomes him to Chicago she is a kinky sight indeed, naked under her gossamer nightgown but topped with a feathered black hat, the veil falling to her breasts. The first, "Pre-Game" section of the novel ends with Roy's shooting, Harriet's bullet cutting a silver line and bouncing into his gut, filling up the hunger with more suffering.

In both sections of the novel Roy makes a journey hoping to begin a new life. In the "Pre-Game" section he starts out as a young man of nineteen going for a big league try-out, hoping to be "the best there ever was in the game"

(*Natural* 33). Yet even at nineteen he's escaping a past of heartache and lost connections. He thinks of his mother as "That bird" (*Natural* 34) and recalls how his father shuffled him from orphanage to orphanage after Roy's grandmother died, "though he did used to take me out of there summers and teach me how to toss a ball" (*Natural* 32) After his hopes for a baseball career are shattered by Harriet's silver bullet, it is fifteen years before Roy makes it back to baseball. At the opening of "Batter Up," the second section of the novel, Roy is thirty-four years old. He has traveled to New York and signed with the Knights. He once again has high hopes and this time they seem unrealistic: he tells Pop Fisher, "I'm good for ten years" (*Natural* 48).

Of all Malamud's displaced heroes, Roy is one of the most displaced. His childhood was a series of moves, his fifteen year absence from big league ball is a series of odd jobs all around the country, and when he signs up with the Knights he spends much of his time traveling to road games. In fact, when Pop Fisher first spots Roy, "although he was sitting here on this step he was still in motion. He was traveling (on a train that never stopped). His self, his mind, raced on and he felt he hadn't stopped going wherever he was going because he hadn't yet arrived" (*Natural* 47). Throughout the novel Roy streams past woods which harbor the image of a boy and a dog, a dim memory of one fulfilling time in Roy's youth within the woodland, "the only place he had been truly intimate with in his wanderings" (*Natural* 22). Roy always seems ill at ease in his surroundings.

In the second half of the novel Roy, like most Malamud heroes, is escaping what he considers a shameful past. For Roy it is the Harriet Bird shooting. Roy avoids the snooping Max Mercy, who realizes Roy seems vaguely familiar and who is trying to dig up some dirt on Roy's past. But other Malamud heroes, like Sy Levin and Yakov Bok, seem more responsible for their failures than is Roy. In the abstract sense, Roy is a knight who fails to give the correct answer when tested by the loathly lady, Harriet Bird. Iska Alter says Roy "defines the heroic ideal selfishly, then materially" (22). Most critics seem to think Roy is a failure when he gives Harriet the wrong answers because he does not understand her allusions to Homer, the Bible, Freud, or the Grail legends. Roy does feel that he has just "flunked a test" (*Natural* 34). But the real failure here is the uneasy imposing of the myth. After all, in what way can or should a baseball player's drive be altruistic? Because baseball is not an altruistic endeavor, Roy's punishment for the wrong answers seems ridiculous. Roy's desire to be the best in the game must be what motivates all professional athletes. Roy may be faulted for not thinking Harriet is somewhat unbalanced, but can he be blamed for not guessing she has a gun in her hat box? The silver bullet that fells the hero is too literary and cannot explain the inordinate shame Roy feels over the incident. Some of his shame might be understood as a reaction to the circumstances of the shooting: on the eve of a big league try-out Roy accepts an illicit rendezvous with a sexy lady.

The shooting and Roy's shame, however, do contribute to his suffering, a suffering that links him with all Malamud's heroes. A lonely, unhappy childhood and then failure in youth are characteristic of these heroes. The sense of years wasted, wandering, working odd jobs, being unsuccessful, is prevalent in Malamud's fiction. All the heroes in Malamud's novels, with the exception of William Dubin, are thirtyish -- most starting out in a new profession or a new place. They are men with no close connections, either single like Roy and Frank Alpine, separated like Yakov Bok, or widowed like Cohn of *God's Grace*. Sometimes their past is sketchy, but always it is suggested as vaguely dissatisfying. They are strangely solitary: Roy is even alone on a baseball team and says, "I want to do it by myself" (*Natural* 74).

Like the other Malamud heroes, Roy has setbacks in his new life. When he first tries on the Knight's blue cap he is moved to tears and feels very "down in the dumps" (_Natural_ 52). He has waited so long to make it to the big league that it gives him little satisfaction. Soon Roy's belief that baseball is all that matters in life will be seen to be one trap or prison Roy suffers from and must learn to overcome.

Roy continues to suffer in his love life, too. And as is often the case with the Malamud hero, Roy's humanity is measured in large part by his relationships with women. Eventually it is through a wise and loving woman that Roy moves toward maturity and becomes something of a _mensch_. But first he falls hard for teammate Bump Bailey's girl Memo Paris. She is another Harriet Bird, a thin, nervous girl in a black dress who spells trouble for Roy. Bump, a practical joker, gets Roy to switch hotel rooms and Roy is visited by Memo. They make love, and when Memo discovers the switch she puts the blame mostly on Roy. Later Bump bumps into the wall and is killed: Memo pounds the wall.

Memo, with her red hair, green eyes, and black panties, brassieres, and dresses, becomes transformed into a lady fish in a dream Roy has while being hypnotized by Doc Knobb, the Knights' mesmerizer:

> Sailing lower into the pale green sea, he sought everywhere for the reddish glint of her scales, until the water became dense and dark and green and then everything gradually got so black he lost all sight of where he was. When he tried to rise up into the light he couldn't find it (_Natural_ 73).

Memo is linked with all that is bad for Roy: Bump Bailey, Gus the "Supreme Bookie," and Judge Goodwill Banner -- the odoriferous owner of the Knights. Memo is physically unhealthy, very thin and complaining of a sick breast. Her silver, jingling bracelets echo her values. She will marry Roy only if he will provide her with such necessities as a maid, a fur coat, and a fancy car. When Roy is in the hospital, late in the novel, "his mind skipped from money to Memo" (*Natural* 197). It is Roy's desire to have Memo at all costs that leads him to accept the Judge's bribe to fix the game.

Memo is associated with Roy's batting slump, a slump that puts the Knights behind in the standings. When she drives his new Mercedes, a gift on Roy Hobbs Day, she has the lights out. Roy thinks they hit a boy and his dog, an image reminiscent of the recurring child Roy in the woods. When he takes over the wheel and returns to look for the boy, he runs off an embankment and into a tree. Roy and Memo get back to the hotel just before dawn. That day Roy does well against the Phillies; the following day his slump sets in.

The slump is Roy's prison: "A whole apparatus of physical and mental pleasures was on the kibosh and without them he felt like the Hobbs he thought he had left behind dead and buried" (*Natural* 132). Both Pop Fisher and Roy wonder if Memo had "maybe jinxed him into a slump" (*Natural* 141). Roy is preoccupied with the unattainable girl and with searching through the newspapers for some news of a hit and run accident in the Long Island woods.

Memo is also identified with Roy's physical suffering, manifest in his insatiable appetite which leads to his food binge. Sexually unsatisfied, Roy begins wolfing down sandwiches, steaks, and slabs of chocolate cake. When Roy is batting well again and the team is close to the pennant, Memo, bankrolled by Gus, stages a lavish supper on the eve of the Reds game. Memo stuffs him: "Now let's mix this lobster meat with hidden treats of anchovies, and here we will lay it on this tasty pumpernickel and spread Greek salad on it, then smear this other slice of bread with nice sharp cheese and put it on top of the rest." Roy correctly adds: "All this needs is a shovel of manure and a forest will grow out of it" (*Natural* 186).

All he eats at the supper, topped off with six hamburgers at the hotel grill, almost kills Roy just as he finally gets in bed with Memo, unromantic sight though she may be, chewing a drumstick and looking at a scrapbook of Bump Bailey pictures. Instead of sex he gets socked by a "thundering locomotive," "a bolt of shuddering lightning," and feels himself sucked under a rush of dirty water, reminiscent of the earlier hypnotic dream (_Natural_ 190-91). He wakes up in a maternity hospital where they pump great quantities of bilge out of his stomach. It is in the hospital, suffering from high blood pressure and what his doctor terms athlete's heart, that he accepts the bribe offered by the Judge and mediated by Memo to throw the Pirates game and lose the pennant.

Malamud uses the humorous hospital scene to undercut the melodrama of the fallen, sick hero on the eve of the big game. The Judge has a money saving contract with the maternity hospital to treat all player injuries. At first the staff try to deliver Roy of his appendix, only to discover he has none. Then Roy, in delirium, hunts through the halls in a nightgown frightening the new mothers by practicing batting with a mop. Memo and the Judge are seen as caricatures: Memo "her hair uncombed, looking like Lola, the Jersey City fortuneteller" (_Natural_ 201) and the Judge in a "hairy black fedora" (_Natural_ 202), wrinkled pants and a thick black wig.

By this time Memo appears so ghoulish and unappealing that it is difficult to understand what Roy ever saw in her. Roy is certainly a slow learner in his wrong-minded pursuit of Memo and all she leads to, including the fix. However, throughout the novel Malamud is also developing another side of Roy, his capacity to reach out to others, to be a _mensch_. This trait in Roy directly opposes Roy's connection to Memo and the Judge.

A more substantial side of Roy does run throughout the novel. Early in the novel he is close to Sam Simpson. Later, in a dream before he is offered

the fix, Roy recalls Sam who warns, "Don't do it" (*Natural* 196). His relationship to Sam is duplicated in his affection for Pop Fisher, another father figure
who has had some rough times, including "Fisher's Flop," a fall on the way to
home plate, and who deserves better than the losing side of his partnership
with the Judge. When Roy is up at bat in the Pirate's game, half-heartedly
planning to stick to the fix, he steals a look at Pop Fisher: "It seemed to Roy
he had known the old man all his life long" (*Natural* 222). He begins to
consider quitting the deal.

Earlier, in Chicago for a Cubs game, Roy's response to two people who
show faith in him is what lifts him out of his slump. The first is Mike Barney,
who begs Roy to hit a homerun for his son who has been hurt in an accident
and is hospitalized. Roy is afraid of the responsibility but promises to do his
best. Mike Barney's boy is an echo of the boy Roy saw or thought he saw in
the woods. The second person Roy responds to and who has faith in him is
Iris Lemon, the dark haired woman in the red dress who rises in the stands and
inspires Roy to hit a homer, that shoots through the pitcher's legs and up into
the dark "like a white star" (*Natural* 147). Mike Barney's boy gets well and
Roy's relationship with Iris begins. It is Iris Lemon who will speak from
Malamud's values, much as Morris Bober will in *The Assistant*.

Memo and Harriet stand for all that is warped in *The Natural*; Iris stands
for all that is life affirming. When Roy and Memo go for a drive and stop at
a stream, the water is polluted, rain clouds form, and the moon sinks. When
Roy and Iris drive to the beach the scene is idyllic. Harriet imitates a "twisted
tree" when Roy tweaks her breast (*Natural* 35). And both Memo and Harriet
are superficially sexy in black dresses, underwear, and nighties; but they
promise more than they deliver. In contrast, Iris has a more natural kind of
sexuality that causes a stranger next to her in the stands to conceal his urge
"behind an impatient cigarette" (*Natural* 145).

The name Iris Lemon does link Iris to what is natural, but like other names in the book it has an ironic connotation, too. The Judge has no Goodwill; Gus, the bookie, is not Supreme; and Max, the sports writer, has no Mercy. Iris is no Lemon: she is the only woman in the book who can bring Roy happiness. Lemons also appear three times in the novel. Roy gets six crates of lemons as part of his haul on Roy Hobbs Day. When Roy and Memo first begin their Long Island drive the night is lit up by "a full moon swimming in lemon juice" (*Natural* 116). Soon it is clouded over. When Roy is on his food binge he tries to drown his horrid sandwich with three bottles of artificial tasting lemon pop. So when Roy is not with Iris the lemons signal trouble for him.

Iris, like Roy, has had some hard times. At thirty-three she is already a grandmother, a fact that drives Roy away for a time because he still wants to think of himself as young and no grandpa. She became pregnant at sixteen after her first sexual encounter, with a man twice her age: "She offered herself in a white dress and bare feet and was considerably surprised when he pounced like a tiger" (*Natural* 150). She raised her daughter alone and was a devoted mother: she writes to Roy, "all the tender feelings I had in my heart for her made up for a lot I had suffered" (*Natural* 210). She nursed her baby and her physical nature stands in contrast to Memo who suffers from a sick breast.

When Iris and Roy take their drive to the beach, the "new moon climbed higher," and "the wind was balmy and the water lit on its surface" (*Natural* 153). Iris speaks of heroes, suffering and life. She says that she hates to see heroes fail and that she stood up for him so that he would regain his power: "Of course I was embarrassed but I don't think you can do anything for anyone without giving up something of your own" (*Natural* 155).

Their conversation echoes Harriet Bird's testing of Roy earlier. Roy says he has a lot to give to this game; Iris asks, "Life?" and he says, no, "Baseball" (*Natural* 156). He wants to break all the records and she says, "Are your values so--" (*Natural* 156). At that moment he hears a train hoot and Iris says, "It must have been a bird cry" (*Natural* 156). It is a rerun of the Harriet Bird conversation on the train minus the literary and mythic allusions, and Roy gazes at Iris suspiciously for a moment.

After he pours out his past, the shooting and his suffering, he wonders what he did to deserve it all. The conversation will be reworked in an exchange between Morris Bober and Frank Alpine. Iris says:

> "Experience makes good people better."
> She was staring at the lake.
> "How does it do that?"
> "Through their suffering."
> "I had enough of that," he said in disgust.
> "We have two lives, Roy, the life we learn with and the life we live with after that. Suffering is what brings us toward happiness. . . . It teaches us to want the right things" (*Natural* 158).

Iris is the first of many Malamud women who will be associated with the emotional development of the heroes. In some ways she is the most perfect one, an earth mother who gives herself so freely, who seems to have known the hero all his life. When they make love, "He smiled, never so relaxed in sex" (*Natural* 163). She literally stands up for Roy at the game; and later when his foul ball hits her rather than Otto Zipp, she is the reason he gives up the fix and tries to win the Pirates game.

Perhaps Iris is too good to be true, the same way those wicked soul sisters Harriet and Memo are a little too ghoulish. And they all exist to impede or advance the development of the hero. On their own they exhibit some of the qualities of characters in adventure novels or comic books; they are one dimensional caricatures, like the minor characters in *The Natural*. Iris is an angel; Harriet and Memo are witches. In Helen Bober of *The Assistant* and Pauline Gilley of *A New Life* Malamud will draw women who are more complex.

However, Malamud does add some humanizing touches to the encounter between Roy and Iris which keep their affair from being a mere idealization. Both are slightly disappointed in each other when they start out. In his street clothes Roy appeared to Iris, "like any big-muscled mechanic or bartender on his night off" (*Natural* 152). Iris is heftier than Roy thought and her soft, brown dress excites him less than the red one she wore when she stood up in the stands at the first game. Iris also has big feet, but we are told, "Her movements were graceful, she made her big feet seem small" (*Natural* 153).

After their initial encounter Roy does not see Iris until he hits her with the foul ball. What happens between Roy and Iris at the conclusion is a matter of dispute. Malamud generally seemed to have difficulty with endings. Some endings are sudden, others unclear. Critics often interpret the endings in a number of contradictory ways. In the case of *The Natural*, some believe it ends dismally, with Roy failing as a baseball star and abandoning Iris and the child she is carrying. Iska Alter suggests Iris has simply repeated her earlier mistakes and is likely being abandoned by Roy as she is taken to the hospital (23). On this side of the argument is Iris' own fear as she gets in the ambulance: "How like the one who jumped me in the park he looks" (*Natural* 225). Others, like Sandy Cohen, believe Roy will start a new life with Iris and their baby (20). Malamud suggests it is possible for Roy to go back to Iris. When she tells him that she is pregnant and that he must win for their son, "He kissed her hard belly, wild with love for her and the child" (*Natural* 225). And when he leaves her side he is a new man, determined to win the game he had agreed to throw. For a second time Roy tries to win a game for a boy, for the lost innocence of his own boyhood.

The Natural, like most of Malamud's work, really ends on what is intended to be an affirmative note. The pieces of Roy's character that stand for something, that show his depth, finally come together at the end of the novel, even though Roy's recognition of what is important comes, literally, late in the game.

After he goes back to the game, determined to win, Roy thumbs his nose at the tower where the Judge and Memo sit. But Roy is not a simple homerun machine. He has wasted time hitting fouls at Zipp; he strikes out, and the Knights lose the game and the pennant. When Roy drags the broken bat Wonderboy out to left field and buries it, he is burying his baseball life. He wishes the bat "would take root and become a tree" (*Natural* 234). Roy finally wants something good to come out of all his suffering. And when Roy discovers the fix money in his pocket, $35,000, he visits the judge in the tower. Roy goes on a rampage, knocking out Gus' glass eye, calling Memo a whore, and showering the thousand dollar bills on the Judge's "wormy head" (*Natural* 236). Then he tweaks the Judge's nose and beats him till he squeals like a pig and has a bowel movement in his pants. In this wild scene all three of them get what they deserve.

But Roy finally does realize that he has himself to blame for much of his suffering: "He thought, I never did learn anything from my past, now I have to suffer again" (*Natural* 236). At the end of the novel when the newspaper boy asks him to deny the fix, Roy weeps many bitter tears. He has let the boy down, denied the promise of his own lost youth; but now he is a more mature person, more of a *mensch*. Malamud ends the novel, leaving open the possibility of a new life for Roy with Iris and the baby.

Malamud often wants to suggest a better future for his heroes but stops short of depicting that future. He leaves off with a sense of what is possible, what is dramatic. When speaking about the ending of the later novel *The Fixer*, Malamud commented to Haskel Frankel:

> As a writer I want uncertainty. It's part of life. I want something the reader is uncertain about. It is this uncertainty that produces drama. That is enormously important to me. A good writer is an imaginative writer (39).

Depicting Iris with Roy, or later in *The Assistant*, Helen with Frank, would seem anti-climactic, too pat. Malamud usually has the hero still maturing as he sends him on his way.

In *The Natural* Malamud displayed his talents and suggested what was to come for the Malamud hero. The book is uneven, with the odd sampling of fans who seem to have escaped from a Nathanael West novel, the too numerous mythic allusions, and the development of Roy Hobbs in an uneasy balance. *The Natural* might be remembered as a greater achievement if it had not been followed by much finer books showing more depth and range. In *The Assistant* and *The Magic Barrel* Malamud finds a balance and material that seems more suited to his considerable talent.

Much that is charming in *The Natural* is its depiction of a baseball hero; a man who is a hero in the popular sense. In the novel Roy Hobbs is a sports giant with a golden nimbus, much as Robert Redford depicted him in the recent movie version of the novel. While Roy, the man, does serve as a map for many of the traits which appear repeatedly in the later Malamud heroes, he is never depicted from the inside out, the way Frank Alpine and most of the other heroes are. Roy remains somewhat distant and unreal. Though Frank Alpine shares many of Roy's characteristics, his private, personal struggle is writ large in *The Assistant*; and in the end Frank's struggle is more dramatic and heroic than Roy's.

THE ASSISTANT: THE MALAMUD HERO AS DISCIPLE

In *The Assistant*, published in 1957, Malamud created a near perfect blend of setting, theme, characters, and Yiddish idiom. The novel still seems quintessential Malamud. It is quiet and graceful. The external conditions of the characters' lives, poverty, confinement and isolation, mask the soaring of spirit and profound optimism in the novel. Malamud, who always professed his belief in man's possibilities, in *The Assistant* chronicles the story of a bum, "holdupnik" rapist becoming a man of character and discipline -- a follower of Saint Francis of Assisi and a convert to Judaism. In the confines of a failing Brooklyn grocery, Malamud works out a parable of Morris Bober as Christ in the modern world, minding the store, giving shelter and moral instruction to his struggling assistant Frank Alpine.

Critics often see Morris as a failure because he is so poor and his life as a grocer seems limited to them. But poverty has esthetic value for Malamud; at times he practically glorifies poverty. As Alfred Kazin has pointed out, "Poverty as a total human style is so all-dominating an esthetic medium in Malamud, coloring everything with its woebegone utensils . . ." (*Bright Books of Life* 140). And the characters in Malamud who prosper financially usually do so at an expense of spirit, like Julius Karp, the liquor store owner of *The Assistant*, who seems limited by his material successes. Malamud said of his own upbringing and his immigrant, grocer father: "Though my father always managed to make a living they were poor, especially during the Depression, and yet I never heard a word in praise of the buck" (Stern 43). Though Morris Bober is always hoping to make a decent living for his family, there is no "praise of the buck" in the novel.

Malamud acknowledged drawing material for his characters in *The Assistant* from three of his earlier short stories (Stern 53). The first story, "The Place is Different Now," was published in the spring of 1943 and reprinted in *The People and Uncollected Stories*. The main character, Wally Mullane, is an alcoholic, diabetic bum who visits his old neighborhood only to be beaten up by his brother, a policeman. He is taken in for a shave by the barber Mr. Davido, whose own son has left town for good. The Davido-Mullane relationship suggests Morris and Frank, though in general Mullane is more a model for Ward Minogue, Frank's partner in the hold-up of the grocery. "The Cost of Living" was published in 1950 and later appeared in *Idiots First* in 1963. In this second story an older storekeeper Sam Tomashevsky, who bears some similarities to Morris Bober, suffers competition from a neighboring supermarket. The third story, "The First Seven Years," was first published in 1950 and later appeared in *The Magic Barrel* in 1958. In this story Sobel, a shoemaker's assistant, labors for seven years to ask Miriam, the shoemaker's daughter, to marry him: it parallels Frank's assistantship to Morris and his struggle for Morris' daughter Helen. Malamud drew elements from all these stories to form the heart of *The Assistant*: the relationship between Morris and Frank.

The Assistant is an especially moving, beautiful novel. As Jonathan Baumbach has pointed out, "much of the beauty of *The Assistant* is in Malamud's marvelous evocation of the grocery which, conducted by ritual, has the aura of a sacred place, Morris' tomb, Frank's monastery -- the church of redemption" ("Malamud's Heroes" 97-99). Irving Howe has attributed the beauty of the novel to "its hum of contemplativeness, its quiet humane undertone" ("The Stories of Bernard Malamud" 33).

The moral vision of the novel springs in large part out of the relationship between the two heroes of the novel, Morris Bober and Frank Alpine. Both share many qualities with other Malamud heroes: a sense of displacement, of disappointment in youth, lives characterized by suffering and feelings of entrapment. Frank, though, undergoes a major change and is the Malamud hero who proves that anything is possible. Together Frank and Morris form the father-surrogate son pattern so common in Malamud. It is in part Morris' longing for his dead son Ephraim that makes him accept Frank so readily, and the fact that Frank is an orphan that causes him to be drawn to Morris.

Like many Malamud heroes, both Frank and Morris are geographically displaced. Morris fled Russia as a young man to avoid conscription in the Tsar's army, leaving his father and family behind. In America he spends his life in a gentile neighborhood, a Jewish grocer among a handful of Jewish storekeepers. Frank Alpine is an "Italyener" among the Jewish storekeepers, an orphan from the West with no family ties, a drifter. He tells Morris he has a sister and later confesses it is a lie: "I am alone by myself . . . I didn't want you to think I was a bum" (*Assistant* 51).

Morris and Frank share youthful disappointments. Morris hoped to be a druggist but gave that up when he met Ida, his wife, who talked him into the grocery business. Then as a young man Morris lost four thousand dollars in partnership with Charlie Sobeloff. Charlie kept the books and when the business collapsed managed to repurchase and restock the store, turning it into a thriving concern. Frank also abandoned plans for a college education when something else turned up, something that didn't work out. As he says, "With me one wrong thing leads to another and it ends in a trap" (*Assistant* 36). Like

Roy Hobbs, Frank has spent some time with a carnival: he tells Helen about the girl acrobat he fell in love with who later died in a car crash. His life has been hard and though he is only twenty-five Morris tells him, "You look older" (*Assistant* 36). Frank comes East hoping for a career in crime: "He shivered with pleasure as he conceived robberies, assaults -- murders if it had to be -- each violent act helping to satisfy a craving that somebody suffer as his own fortune improved" (*Assistant* 92). Ward Minogue talks him into a robbery, but once they get inside the grocery, after abandoning plans to hold up Karp's liquor store, Frank finds the whole idea senseless. "His plans of crime lay down and died" (*Assistant* 93). All these disappointments unite Morris and Frank. As Morris says of Frank, "I am sixty and he talks like me" (*Assistant* 93).

Morris and Frank share the suffering so characteristic of the Malamud hero. Morris mourns his long dead son Ephraim and grieves that he accepts money from his daughter Helen and that he can't offer her a college education. His life is marked by suffering: his twenty-one year struggle in the grocery; his ailments, a cough and spots on his lungs; his head wound from the robbery; his near deaths from the gas heater he leaves unlit and from the "celluloy" fire he sets.

But much more than Morris, Frank is the maker of his own suffering. The drama in the novel hinges largely on the battle within Frank Alpine between his desire for a new, moral life and his compulsion to do things which poison his chances. He tries to atone for the robbery by working in the grocery but he pilfers from the register. He falls in love with Helen; but he spies on her in the shower, and after rescuing her from Ward Minogue in the park, he rapes her. These incidents bring on fits of self-loathing. The "snitching" from the store leaves him "afraid to look in the mirror for fear it would split apart and drop into the sink" (*Assistant* 85). Of spying on Helen, "he was forcing her out of reach, making her into a thing only of his seeing, her eyes reflecting his sins, rotten past, spoiled ideals, his passion poisoned by shame" (*Assistant* 75-76). After the rape, "His thoughts were killing him. He couldn't stand them" (*Assistant* 174). And he becomes convinced that he smells like garbage. When the tenant Nick Fuso smells the gas Morris has left on and knocks on Frank's door, this wild exchange follows:

> "Do you smell anything?" Nick said, staring at the eye in
> the crack.
> "Mind your goddamned business."
> "Are you nuts?" . . . (*Assistant* 177).

Frank imagines Nick smells the stench of his guilt resulting from the rape. When Nick explains it's gas he smells, Frank rushes to Helen's door, perhaps fearing she has killed herself.

Frank's road to a new life is the most zigzag road in all of Malamud's fiction. He takes one step backward and one step forward over and over again. But even his most serious mistakes are mixed with something positive. When he takes part in the robbery, he rinses a cup and offers Morris a drink of water. His stealing from the register is mixed with his sneaking money back in, including the original robbery money. When he watches Helen from the air shaft he is an unusual voyeur indeed, "crossing himself" (*Assistant* 75) as he climbs the dumbwaiter ropes, teary eyed and filled with love as he looks in the window. Even when he rapes her he is distressed by the memory of spying on her; he speaks of love and stops her pleas "with kisses" (*Assistant* 168). For Malamud, these pleas do not lesson the violence of the rape; they merely suggest that even when Frank is at his worst, something in him longs for love, for a better life.

Malamud provides one important clue as to why Frank hurts those he loves: he sees himself as unworthy of love. By transgressing he matches himself up to this negative image, hoping he will still be loved. After the rape he wants to apologize to Helen: "It wasn't asking too much. People forgave people -- who else? He would explain if she would listen. Explaining was a way of getting close to someone you had hurt; as if in hurting them you were giving them a reason to love you" (*Assistant* 174).

Malamud does seem to believe in a fortunate fall. Frank's mistakes and his ensuing guilt motivate him to be a better person. The guilt is beneficial. With each transgression, Frank has new resolve. After the rape for example, he thinks of killing himself, but has an insight: "he was really a man of stern morality" (*Assistant* 176). He does become a new man: he no longer steals from the register, and he begins the long fight to win back Helen's respect. At the end of the novel his suffering has a purpose: he is trying to make a better life for Helen and he offers to put her through college. He suffers long hours at the grocery and at his night job as counterman but not from his old shame.

Both Morris and Frank suffer types of imprisonment. Frank's prison is similar to Roy Hobbs' prison: a sense of bad luck, defeat, disappointment, of being caught on "the inside of a circle," always doing "the wrong thing," as Frank tells himself (*Assistant* 174-75). Both Roy and Frank are largely responsible for the traps they fall into and their resulting misery. Both have some good instincts but they are slow learners. They share a desperation born of lonely, sad childhoods in orphanages. But Morris' prison is more literal -- the store. In the beginning of the novel he recalls his boyhood, running in the streets and fields of his village; but "in America he rarely saw the sky . . . In a store you were entombed" (*Assistant* 6). Later he tells Frank, "A store is a prison. Look for something better" (*Assistant* 33). And Al Marcus warns

Frank of Morris' store: "This kind of store is a death tomb, positive . . . Run out while you can" (*Assistant* 60). Ida and Helen share the view of the store as a trap for Morris. At his funeral Helen thinks of the store: "He buried himself in it; he didn't have the imagination to know what he was missing. He made himself a victim" (*Assistant* 230). And Ida tells herself, "If he had money he had bills; and when he had more money he had more bills" (*Assistant* 230).

But Malamud imbues the store with positive qualities, too. It may be Morris' cross, but it is also a sanctuary for Frank and others. In the store-- "Frank was content . . . safe from cold, hunger and a damp bed . . . The store was fixed, a cave, motionless. He had all his life been on the move, no matter where he was; here he somehow couldn't be. . . It wasn't a bad life" (*Assistant* 58).

Others seek out refuge in the store and in Morris' company: Breitbart, the bulb peddler, sits down for a thick glass of tea served with lemon; Karp, the liquor store salesman, still visits, "more than his welcome entitled him to" (*Assistant* 22). And in the store customers are dealt with generously, honestly. Though Morris suspects the "Polisheh" of anti-Semitism, he rises early every day to sell her a three cent roll. He gives a ten-year-old girl groceries though he knows her drunk mother will never pay.

Although the lives of Morris and Frank are marked by disappointment, imprisonment, and suffering there are many comic touches in the novel. The comedy functions nicely, lightening material that could easily become heavy and dreary. It humanizes the characters and draws them together. These comic touches often involve small deceptions. In the store Frank eats "crackers, macaroons, cupcakes and doughnuts, tearing up their wrappers into small pieces and flushing them down the toilet" (*Assistant* 60). He marks down all the money he takes from the register on a small card he hides in his shoe.

While Frank hides things from Morris, Morris hides things from Ida. He reduces the amount written under "Drunk Woman" on a worn spot on the counter so Ida won't "nag" (*Assistant* 4). He pilfers from the register so he can give Frank a raise to fifteen dollars without telling Ida. Later in the novel he "guiltily" takes a "half-pint bottle of whipping cream" and starts soaking it up with "stale white bread" (*Assistant* 210). When he hears a noise he is so guilt ridden that he hides the bread and cream in the gas range.

The noise turns out to be the "macher," the wildest character in the book, who enters speaking of "a gut shabos," "insurinks," and "celluloy" -- a "macher" of fires (*Assistant* 211-12). He offers to make a Friday fire saying, "I am not kosher" (*Assistant* 212). The next night Morris sets a fire himself, but his clothes catch fire and Frank arrives just in time to save him.

Much of the beauty and humor in *The Assistant* comes from Malamud's handling of the Yiddish accent, though usually with a very light touch. *The Natural* had no accent, just some baseball jargon. In this second novel Malamud allows even the narrator a light Yiddish accent. The accent often has a humorous and touching ring, as in Morris' admission to Frank that he knows about the hold up: "Frank is the one that made on me the hold up" (*Assistant* 199). Malamud uses the accent to lighten and to humanize scenes that could be melodramatic: Morris with the arsonist and Morris recognizing Frank.

Morris and Frank are identified in their taking money from the register and in Morris' accepting Helen's check and slipping it under his apron the way Frank slips money from the register into his pockets. In fact, everyone in the novel does some sneaking around and Malamud uses the sneaking to underline their humanity and their vulnerability. Ida trails Helen to find out if she is seeing Frank, and she spies on Frank to see if he is stealing from the register. Helen sneaks out to see Frank and once has him carry her up the stairs to his room, undetected by her parents. Morris hides from Ida and also spies on the German, his competition, as Frank will later spy on the Norwegians. When the poor refuge Podolosky comes to perhaps buy the store, Morris hides in the cellar. Frank hides in the same cellar earlier in the book. Morris also hides behind the hall door to catch Frank stealing from the register. All these tricks and deceptions are very human, very believable. Malamud makes it easy to identify with the characters.

The _mensch_ theme is important in Malamud's handling of both Frank and Morris. Throughout the novel Morris has many of the qualities of a _mensch_ -- goodness, gentleness, humility, love. Frank is a more typical Malamud hero who does not start out as a _mensch_ but who undergoes a transformation over the course of the novel and by the end of the book embodies many qualities of a _mensch_. From Morris, Frank learns what it means to have a good heart, to be honest. The love and concern Morris shows Frank initiates Frank's transformation; but by the middle of the novel it is Frank's growing love for Helen that is working big changes within him.

As with most Malamud heroes, Frank's relationship to a woman inspires him and turns him into a better person. Helen is clearly a woman in the Malamud mold. Though she is less abstract than the women in _The Natural_, both Helen and Iris Lemon are physically flawed: Iris is a little heavy and has big feet; Helen is bowlegged. Malamud often gives his ladies these little flaws and then forgives them the flaws. Frank even wonders if Helen's bowed legs might be the "sexy part" of her walk (_Assistant_ 62). Malamud presents Helen's longing for a college education and a better life as important, worthwhile desires. He clearly respects what education can be, though he will later satirize Cascadia College in _A New Life_ for all that education sometimes is not.

Curiously, in Malamud's fiction, people who do get an education, like Nat Pearl, don't seem to grow from it, and more sensitive people like Helen have a hard time getting an education. Generally in Malamud's fiction people who have to struggle are the ones who grow up. Helen wants more than her job as a secretary in an underwear concern: She wants to be a social worker or maybe a teacher. As she tells Louis Karp, "I want a larger and better life" and "We die so quickly, so helplessly. Life *has* to have some meaning" (*Assistant* 43). If Helen sounds a bit melodramatic at times, she is young; but Malamud does not cheapen her dreams. It is important to see that Helen's aspirations are worthwhile or the conclusion of the novel, with Frank helping her through college, becomes ridiculous.

Frank's love for Helen is the most intense, obsessive, and idealized love in the Malamud novels. It feeds on the trouble they have getting together and later on Frank's guilt over the rape. He thinks of her constantly and associates her with all that is positive -- birds, flowers, a new life, a life of discipline. Early in the novel he pretends she has a phone call just to get her down to the store. He waits all day for brief glimpses of her as she comes home from work. The rape takes place in February and it is not until the following January that Helen has any kind words for Frank. Still he works long hours and denies himself necessities so he can give Ida the ninety a month in rent for the store, hoping Helen will be able to return to college.

Malamud gives Frank so little, less than he gives most of his heroes; yet he demands a great deal of him. While Roy Hobbs and Frank share similar pasts, Frank lacks Roy's magical baseball talent. And most of the heroes have at least some sort of career: Sy Levin of *A New Life* is a teacher; Lesser and Willie of *The Tenants* and Dubin of *Dubin's Lives* are all writers. But Frank starts out with nothing; he is an alcoholic, a drifter, an orphan, even a lousy criminal. Yet by the end of the novel Frank is almost a saint.

The Saint Francis of Assisi and Christ parallel in the Frank and Morris relationship is the dominant image of the book. Some suggestions of this parallel are obvious: Assisi-assistant; Frank A., Alpine, an Italian Catholic from San Francisco; and all the references to Saint Francis in the novel. A few critics have touched on the St. Francis motif, including Peter Hays (224-25), Walter Shear (213-15), Joan Zlotnick (22-23) who notice the bird, snow and moon imagery associated with St. Francis in the novel. Both Morris and Frank refer to birds in descriptions of Helen; and when Frank finally confesses his part in the hold up to Morris, Frank feels as though a treeful of birds are breaking into song. In addition, Frank uses expressions like "for the birds" (*Assistant* 67) and thinks of Morris as "the wet-eyed old bird, brooding over him" (*Assistant* 83). Sheldon Hershinow notes, "Frank senses Saint Francis's gentleness and associates it with Morris's Jewishness" (36). And Robert Ducharme says, "If Morris embodies the moral qualities of Christ, Frank is cast in the role of one of his most celebrated imitators, St. Francis of Assisi" (16). However, the degree of similarity between Frank and St. Francis has not been noted.

St. Francis worked at a store too, his father's dry goods store (Bishop, *Saint Francis of Assisi* 13). At twenty-four Francis considered himself a failure: he had twice failed to be a heroic knight and he had no appetite for his father's business (Bishop 27). Like Frank, St. Francis started out on his moral pilgrimage by stealing. He stole from his father's shop and sold the cloth in the neighboring town of Foligno, in order to get funds to repair a chapel dedicated to St. Damian (Bishop 35-37). With this theft Francis began his service to God in his mid-twenties, the same general age as Frank Alpine.

St. Francis wore a patched, ragged robe with a knotted rope belt and dedicated himself to Lady Poverty: Frank dons the apron of a storekeeper and offers his services for nothing, tying "the apron strings around him" (*Assistant* 41). The apron is mentioned repeatedly in the novel and identified with Frank's service. Frank even thinks of the store in terms similar to those a monk might use in describing his order: "In the store he was quits with the outside world" (*Assistant* 58).

Frank's relationship to Helen parallels St. Francis' to Lady Poverty. And Arnold Goldsmith compares Frank and Helen to St. Francis and St. Clare (211-23). In the early days of their association, Clare and Francis spent hours conversing, hiding their meetings from her parents (Bishop 81). Helen and Frank must hide their relationship from her parents, too. Throughout her life St. Clare saw St. Francis as her ideal; Frank tends to look upon Helen as an ideal.

The general movement of the life of St. Francis was toward more and more simplicity, poverty, self-denial. By the end of *The Assistant* Frank is living on air, his clothes falling apart; but he gives ninety dollars to Ida every month so Helen can continue night school. He is even beginning to resemble the Giotto portraits of St. Francis: "He grew thin, his neck scrawny, face bones prominent, his broken nose sharp" (*Assistant* 241). He shares St. Francis' goal of conquering the self, of discipline (Bishop 145). In St. Francis this self-denial comes close to an idealizing of suffering, culminating in the stigmata. Near death from his wounds, he commanded his followers to strip him naked and lay him on the cold ground (Bishop 195). Curiously, Frank's hands are described as "scarred" (*Assistant* 33). In a fit of remorse over the rape, Frank "stepped on the lit match and danced in the pain" (*Assistant* 174). In a dream Frank stands bare foot in the snow, frozen, hoping Helen will open her window to him. When he realizes Helen is returning his gifts, the scarf and the volume of Shakespeare, "His fists were clenched, the nails cutting his palms" (_Assistant_ 112). Perhaps the circumcision of the final page is Frank's stigmata. St. Francis' identification with Christ, even in the wounds of his death, is also echoed in the novel when Frank falls into Morris' grave.

Frank reads magazines and books about St. Francis and talks to Helen about stories of the saint he heard in the orphanage, including the story of St. Francis fashioning himself a family out of snow. He tells Sam Pearl, who owns the candy store, of his admiration for the saint who had the "nerve to preach to birds," who "enjoyed to be poor," and who "took a fresh view of things": "He was born good, which is a talent if you have it" (_Assistant_ 31). Once Helen spots him in the park feeding peanuts to the pigeons: "When the man rose, the pigeons fluttered up with him, a few landing on his arms and shoulders, one perched on his fingers, pecking peanuts from his cupped palm. Another fat bird sat on his hat" (_Assistant_ 118).

The life of St. Francis was marked by little concern for theology, philosophy, dogma, or strict observance of religious ritual. He was in general anti-intellectual (Bishop 57). This concern for the spirit rather than the letter of the law is also a theme in _The Assistant_. Helen feels "loyal to the Jews, more for what they had gone through than what she knew of their history or theology" (_Assistant_ 132). Joan Zlotnick has noticed that like St. Francis, Morris is "unlettered" and has a "meager religious education" (22). When Morris and Frank talk of what it means to be Jewish, Morris says, "My father used to say to be a Jew all you need is a good heart" (_Assistant_ 124). For Morris the real "Law" is "to do what is right, to be honest, to be good. This means to other people" (_Assistant_ 124). And Morris tells Frank, "I suffer for you, . . . I mean you suffer for me" (_Assistant_ 125).

As Frank's life parallels St. Francis, Morris' life parallels Christ. The notion of Morris' suffering in the store as sacrificial, a suffering for others, in itself suggests Morris as a Christ figure; and there are many other clues in the novel to suggest Malamud had this parallel in mind. On the simplest level Frank uses the name of Christ or Jesus too many times when speaking to Morris for it to be an accident on Malamud's part. When Morris first feeds Frank, Frank says, "Jesus, this is good bread" (*Assistant* 33). When Morris discovers Frank in the cellar and asks him if he has ever been in prison, Frank says, "Never, I swear to Christ" (*Assistant* 51). And later, when Morris comes down to the store after he has recovered from his near asphyxiation, Frank falls on one knee as he lights the gas heater, in the pose of a supplicant, and in a moment confesses his part in the hold up. He says, "I swear to God I didn't want to once I got in here" (*Assistant* 198). Then when Frank saves Morris from the fire he again calls Christ into the picture: "For Christ's sake," Frank pleaded, "take me back here" (*Assistant* 214). And when Frank confesses his part in the hold up to Helen, after Morris is dead, he asks her to forgive him, "For Christ's sake" (*Assistant* 240).

Like Christ, Morris is surrounded by two thieves, one who will find redemption and one who will not. Ward Minogue dies trapped in a fire he starts accidentally while vandalizing Karp's liquor store. Morris' physical deterioration, leading to his death, begins when Ward hits him on the head with the gun during the hold up. Frank, however, shows Morris kindness during the robbery; filling a cup with water, "He brought it to the grocer, spilling some on his apron as he raised the cup to his lips" (*Assistant* 26). This gesture suggests the sponge filled with vinegar offered to Christ on the cross (Matthew 27:48).

When Morris wakes up on the last Sunday in March he imagines "a wound, a gap in his side" (*Assistant* 219) which parallels Christ's wound. He is moved by watching the snow and recalls himself as a young boy, "whooping at blackbirds as they flew from the snowy trees; he felt an irresistible thirst to be out in the open" (*Assistant* 221). This time the snow and birds suggest a connection between St. Francis and Morris. Morris goes out to sweep for the customers, "the goyim" to Ida (*Assistant* 221), neglecting to wear a coat or galoshes. Nick and Tessie Fuso, the tenants warn him of the cold, but he says, "I'm almost finished" (*Assistant* 222). And when Ida discovers him and shouts down, twice he tells her "Finished" (*Assistant* 222), echoing Christ's words on the cross. He wakes up that night feeling sick; again, "his left side pained him" (*Assistant* 225). Three days later Morris dies in the hospital.

Morris also seems to possess some supernatural powers that are almost godlike. Schmitz, his German competitor, gets a blood disease and must sell off the store. And Morris wishes on Karp "some small misfortune" (*Assistant* 22), and later he wishes "the liquor store would burn to the ground" (*Assistant* 206). The liquor store does burn and Karp suffers a heart attack.

But in general it is Morris' character that most closely identifies him with Christ. Like Christ, Morris is not a success in the world's eyes; still he keeps the store open, serving humanity. He offers concern for others throughout the novel: for his dead son Ephraim, for Helen, for Brietbart, for Al Marcus, the paper products salesman who is dying of cancer, even for the father of Ward Minogue. But most especially he shows love for Frank. From the outset his concern for the fellow who will become his assistant is striking. When Frank is still a stranger, Morris is quick to offer him coffee and rolls; Morris "knew a poor man when he saw one" (*Assistant* 34). A little later, after finding out Frank has been hiding in the cellar and stealing milk and rolls, Morris still offers him a meal; and when he sees how hungry Frank is, how his hands tremble, "The grocer had to look away" (*Assistant* 51). He apologizes that the bread is stale, and he won't let Frank sleep in the cellar because it is too cold and drafty, "Also rats" (*Assistant* 53). Even after he catches Frank stealing from the register and dismisses him, it is despite "tears in his eyes" (*Assistant* 163) for his assistant. And after Frank is gone Morris wonders if he has done the right thing. Later when he dismisses Frank for the last time after he realizes Frank is the one who held him up, still "he pitied the clerk" (*Assistant* 199). Morris, the keeper of the store, embodies love and charity and, like Christ, he is a Jew.

The St. Francis-Christ parallel is intricately worked out and many have noted that the book seems like a parable. But are Morris and Frank believable heroes? In an early review Alfred Kazin was critical of certain aspects of *The Assistant*, claiming "the moral is too pointed to convince me," and "Bober himself remains too generalized a Jew, as Frank is too shadowy and unvisualized the Gentile, to make their symbolic relationship felt" ("Fantasist of the Ordinary" 92). And Philip Roth has said that the Jews of *The Assistant* and *The Magic Barrel* are not the Jews of New York or Chicago: "They are a kind of invention, a metaphor to stand for certain human possibilities and human promises . . ." ("Writing American Fiction" 68).

However, these judgments are unjust and stem from a distaste for what Kazin and Roth see in Morris Bober -- a negative stereotype of the unassimilated Jew. But Malamud glories in Morris Bober's immigrant English, in his Old World values and ways: he does not find Morris quaint or ridiculous. Morris is not like the middle class Patimkins of Roth's *Goodbye Columbus*, nor does the subject of suburbia hold much appeal for Malamud.

Morris is no mere stereotype. From his misshapen shoes to his thick pelt of hair, he is visualized in the most concrete of terms. While his Jewishness is central to his character and to the theme of the book, it does not detract from Morris the man. And Morris is anything but the image of a conventional Jew: he seldom goes to temple, he is not kosher, and his own description of what it means to be a Jew is so generalized as to be more a definition of humanism -- to have a good heart, to be good to others. Morris' suffering is not abstract or unvisualized either: he suffers from physical ailments, from a nagging wife, from the loss of a son, from a failing business, from many human disappointments.

Frank is not the "shadowy and unvisualized" Gentile Kazin claims either. Frank is clearly drawn throughout the book, and other than his admiration for St. Francis there is little about him that is especially Gentile. He is referred to as an "Italyener" several times and he even thinks of himself as a "sentimental wop." But as Malamud has pointed out, this is simply how these people talk (Field 15). Other than his cooking pizzas, ravioli, and lazagne, Frank is not even depicted as especially Italian. He, in fact, has many affinities to Sy Levin of _A New Life_ who is Jewish. Both have unhappy childhoods, bouts of alcoholism as young men, and most importantly a drive to achieve a love that seems impossible and to take on weighty responsibilities for the loved one. And though Frank allows Ward Minogue to talk him into the hold up because Morris is a Jew, Frank's anti-Semitism does not run deep. He is not a stereotype of an anti-Semitic Gentile, and after he has gotten to know the Bobers he wonders why he blamed the Jews for anything. "What the hell are they to me that I gave them credit for it" (_Assistant_ 70).

However the whole question of Jewishness in the novel and the relationship between Jews and Gentiles is a complex one, especially considering the last page of the novel -- Frank's circumcision and conversion. In what way is Morris a Jew and in what way is Frank converted?

Several critics have noted that the Jewishness in *The Assistant* is more a metaphor than a religion. Norman Podhoretz claims: "To Malamud, the Jew is humanity seen under the twin aspects of suffering and moral aspiration" ("The New Nihilism in the American Novel" 589). And Theodore Solataroff notes: "Malamud's Jewishness is a type of metaphor -- for anyone's life -- both the tragic dimensions of anyone's life and for a code of personal morality and salvation that is more psychological than religious" ("Bernard Malamud's Fiction" 237). Philip Rahv claims that for Malamud, "Jewishness as he understands it, above all feels it, is one of the principal sources of value in his work as it affects both his conception of experience in general and his conception of imaginative writing in particular" (viii). For Malamud, Jewishness is associated with a life of suffering and with the possibility of finding value amid the suffering, of finding a life of meaning.

Morris is a Jew because of his suffering and his values, not because he observes any religious rituals. Throughout the novel Frank moves toward salvation as he identifies with Morris' decency and sacrifice. After Morris' death Frank's behavior becomes more and more similar to the grocer's: he lets his hair grow thick to save the cost of a hair cut; he watches as Nick Fuso, the tenant, buys his groceries elsewhere; he serves tea with lemon to Brietbart, the bulb peddler. This identification with Morris culminates in Frank's circumcision and conversion. Philip Rahv has noted:

> Frank's act is not to be understood as a religious conversion. Within the context of the novel, what Frank's singular act stands for is the ultimate recognition by this former hold up man and thief of the humanity that he had long suppressed within himself (xi).

But not everyone has seen the circumcision in such benign terms. Kingsley Widmer says: "Despite some incongruity with his realistic manner, the author develops the motif for his concluding grotesque metaphor of the castrated goy" (468). Sanford Pinsker sees Frank's suffering as "his penchant for masochism. The old guilts must be punished and what better way than by circumcision" ("The Schlemiel as Moral Bungler" 53). Ruth Wisse sees Frank's acceptance of himself as a Jew as his acceptance of failure (114).

The most interesting member of the "castrated goy" school of thought is Philip Roth. In an essay "Imagining Jews," written in 1974, partly in response to the lack of righteousness and moral restraint readers found in Roth's own _Portnoy's Complaint_, he explores the heroes imagined by other contemporary Jewish writers, especially Bellow and Malamud. In general he claims that the fictional Jew is associated with all that is ethical; the fictional Gentile, with appetite and aggression. Roth says:

> For Malamud, generally speaking, the Jew is innocent, passive, virtuous, and this to the degree that he defines himself or is defined by others as a Jew; the Gentile, on the other hand, is characteristically corrupt, violent, and lustful, particularly when he enters a room or a store or a cell with a Jew in it ("Imagining Jews" 230-3).

Roth believes _The Assistant_ is Malamud's best book, as of 1974, because it adheres so closely to the images of a good Jew and a bad goy, "the classic Malamudian moral arrangement" ("Imagining Jews" 231). The turning of Frank into "another entombed, impoverished, and suffering Jewish grocer . . . shall constitute an act of 'assistance,' and set Alpine on the road to redemption -- or so the stern morality of the book suggests" ("Imagining Jews" 231). And Roth on the circumcision: "It is precisely with an attack upon the body -- upon the very organ with which Alpine had attacked Bober's daughter.

. . . So penance for the criminal penis has been done" ("Imagining Jews" 234). Roth notes that Frank takes on responsibility for Helen's college education, "rather than the orgasmic, no-holds-barred, time-of-her-timish education" ("Imagining Jews" 234).

Roth makes a good case for this Puritanical strain in Malamud's "stern morality," but Roth and the others who see a castrated Frank are somewhat mistaken. Certainly Malamud did intend for the circumcision and the rape to be connected: it is inevitable that when reading of the circumcision one is reminded of Helen's accusation after the rape, "Dog -- uncircumcised dog" (*Assistant* 168). However, I do not think Malamud intended the circumcision as a denial of sexuality or a castration. For one thing, circumcision does not equal castration. If it is connected directly to sex in the novel, it is a way for Frank to make himself more acceptable to Helen and a way to apologize. The circumcision comes in the paragraph following Frank's vision of Helen's final acceptance of his love. He imagines St. Francis turning the wooden rose he carved into a real rose and presenting it to Helen "with the love and best wishes of Frank Alpine" (*Assistant* 246). Though this vision is not a sexual one, throughout the novel Frank's love for Helen has been characterized by a persistent physical longing.

In general, Malamud does associate love with sex in a way that might strike many as old-fashioned. The Malamud hero does not cavort easily in and out of bed. The one mutually satisfying sexual episode in *The Natural* eventually results in love. The heroes like Sy Levin, Fidelman, and Dubin who try for simple sex find difficulties. But this reflects something other than prudishness in Malamud. All of his fiction reflects the desire for connection, for relationships and commitments. It is not surprising that the sexual relationships reflect these concerns, too. And as Malamud often uses the hero's relationship to a woman as the vehicle for his moral transformation, it seems natural that the man-woman connections are not simply physical.

Helen's feelings about her sexual relationship with Nat Pearl perhaps best reflect Malamud's attitude toward sex in _The Assistant_. She had satisfaction in sex with Nat, "had felt very moving the freedom of fundamental intimacy with a man"; her "sense of waste" comes later because she wanted more, "simply a future in love" (_Assistant_ 14). Both Helen and Nat are Jews not immune to "lustful" physical pleasure that Roth claims Malamud reserves for goyim. In Helen's Jewishness, Malamud does not present a denial of sexuality; she will later desire Frank, too. Malamud simply presents sex without love as disappointing.

Neither does Malamud present the Jews of _The Assistant_ as entirely innocent or virtuous as Roth claims. The sneaking around that Ida, Morris, and Helen do, the spying, the little deceptions serve to make them more human and to bring them closer to the sneaking Frank Alpine. And some of the other Jews are not models of virtue: Louis Karp steals from his father Julius; Julius Karp got his liquor license by bribery; Charlie Sobeloff stole from Morris; and the "macher" is an arsonist.

In _The Assistant_ Malamud does not reduce anyone to stereotype. He draws convincing portraits of real people. Even the minor characters like Brietbart the bulb peddler and Podolsky the prospective buyer for the store seem to jump out of the pages and have a life of their own. What concerns Malamud is each man's humanity, what each has made of his life, of the often lousy hand each has been dealt.

Frank and Morris are heroes clearly in the Malamud mode. They fail, they suffer, forces conspire to imprison them, isolate them, limit them. But they do not give up. They are tenacious in typical Malamud style: they seem glued to the very floor boards of the store. Yet what a world Malamud creates in one small grocery. Who walking by this Brooklyn store would guess the disappointments, the longings of a Morris Bober -- the struggles and dreams of a Frank Alpine? Malamud chooses characters and a setting that seem so commonplace; but he leaves the reader with a sense of the beauty, the intensity of life -- with a sense that the most moving lives might be those that appear the most ordinary.

What makes *The Assistant* so impressive is that Malamud created characters well-suited to his theme, the making of a *mensch*. In the dignity and humanity that Morris brings to his humble role as grocer, Malamud strikes the deepest of chords. From beginning to end Malamud draws sharp Christ parallels into his portrait of Morris Bober; but he never forgets that his grocer is a grocer, with a poor grocer's economic hopes and worries: will I pull in some real money today, will I be able to pay for new merchandise, where are my customers going, to the new store down the block? Suffering has molded Morris into a man so sensitive that no sigh is lost on him. What Malamud presents as most Christlike in Morris is his adherence to the Golden Rule, his willingness to be more than fair with others.

But Malamud is not really a religious writer: he is a humanist. In a novel that suggests such interest in Jewishness and in the figures of Christ and St. Francis, curiously God has absented himself. He does not intervene in the characters' lives, nor do they call upon him to. If he exists at all he is hiding among distant clouds while life metes out its Job-like afflictions on man. What gives life beauty for Malamud is man in communion with other men.

And while Frank is identified with St. Francis, Frank is still more man than saint. As D. H. Lawrence said, "Even Francis of Assisi turns himself into a sort of angel-cake, of which anyone may take a slice. But an angel-cake is rather less than man alive" (104). Frank is more "man alive." He is most definitely of this world in his appetites and longings. His physical presence in the store is so strongly felt that Ida uses all her wiles to keep Helen away from him. From beginning to end of the novel Frank is depicted in very human terms. In August, five months after Morris' death, Frank offers to support Helen if she will quit her job and go to school full time: still "the sight of her struck him with renewed hunger" (*Assistant* 238). He confesses his part in the hold up and though Helen runs from him then, by January, after spotting him at his counter job and realizing it is because of him that she has been able to return to school part time, "It came to her that he had changed" (*Assistant* 243). "What he did to me he did wrong, she thought, but since he has changed in his heart he owes me nothing" (*Assistant* 243). And the last time he sees her in the book, he still desires her and those bowed legs: "She was wearing flat-heeled shoes, making her legs slightly more bowed, which for some reason he found satisfying" (*Assistant* 244).

Frank is not a neutered saint. In the circumcision and conversion he is identified with Morris and with what a Jew means to Morris, someone with a "good heart." Frank still hopes for a future with Helen, a future that once again seems possible. And it is partly with that future in mind that he converts to Judaism. "The pain enraged and inspired him. After Passover he became a Jew" (*Assistant* 246).

THE MAGIC BARREL: OF HUMAN COMPASSION

The Magic Barrel, Malamud's first collection of short stories, received the National Book Award in 1958 and has remained over the years one of the most highly praised of his works. In these twelve stories Malamud presents his distinctive heroes in typical predicaments: oppressed by poverty, disease, and failed loves, they somehow manage to persevere. And while there is not the extended character development that occurs in the novels, in the short space of many of these stories the heroes do change, recognize their isolation, and move toward human communion and commitment.

In general critics have seen these stories as affirmative, in spite of the pervasive suffering depicted in them. In an early review William Peden said, "The atavistic identification with grief permeates all these stories. Yet Malamud's fiction bubbles with life" (5). And Irving Howe noted, "The settings contribute to an atmosphere of limitation, oppression, coercion: man is not free. The action and language preserve, through the renewing powers of imagination, the possibility of freedom" ("Stories of Bernard Malamud" 34). Dan Jacobson noted that in these stories Malamud "has the capacity to do what has baffled greater writers: the capacity to make goodness of the most humble and long-suffering kind real, immediate and attractive" ("Magic and Morality" 360).

Many of the characteristics of Roy Hobbs, Frank Alpine, and Morris Bober appear in these heroes from *The Magic Barrel*. Several are seeking new lives

and fighting the burdens of old guilts, failures and prisons. Many are molded
by suffering that sometimes results in a sensitive heart. Often these heroes
seek a new life in the love for a woman. Again, as in *The Assistant*, Malamud
exhibits his talent for pairs of characters. As Theodore Solotaroff has noted,
Malamud has an "uncanny sense of what types of people belong in the same
story . . ." ("The Old and The New" 241). These pairs often repeat the
teacher-disciple pattern of Morris and Frank, though here the teachers are
fantastic, wild, almost Jewish leprechauns. Henry Popkin has called Susskind
of "The Last Mohican," Bevilacqua of "Behold the Key," and Salzman of "The
Magic Barrel" all *luftmenschen* for their ability to live on and travel on air
(640). To their company I would add the angel-in-waiting of "Angel Levine."
The students of these raggedy mentors are often unwilling, reluctant, even
suspicious: but they are up against sorcerers who will inflict changes on them
nevertheless. And in general the changes are toward more self-knowledge,
faith, and brotherhood.

Three of the stories are set in Italy: "Behold the Key," "The Lady of the
Lake," and "The Last Mohican." "The Last Mohican" is the first of a series
of stories that were eventually collected in *Pictures of Fidelman*. Ihab Hassan
has found the Italian stories of *The Magic Barrel* the weakest, claiming they
have a "glossy" quality ("Qualified Encounter" 200). But, in fact, these stories
have held up well and can be seen as directly related to the American stories.
Most of the American stories in *The Magic Barrel* are similar to *The Assistant*
in setting and tone.

Like many of Malamud's novels, these stories have vibrant, sudden, and
sometimes confusing endings. "The Magic Barrel" and "Take Pity" in
particular have led to several disparate readings. And Irving Howe has
complained: "In his inferior stories Malamud depends too much on hard and

flashy climaxes . . ." ("Stories of Bernard Malamud" 33). But understanding these endings is crucial to see where Malamud finally leaves his heroes.

Taken together these stories contribute to the picture of the Malamud hero. Four of the stories show this hero in search of love: "The First Seven Years," "The Girl of My Dreams," "The Lady of the Lake," and "The Magic Barrel."

The first story in the collection, "The First Seven Years," is a reworking of the Jacob and Rachel story of the Bible. In the biblical account Jacob agrees to work for seven years for Laban in order to marry Laban's daughter Rachel: "And Jacob loved Rachel; and said, I will serve the seven years for Rachel thy younger daughter" (Genesis 29:18). Jacob must wait longer than seven years and is first tricked by Laban into marrying Leah, the older daughter. In Malamud's story, the shoemaker's assistant Sobel must work for seven years for the privilege of asking the shoemaker's daughter to marry him. The story also has many similarities to *The Assistant*. The assistant loves his employer's daughter and her father at first hopes for a better life for his daughter in marriage to a college man -- here Max the accountancy student, in *The Assistant* Nat the law student. The shoemaker, like the grocer, depends on his assistant for his livelihood. But in "The First Seven Years" there is a twist: it is the younger man Sobel, the assistant, who teaches Feld the shoemaker to have heart. Feld ignores Sobel's love for Miriam though it is right under his nose. Feld has a heart condition but he must be taught to recognize the condition of Sobel's heart. Here it is the younger man who is the *mensch*-teacher. Sobel cares nothing for wages, living only for love. At the conclusion of the story he works, "seated at the last, pounding leather for his love" (*Barrel* 16).

Miriam, the object of this love, knows Sobel largely through the copious notes he sends her to read along with the classics. Since she was fourteen she has read these notes, "page by sanctified page, as if the word of God were inscribed on them" (*Barrel* 8). For Malamud these notes reflect the word of God: the truth of great literature and the love in Sobel's heart. Feld incorrectly believes a better life for Miriam would be gained by a college education or at least marriage to a man with a college education. He does not realize what an education Miriam is getting from Sobel, and he incorrectly explains Sobel's continued presence in the store as evidence that he was "afraid of the world" (*Barrel* 8).

Again, as in *The Assistant*, Malamud associates a love of learning and of great literature with a life of value. Sobel reads constantly. During his worst moment, when he has refused to return to the shop and Feld has said of Miriam, "She will never marry a man so old and ugly like you" (*Barrel* 14), Sobel stands at the window reading. Even Feld must admit of Sobel, "it was curious that when he read he looked young" (*Barrel* 15). Max, with his practical education, is another Malamud character like Nat Pearl who does go to college but does not learn about life. As Miriam says about Max, "He has no soul. He is only interested in things" (*Barrel* 11).

Several qualities link Sobel and Feld to each other and to other Malamud heroes. Sobel, like Frank Alpine, is young but looks old. He is only thirty but he already knows suffering: he barely escaped Hitler's incinerators. He is alone in the world and lives in a bare boarding house room. He is tenacious and determined in his love for Miriam. She was only fourteen when he first arrived at the store, and when the story opens he has already waited five years for her to become a woman. Sobel's love for Miriam is idealized and romantic, and like several Malamud heroes he must wait and work hard to achieve that love. The struggle and suffering that Sobel has endured has not been wasted on him: he is a true *mensch*. His "soft blue eyes prone to tears over the sad books he read . . . " (*Barrel* 7) reflect the degree to which he can empathize with other people's suffering. He is easily moved to human sympathy.

Like Sobel, Feld is a displaced person, an immigrant. Feld thinks of his boyhood in the Polish village "where he had wasted his youth" (*Barrel* 3). Like most of Malamud's older protagonists, Feld is in poor physical shape. He has a heart condition. Many of Malamud's characters are softened by their suffering; Feld is not. Though he has had a rough life struggling in the shoe repair shop, Feld is not easily moved: "Feld, if anything, was a practical man" (*Barrel* 3). But in spite of Feld's practical concern that Miriam not live the lowly life of a shoemaker's wife, the story still emphasizes the molding value of poverty and struggle in the lives of both Feld and Sobel.

The conclusion of the story is both moving and hopeful. When Feld finally realizes Sobel's feelings for Miriam and thinks of all Sobel has been through, "His teeth were on edge with pity for the man, and his eyes grew moist" (*Barrel* 15). He asks Sobel to wait just two years, till Miriam is twenty-one to ask her to marry him. This is a common final note in Malamud's fiction: one man moved by the grief of another.

Yet Malamud does leave a small element of doubt that Sobel will wed Miriam in the two years. The presence of the word "first" in the title suggests there may be more years of waiting ahead. And while Feld claims that Miriam at nineteen is too young to marry, he did not seem to feel she was too young to marry Max. As in the conclusion of *The Assistant*, the reader feels the man will get the girl he loves but his fate is not completely sealed.

The second story on the theme of love is "The Girl of My Dreams." This story is a good deal less romantic than "The First Seven Years" and Mitka, the main character, is a good deal less sympathetic than either Sobel or Feld. It is the first of a number of struggling failed artist stories Malamud will write. As the story opens, Mitka is burning his novel after the twentieth publisher has sent it back. In despair, he closets himself for months in his room at Mrs. Lutz' boarding house. One day Mrs. Lutz brings him a bowl of soup and the morning *Globe*. In the paper, where he had first published his own stories, he reads a story by a Madeleine Thorn about a young woman whose landlady carelessly burned the girl's novel in a barrel. Mitka is convinced the story is autobiographical and starts up a correspondence with the author.

In his loneliness he imagines that she will be the girl of his dreams. Malamud is likely echoing Keats' "The Eve of St. Agnes" (524-35) where Madeleine dreams of her Porphyro who appears complete with a sumptuous feast. But here Madeleine and Mitka meet in a library and she is a heavy, dowdy, middle-aged woman whose real name turns out to be Olga -- hardly Mitka's dream girl. She does bring quite a picnic with her though, which Mitka wolfs down at a neighborhood bar. When they part, he has eaten so much "he could live for a week. Mitka, the camel" (*Barrel* 41).

Mitka has several characteristics of the typical Malamud hero. He seems to be thirtyish though his exact age is not given. He is a failure as a writer and a failure as a person. A loner, he is withdrawn from the world. But unlike most Malamud heroes, he does not undergo any great changes at the end of the story. After he says a cool goodbye to Madeleine/Olga he is gripped by the spring air and plans to go back to the boarding house, dress Mrs. Lutz in white, and "swing her across the threshold, holding her where the fat overflowed her corset as they waltzed around his writing chamber" (*Barrel* 41). But he is not awakened to giving love so much as to the convenience of receiving it from Olga or from Mrs. Lutz. He will let the doting mama Mrs. Lutz care for the struggling artist.

It is Madeleine/Olga who is the *mensch* in this story who speaks for Malamud's values. She has had a rough life. Abandoned by her husband, she struggled to raise two children. Then her daughter Madeleine, her greatest joy, died at the age of twenty. Still Olga goes on, adopts Madeleine as a pen name and struggles with her writing. She counsels Mitka, who is struggling with writer's block, on the virtues of work: "You'll invent your way out," said Olga, "if you keep trying" (*Barrel* 39).

Iska Alter observes that Mitka "is foolish enough to select bad art over living in the world" (126) and notes that Mitka's withdrawal is part of his problem: "To write or paint requires discipline and dedication but never to the point of egocentric isolation. Such withdrawal attenuates the creative impulse" (126).

In general this story is less satisfying than most of the others in the collection because the hero and his problems are not too compelling. Malamud also faces the problem of writing about a writer who is not writing, usually a dull business. And Mitka's struggles do not mold him; he does not seem to profit from his experience except in that he is realizing he cannot write. What separates him from most of Malamud's heroes is his insensitivity to others and his inability to change. The barrel of his burning manuscript does not shed light; it merely withers the apples on the tree. He is no true *mensch* and the story suffers from this lack.

The hero of the next love story "The Lady of the lake" is Henry Levin, alias Henry R. Freeman, an ex-floorwalker from Macy's book department who after receiving a small inheritance has gone to Europe in search of romance. Like a number of Malamud heroes he is thirty, he is alone in the world with no close family, and he is seeking a new life in the love of a woman. While he is not a product of deprivation and suffering, he is dissatisfied with his life, "tired of the past -- tired of the limitations it imposed on him" (*Barrel* 105). Malamud suggests that Henry may be responsible for his past failures with women, perhaps because he was overly romantic and was looking for an ideal woman: "he had sometimes in the past deceived himself about women, they had come to less than he had expected" (*Barrel* 105).

When Henry goes to Europe seeking romantic love, it is romance, rather than the lasting connection of a deeper love, that he finds. He sets off on an unreal footing by camouflaging himself as Henry R. Freeman, non-Jew, suggesting that he associates his past failures with his Jewishness and that he is ashamed of being a Jew. And when he first sees his dream woman Isabella, he is unsure of whether she is a statue or a woman. At the end of the story he embraces "moonlit stone" as Isabella vanishes (*Barrel* 133). Henry cannot tell a real woman from a statue or the real art in the Del Dongo palace from the forgeries because he has rejected his true self.

Isabella is the sufferer, the woman still bearing the numbers the Nazis tattooed on her breast when she was in Buchenwald as a child. At the conclusion of the story she rejects Henry's proposal of marriage saying: "I can't marry you. We are Jews. My past is meaningful to me. I treasure what I suffered for" (*Barrel* 132). She believes Henry who has told her three times that he's not hiding anything, that he is not a Jew. But she, too, has lied, pretending to be an aristocrat, a del Dongo, rather than a della Seta, daughter of the caretaker and guide Ernesto. Yet when she confesses her deception and Henry has the perfect opportunity to admit he is Henry Levin, a Jew, he says only, "So you had to pretend" (*Barrel* 129). He feels "hurt where it hurts -- in his dreams" (*Barrel* 130). Even at her final admission that she is a Jew his first reaction is, "Oh, God, why did you keep this from me, too?" (*Barrel* 132). He is quicker to blame her than to confess his own deception. When he does start to tell her he is Jewish she has already "stepped among the statues" (*Barrel* 133).

The lesson of this story is a pointed one: accept yourself, be proud of who you are. Henry learns the lesson but it costs him Isabella. In denying that he is a Jew, Henry denies his connection to all the victims of the Holocaust and, therefore, to all human suffering. He is not a *mensch* because he fails to accept suffering as the very foundation of life. He seeks to rise above suffering, above what is human.

The last love story, "The Magic Barrel" starts out with Leo Finkle, rabbinical student, in practical pursuit of a bride; but it turns into one of Malamud's most moving love stories. Again Malamud creates an interesting pair of characters in Leo Finkle, the sheltered student from Yeshiva University, and Pinye Salzman, the marriage broker. Here it is the older man Salzman, the salt of life man, who must teach the younger man Leo to have heart. Salzman, who "smelled frankly of fish which he loved to eat . . ." appears to be a little shady or fishy himself (*Barrel* 193). When he talks of his female clients their ages are always understated, and he tries to avoid mentioning drawbacks like their lame legs. Yet Salzman has an "amiable manner" and he has almost magical powers. He appears when Leo needs him and his wife says his office is "In the air" (*Barrel* 210). He travels "as if on the wings of the wind" (*Barrel* 207). He may be an angel.

Leo at twenty-seven has eyes "heavy with learning" (*Barrel* 195). His scholarly life has left him with few close human connections. He is somewhat embarrassed by calling in a marriage broker, but he is incapable of finding a wife on his own. His very search for a wife begins when "an acquaintance" suggests to Leo that "he might find it easier to win himself a congregation if he were married" (*Barrel* 193). On this unromantic note Leo calls upon Salzman.

In his early dealings with Salzman, Leo's lack of warmth is apparent; yet the marriage broker draws him out gradually. Here Malamud uses the serving of food as a measure of human sympathy. On Salzman's first visit to Leo, Leo offers him nothing to eat or drink. On his second visit Salzman asks, "A sliced tomato you have maybe?" (*Barrel* 200). Leo says no and Salzman eats the smoked whitefish and roll he brought with him and then asks, "A glass of tea you got, rabbi?" (*Barrel* 200). He is drawing Leo out, making him show some hospitality. "Conscience-stricken, Leo rose and brewed the tea. He served it with a chunk of lemon and two cubes of lump sugar, delighting Salzman" (*Barrel* 200). By the final time Salzman arrives at Leo's, Leo fixes him tea and a sardine sandwich; Salzman did not need to ask. The importance of Leo's feeding Salzman is emphasized by the fact that Salzman is very thin, "a skeleton" (*Barrel* 206).

Like other Malamud heroes Leo is a loner, a personal failure, a man seeking a new life. But unlike many of these heroes who have failed in the world, Leo has insulated himself from the world. His sheltered life is his failing. Leo's awakening to others is accompanied by some painful discoveries about himself. This increasing self-awareness has several stages. First, when he is out with Salzman's client Lily Hirschorn, he says, when provoked by her questions, "I came to God not because I loved Him, but because I did not" (*Barrel* 204). Then when he returns he realizes "that apart from his parents, he had never loved anyone" (*Barrel* 205). At this stage he weeps into his hands, a gesture that indicates he is not dead to feeling. Soon he decides that love is most important: "Perhaps love would now come to him and a bride to that love" (*Barrel* 206). It does come in the form of a picture of Stella, Salzman's fallen daughter, a picture from the magic barrel.

Leo's rush to Stella and Salzman's prayers for the dead on the final page of the story have resulted in a variety of critical interpretations. Sanford Pinsker says, "It is the movement toward Stella which makes a *schlemiel* out of Finkle . . ." ("Bernard Malamud's Ironic Heroes" 49). But Pinsker's interpretation misses two critical elements in the story. First, after falling for Stella's picture, Leo says, "love has at last come to my heart" (*Barrel* 213). The whole movement of the story is toward Leo's emotional awakening, not toward his *schlemielhood*. And second, when Leo tells Salzman of his love, Malamud says Leo's "eyes were weighted with wisdom" (*Barrel* 213). Wisdom is not an attribute of the *schlemiel*. Mark Goldman sees in Leo's rush for Stella an echo of the Hosea story of the Old Testament (156). God commanded Hosea to marry a whore because "the land hath created a great whoredom, departing from the Lord" (Hosea 1:2). Malamud does suggest Stella has been a whore, or at least a whore in Salzman's eyes, "a wild one--wild, without shame" (*Barrel* 214). But when she stands under the street lamp waiting for Leo she wears a white dress; only the shoes are red. Leo sees a "desperate innocence" in her eyes (*Barrel* 214). Leo "pictured, in her, his own redemption. Violins and lit candles revolved in the sky" (*Barrel* 214). The scene is so poetic, so romantic: it hardly seems a reworking of Hosea's marriage which was basically a punishment.

But Salzman's attitude toward Leo and Stella does raise several questions. When Leo first asks him about Stella's picture, Salzman claims that it was a mistake that the picture was in with the pictures of the other clients and that Stella is no bride for a rabbi. But after Leo badgers him, he agrees to arrange a meeting. At this point Leo is "afflicted by a tormenting suspicion that

Salzman had planned it all to happen this way" (*Barrel* 213). Several things in the story suggest that Salzman did plan it all. From the first encounter Salzman is continually sizing up the rabbinical student in a way that suggests a prospective father-in-law: "he heartily approved of Finkle" (*Barrel* 194). And Salzman is so wily that it is hard to imagine he would have mistakenly included Stella's picture in the packet. Salzman also realizes that Leo is stubborn and somewhat perverse: for instance, Leo says he is not interested in school teachers when Salzman is recommending some clients. So Salzman may be exercising some reverse psychology when he claims Stella is not for Salzman.

The most confusing element in the story is Salzman's final Kaddish, or prayer for the dead, when Leo and Stella do meet. Ben Siegel has said, "But what has died may be Salzman's honesty, Leo's innocence, or Stella's guilty youth: all merit lamentation" ("Victims in Motion" 133). Several others see the prayers as affirmative. Marc L. Ratner claims, "Finkle pictures his own redemption in Stella the prostitute, Salzman her father mourns both guilt and the loss of innocence, but the belief in salvation overcomes the ironies of the conclusion" (665). Richard Reynolds notes that a Kaddish is "a plea for the resurrection of the dead," and that "Leo and love are to effect her [Stella's] resurrection. The understanding and art of Salzman have brought about a prospect of happiness" (102). Theodore C. Miller associates the Kaddish with Leo's rebirth and with Salzman's claim to Leo of Stella, "If you can love her than you can love anybody" (*Barrel* 191). As Miller says:

> If Salzman has planned the whole episode, then the matchmaker is commemorating the death of the old Leo who was incapable of love. But he is also celebrating Leo's birth into a new life . . . Salzman is suggesting if Leo can love Stella, he has unlocked his heart to mankind and God (44).

It is also important to realize a Kaddish is a prayer that the souls of the dead will find peace. Salzman has already told Leo of Stella, "to me she is dead now" (*Barrel* 212). Malamud is suggesting in the conclusion that Leo and Stella may give each other a new life. Malamud has no respect for the sheltered, untested goodness of Leo: the loss of his shallow innocence is a good thing. At the conclusion Leo has even grown a pointed beard; he has become a bit of a devil. And as Leo notes of Stella in the picture, she "had lived, or wanted to -- more than just wanted, perhaps regretted how she had lived -- had somehow deeply suffered" (*Barrel* 209). Stella is one of the many Malamud characters who has failed, suffered, and grown from it all. Together Stella and Salzman work changes on Leo Finkle: he is learning to be a *mensch*.

While four of the stories are concerned with finding love, five others are concerned with the general theme of man as his brother's keeper. "The Mourners," "Take Pity," "The Prison," "The Bill," and "The Loan" all deal with man's responsibility to others and with the giving and receiving of trust.

The first of these stories, "The Mourners," reflects several common Malamud themes. Again one man teaches compassion to another. Again it is suffering that brings out the *mensch* in man. And again it is guilt and remorse that instigate change. But the story has an ironic twist: the teacher is a man named Kessler who has lived a very selfish life, and when Kessler's grief changes Gruber, the landlord, it is because Gruber mistakenly believes Kessler is mourning him.

Kessler is an unusual Malamud hero. He has not simply wasted his youth; his whole life has been a failure. Though he is an excellent egg candler, no one will hire him now because he is a quarrelsome troublemaker. Over sixty-five, he is all alone, as he has been since he deserted his wife and children

thirty years ago. He knows most of the other tenants in the building but has
"contempt for them all" (*Barrel* 18). Though Ignace the janitor really wants to
evict Kessler because Kessler has beaten him in pinochle, there seems to be
some truth to his charges that Kessler is unclean. In general, Kessler is one of
Malamud's least appealing heroes.

Though Gruber knows that Ignace is exaggerating the charges against
Kessler, he decides to evict the old man so he can paint the flat and rent it to
someone else for five dollars more. Gruber is "a fat man with a consistently
worried face" (*Barrel* 18), and high blood pressure due to financial worries,
though he carries a "bulky wallet" (*Barrel* 20). Malamud suggests that the
landlord Gruber has final say over what happens to the Job-like Kessler. But
Kessler's suffering slowly teaches Gruber what it means to be a human being
and what his responsibilities to his fellow man are.

The change in Gruber is gradual. At first he is very tough with Kessler and
orders "a dispossess" (*Barrel* 21). Then after the gentile tenants have cut the
lock on the apartment and moved Kessler and his goods in out of the snow,
Kessler says to Gruber, "Who hurts a man without a reason? Are you a Hitler
or a Jew?" (*Barrel* 23). The next morning Gruber decides to offer to get
Kessler into a public home. But when Gruber enters the apartment, "Gruber
was frightened at the extent of Kessler's suffering" (*Barrel* 25). He considers
letting Kessler stay.

The conclusion has bothered some critics. Sidney Richman said, "The
weight of despair is so intense, in fact, that the resolution, despite numerous
anticipatory clues, offers less relief than a weird shock" (104). And Sheldon
Hershinow claimed that "Malamud strains the plot line in the direction of
symbolic meaning" (122).

Nevertheless, though the conclusion seems sudden at first, it is justified and fits the story well. Kessler's suffering has changed him. He suddenly regrets his miserable life and mourns leaving his wife and three children. He thinks, "How, in so short a life, could a man do so much wrong?" (*Barrel* 25). When Gruber sees Kessler in the act of mourning, he first thinks someone has died. Then he believes Kessler is mourning him, "it was *he* who was dead" (*Barrel* 25). Gruber has been dead to human feeling and Kessler's grief awakens him. After nearly having a stroke Gruber gazes around the room, "it was clean, drenched in daylight and fragrance" (*Barrel* 26). It has been washed clean by human sympathy. Gruber feels guilty for the way he treated Kessler and joins Kessler as a mourner. Both men have changed and both regret their failure to have compassion for others. Kessler's humanizing humanizes Gruber. They have both realized their responsibilities.

The second story on the theme of man as his brother's keeper is "Take Pity." But here the theme is twisted: the ex-coffee salesman Rosen tries to give help to the struggling Eva and her two daughters, but Eva refuses the help.

The "pisher grocery" (*Barrel* 87) that Eva's husband Axel Kalish buys is a grave, like Morris Bober's store in *The Assistant*. Axel dies just as Rosen has convinced him to sell the store in auction. Rosen then advises the widow Eva to take the thousand dollars insurance money and flee the store. She refuses and his efforts to help her begin. He extends credit, offers to restock the store, offers to let her live free in a house he owns, and finally offers to marry her. When she refuses all this, he offers to take her to a marriage broker and to provide the dowry. Though she and the girls are near starvation, she refuses Rosen on every score and won't even let the girls accept cakes from him.

Though Eva has suffered all her life, the suffering has not softened her. She is hard and proud. Much of her bitterness reflects her solitary struggle. She is alone when Axel dies. She says, "My relatives Hitler took away from me" (*Barrel* 88). She is bitter and sees no better prospects for the future: "Nobody wants a poor widow with two children" (*Barrel* 89).

In spite of Eva's resistance, Rosen is determined to help her. He finally leaves everything to her in his will, turns on the gas, and puts his head in the stove. His drive to be Eva's protector and provider is not completely explained in the story. But he is a bachelor, alone in the world. Perhaps his insistence on helping Eva is, in part, an effort to make up for a life of lost connections. There is also a large element of pride in Rosen's charity. When she refuses him the last time he says, "I felt like to pick up a chair and break her head" (*Barrel* 93).

The story is told in some after-life where Rosen is interviewed by Davidov the census-taker. The furnishings suggest an institution. Laurence Perrine is close to the mark when he calls it "a kind of purgatory" (86).

The conclusion of the story is sudden, flashy and full of ironic reversals. Perhaps Malamud began with a tricky conclusion and constructed a story to fit it. As Rosen finishes telling Davidov the story, Davidov "got up and before Rosen could cry no, idly raised the window shade" (*Barrel* 94). Eva stands there beseeching Rosen: "She raised her arms to him" (*Barrel* 98). But now that she appears willing to accept the sympathy he has offered all along, he has hardened his heart toward her. "Whore, bastard, bitch," he shouted at her. "Go 'way from here. Go home to your children" (*Barrel* 98). He rams down the window shade. She has apparently killed herself, too, perhaps in grief that he committed suicide for her.

But as is nearly always the case in suicides, these deaths have a quality of revenge about them. In truth, both Rosen and Eva are killed by their pride. Their suffering links them to other Malamud characters, and Rosen's attempt to break out of his isolation is typical of a Malamud character. But the suffering of Rosen and Eva goes nowhere: it leads only to more grief.

"The Prison" and "The Bill" deal with characters getting something for nothing from struggling storekeepers. Both stories have qualities of *The Assistant*. And in both stories the theme of man as his brother's keeper has a twist: the storekeepers offer sympathy and trust but the recipients are ungrateful.

Tommy Castelli, the hero of "The Prison," has many qualities of the typical Malamud hero. At twenty-nine he already feels he is a failure; he has "this sick-in-the-stomach feeling of being trapped in old mistakes . . ." (*Barrel* 97). As a teenager he had taken part in the hold-up of a liquor store. After the hold-up, his father arranged with Rosa Agnello's father that Tommy marry Rosa and open a candy store, bankrolled by Mr. Agnello. But this new life that is planned for Tommy is a prison to him. He cares for neither Rosa nor the store. Like a number of other Malamud heroes, Tommy has had a close relationship with a surrogate father, his Uncle Dom. But Dom ended up in jail and when he got out he took off for parts unknown. In general, Tommy is a lonely, bitter, "old" young man.

One day Tommy glances in the mirror Rosa hung on the back well and he catches a ten-year-old girl stealing two candy bars. "He first felt like grabbing her by the neck and socking her till she threw up . . ." (*Barrel* 100). But he remembers his Uncle Dom, who took him on crabbing trips to Sheepshead Bay, and he is somehow filled with sympathy for the girl. He regrets how his life has turned out, and he is "moved that she was so young and a thief" (*Barrel* 100-101).

Weeks go by as he tries to decide how to talk to her. Meanwhile she keeps stealing. One Monday he puts a note in a candy bar: "Don't do this anymore or you will suffer your whole life." He signs it "Your Friend" (*Barrel* 103). But the girl does not come at the usual time in the morning and Tommy goes upstairs for a nap. When the girl does arrive, Rosa waits on her and catches her stealing. She screams at the girl and shakes her. Then Tommy comes down and slaps Rosa and says of the candy, "I let her take it" (*Barrel* 104).

Tommy slaps Rosa for two reasons: he identifies the girl with his own wasted youth, and he identifies Rosa and the store with his failure, his prison. His feelings for the girl may be his first step in trying to transcend his prison, to have some compassion and some imagination. But unlike most other Malamud heroes, Tommy is not given a chance to change, and his generosity to the girl is not appreciated anyway. Her mother slaps her around and yanks her out of the store. But the girl "managed to turn her white face and thrust out at him her red tongue" (*Barrel* 104). The girl simply feels that Tommy must be a creep.

In some ways this is a smaller, less ambitious story than many in the volume, but the psychology rings true and Tommy is quite believable. In his longing for a better life, Tommy is like Frank Alpine. But Tommy has no Morris Bober to be a moral guide for him. Tommy's service in the store is pointless; the store is his prison. Frank's service in Morris Bober's store became sacrificial and redemptive. Tommy's charity toward the girl who steals the candy is his one attempt to give his life more dignity and meaning.

In the story "The Bill" the Panessas, keepers of a small grocery, are generous, kind people willing to give credit. Mr. Panessa says, "if you were really a human being you gave credit to somebody else and he gave credit to you" (*Barrel* 146-47). Though the Panessas are struggling in their store they are willing to help out Willy Schlegel, the janitor across the street. They let him charge all sorts of items till he owes over eighty-three dollars. But instead of feeling grateful, Willy begins to hate the Panessas. "He felt for Panessa and his wife a grating hatred and vowed never to pay because he hated them so much, especially the humpback behind the counter" (*Barrel* 149). Malamud depicts how easily guilt turns into hate.

Finally Mrs. Panessa writes that her husband is sick and asks Willy to pay ten dollars of the bill. Though times are hard, Willy pawns his overcoat for the ten dollars. But when he goes to the grocery two men are carrying Mr. Panessa out in a pine box. The story ends with a bitter sentence: "Mrs. Panessa moved away to live first with one stone-faced daughter, then with the other. And the bill was never paid" (*Barrel* 153).

"The Bill" is one of Malamud's more grim and realistic stories. Charity is not always appreciated and it does not necessarily bring out the *mensch* in man. The story even has a perverse element: Mr. Panessa is so eager to extend credit that he practically encourages Willy Schlegel to spend beyond his means. But the real impact of the story is in the final mention of the bill that is never paid. Malamud emphasizes the extent of human debt and need. The communion that is found in many of these stories is rare in life. In Mr. Panessa's death, Malamud emphasizes the sour finality of all unmet need.

The final story on the theme of what people owe one another is "The Loan." Kobotsky, an old friend, shows up after many years to ask Lieb, the baker, for a loan. Though these men have suffered in life, suffering has not had the same effect on them both. Lieb, after thirty years of barely making a living, makes something out of his struggles: "One day, out of misery, he had wept into the dough" (*Barrel* 185). Since then his sweet bread has brought in customers from miles away. The tear-filled bread suggests both the sweet, cathartic nature of suffering and the efficacy of the body of Christ. Suffering has not been wasted on Lieb. He is a *mensch*, easily moved by the claims of Kobotsky.

"Though his face glittered with misery" and "suffering had marked him" (*Barrel* 183), Kobotsky is a puzzling character. A close reading of the story suggests he is something of a con man. For one thing he borrowed a hundred dollars from Lieb years ago and then denied it. That broke up their friendship. And though Kobotsky does have hands crippled with arthritis and probably cannot work as a fur cutter anymore, the story he tells when he asks for the loan may not be completely true. He claims he needs the two hundred dollars to buy a stone for his dead wife's grave. But just before he tells this story to Lieb, when Lieb and his wife are in the front of the shop, "He went to the sink, wet half his handkerchief and held it to dry eyes" (*Barrel* 189). Though Lieb is moved to tears easily, Kobotsky fakes his tears.

But Kobotsky does not get the loan because Bessie, a loving wife to Lieb, has had miseries of her own and claims she would need the money if Lieb died. She tells of the Bolsheviki murdering her father, of the death of her first husband to typhus, of the death of her brother and family in Hitler's ovens. At the end of her story Kobotsky "held his hands over his ears" (*Barrel* 191). He probably feels guilty for trying to make a false claim on Lieb.

During this discussion the bread burns. "The loaves in the trays were blackened bricks -- charred corpses" (*Barrel* 191). The suggestion again is of the corpses burned in Hitler's ovens, the same ovens just mentioned by Bessie. The temptation is to see Bessie's hard-hearted attitude toward Kobotsky as deadly, reminiscent of Kessler's accusation to Gruber in "The Mourners":

"Are you a Hitler or a Jew?" (_Barrel_ 13). But as Charles May has noted, it would seem wrong for a dead wife to get what is denied a living one ("The Bread of Tears" 654). And because of the hints in the story that Kobotsky is a fake, Malamud allows Bessie the stronger claim.

Still the story ends with the communion of Lieb and Kobotsky. "Kobotsky and the baker embraced and sighed over their lost youth. They pressed mouths together and parted forever" (_Barrel_ 191). They are united by their grief, by their appreciation of how rough life is.

The story "Behold the Key" stands out as a lesson in failed communion. Carl Schneider has taken his wife and two small children to Rome, Italy, where he hopes to complete the research for a dissertation on the Risorgimento. Although he has studied Italian culture for years and is fluent in Italian, Carl does not fit in easily in Rome. The plot hinges on his difficulty in finding an apartment, but the theme is his difficulty sympathizing with others and being flexible.

Carl is another one of Malamud's young men who at twenty-eight, feels old; he is seeking a new life in a new place, but he finds himself "so dissatisfied in this city of his dreams" (_Barrel_ 57). Unlike most Malamud heroes, Carl has a family. The young heroes are usually single and ripe for change, for a new life. Carl is encumbered by family responsibilities. His connection to his family does not seem especially warm: "He felt unpleasantly lonely for the first time since he had been married, and found himself desiring the lovely Italian women he passed in the street, especially the few who looked as if they had money" (_Barrel_ 57). Like many of Malamud's young heroes, he has a raggedy teacher-guide, an older man who has seen rough times: Bevilacqua -- an Italian real estate agent of sorts who operates an unlicensed business during his afternoon break from a poor paying job as a clerk. He was wounded twice during WWII, "once by the Americans advancing, and once by the Germans retreating" (*Barrel* 66). His father was killed by Allied bombs. Bevilacqua's wry comment is that "Americans dropped bombs everywhere. This was the advantage of your great wealth" (*Barrel* 67). Malamud suggests that Bevilacqua's life has been full of needless, even accidental, suffering -- often inflicted by foreigners.

The contrast between Bevilacqua and Carl is at the heart of the story. While Bevilacqua professes his fondness for Americans, Carl is curiously distant and critical with him and the other Italians he meets. Bevilacqua lives by his wits, using everything he can; but he seems willing to share the little he has. At one point he takes two apples from his briefcase and offers one to Carl who declines. Then after he peels and eats the apples he returns the peels to his briefcase and locks it. Does he have a use for the peels, too? Apple peel soup perhaps? Carl is not so resourceful. And Bevilacqua is willing to try anything that might bring him luck: he rubs a small wooden hunchback and has his wife kiss St. Peter's toe.

When Bevilacqua finally locates a suitable apartment for Carl and his family, the previous occupant, the former lover of the owner, a Contessa, has made off with the key. Though Carl is desperate and running out of time and money, he refuses to pay a bribe demanded by De Vecchis, the lover, for the key, even when the price is lowered to 15,000 lire, a third of a month's rent. Carl claims to be "a student of Italian life and manners" (*Barrel* 80), but he is superior to bribes. De Vecchis argues that Carl is the type that drives the Italians to the Communists: "You try to buy us -- our votes, our culture, and then you dare speak of bribes" (*Barrel* 79). Though De Vecchis is a comical, wild figure reeking of cologne, he speaks some truth. Carl has no right to feel so superior. And after rejecting De Vecchis, Carl turns around and offers the portiere a bribe for the Contessa's last name and new address so he can petition her himself.

The Contessa is unmoved and she reminds Carl again of all the Italians went through during the war. She tells him to come back in two weeks, after her honeymoon. Outside the Contessa's villa Carl meets Bevilacqua who says, "So you've betrayed me?" (_Barrel_ 81). Carl responds, "What do you mean 'betrayed'? Who are you, Jesus Christ?" (_Barrel_ 81). But Bevilacqua is Carl's intercessor with the Italian people; Carl's failure to accept him and to sympathize with him is a symptom of his lack of feeling for others.

When the apartment door is finally opened, the place has been wrecked by De Vecchis. Furniture, crockery, books are all destroyed. One wall has been "decorated with dirty words in six languages, printed in orange lipstick" (_Barrel_ 82). De Vecchis appears and says in Italian, "Behold the key" (_Barrel_ 82). Bevilacqua curses De Vecchis and De Vecchis shouts to Carl, "He lives for my death, I for his. This is our condition" (_Barrel_ 182). The death De Vecchis longs for would appear to be Bevilacqua's, but Carl takes things personally. Carl tells De Vecchis he is lying, "I love this country" (_Barrel_ 183). But De Vecchis throws the key at them and Bevilacqua ducks; "the key hit Carl on the forehead, leaving a mark he could not rub out" (_Barrel_ 83). Italy has made its impression on Carl.

In general the story attests to the difficulties people have in getting along, difficulties magnified by any cultural differences. Malamud is dealing here with failed dreams and poor communications; he is not always the creator of the optimistic ending. This theme of failed communion and cultures in conflict is later dealt with in greater detail in his novel _The Tenants_. And while Bevilacqua is something of a _mensch_-teacher, Carl is a poor student. Like

Mitka in "The Girl of My Dreams," Carl remains self-absorbed and fails to profit from his experience.

The two remaining stories in this collection, "A Summer's Reading" and "Angel Levine," both suggest the importance of people having faith in each other. In each story a character benefits from the belief someone has in him.

The thinner, less powerful story is "A Summer's Reading." George Stoyonovich is another of Malamud's failing young men, a loner. He is an unemployed high school drop-out who lives with his father and sister. In the evenings he walks the streets dreaming of a better life, a job, a house, a girl. But he does nothing to make the dream come true.

A neighbor, Mr. Cattanzara, a change-maker on the IRT who is always reading *The New York Times*, asks George what he does with all his time. George makes up a story that he is reading one hundred great books. Charles E. May has pointed out some ironies here: though George hates made-up stories, he makes up a story for Mr. Cattanzara; though he dislikes story books, he spends most of his time fantasizing ("Bernard Malamud's 'A Summer's Reading' " 12). May also noticed that the central irony of the story is that a made up story about reading becomes the truth ("Bernard Malamud's 'A Summer's Reading' " 12).

When Mr. Cattanzara, in a drunken state, encounters George and asks him about the books, he realizes that George has not read them. But he apparently does not reveal this to the neighbors, who have been looking on George with new respect since the change-maker passed around news of the reading list. Cattanzara's kindness to George, his consideration, links him to many other older characters in Malamud, like Morris Bober, who are willing to have faith in the young heroes and whose faith causes the young men to change. Cattanzara is indeed a change-maker because at the end of the story

George goes to the library and begins his reading, "struggling to control an inward trembling . . ." (*Barrel* 144). George is entering a new life.

In "A Summer's Reading" Malamud once again depicts a young man whose life is without direction who is suddenly given a purpose through his relationship with someone who cares. Again Malamud associates a love of great literature with a life of value. As Helen suggested books for Frank to read and Sobel gave books to Miriam, Mr. Cattanzara initiates George into the world of great books.

"Angel Levine," one of Malamud's finest stories, also deals with the necessity of having faith in someone. Manischevitz, the Job-like, long-suffering tailor, learns to have faith in Angel Levine, the Harlem angel-in-waiting.

Manischevitz is like many other of Malamud's older heroes. He suffers from physical and financial hardships. He has lost his tailor shop to fire, his son to war, and his daughter to "a lout" (*Barrel* 43). He is plagued with severe backaches which limit his ability to work even as a presser. His wife Fanny suffers from shortness of breath that the doctor has diagnosed as hardening of the arteries.

Manischevitz asks God why he has been singled out for all this suffering and then humbly begs for assistance: "Help now or tomorrow is too late. This I don't have to tell you" (*Barrel* 44). Later he questions his suffering again. He felt, "Upon him suffering was largely wasted. It went nowhere, into nothing: into more suffering" (*Barrel* 49).

The accent in Manischevitz' story is on man. In Malamud's world man suffers, but the suffering is not usually wasted, in spite of what Manischevitz may think.

Manischevitz' extreme need makes him susceptible to Angel Levine. Levine shows up one night at Manischevitz' apartment and offers his assistance. Levine is a black, Jewish angel with "a very white part in his black hair" (*Barrel* 40). The white part may reveal a dye job, a halo, or the white feather Manischevitz thinks he sees later as Levine flies off at the end of the story. Levine is on probation, as he says: "How long that will persist or even consist, I admit, depends on the outcome" (*Barrel* 47). He seems to be referring to the outcome of his assistance to Manischevitz.

Malamud has said, "I don't believe in the supernatural except as I invent it" (Field and Field 10). His invention serves him well in this story. Levine is charming and fantastic. And in the relationship between the tailor and the angel, Malamud again exhibits his genius for pairs of characters.

At first Manischevitz considers Levine a faker. But as his suffering continues, Manischevitz reconsiders and calls on Levine in Harlem. He finds the angel in Bella's honkey-tonk, looking "deteriorated in appearance" (*Barrel* 50). "Levine looked straight at Manischevitz with a haunted expression, but the tailor was too paralyzed to move or acknowledge it" (*Barrel* 50-51). Levine winks at Manischevitz and shimmies past the window with Bella.

Fanny's condition worsens, and the tailor dreams that Levine is a true angel. He returns to Harlem looking for Angel Levine. He goes to what he thinks is Bella's, but it turns out to be a black synagogue where he hears a discussion of *Neshoma* or soul. The point of the passage is the brotherhood of all people, united by a God who "put the spirit in all things" (*Barrel* 53), as the boy in the synagogue says -- a spirit that knows no color. These students of the Torah direct Manischevitz across the street to Bella's to find Levine.

This time Levine is dandied up in a derby, a checkered suit, and a pair of two-tone button shoes, and "To the tailor's dismay, a drunken look had settled on his formerly dignified face" (*Barrel* 54). Other patrons of Bella's try to keep Manischevitz out saying, "Exit, Yankel, Semitic trash" (*Barrel* 54). Levine's new sleazy appearance is not accounted for. Perhaps he has gotten involved in some illegitimate ventures. But most important, Malamud is suggesting that Levine and Manischevitz need each other; both do poorly on their own.

In spite of Levine's barbs and insults, Manischevitz decides to state his belief: "I think you are an angel from God" (*Barrel* 55). And abracadabra, Levine is a changed man. After saying, "How you have humiliated me" (*Barrel* 55), Levine goes to the men's room and returns in his old clothes. They go back together to the door of Manischevitz' flat and Levine says, "That's all been taken care of" (*Barrel* 56). Manischevitz chases the angel up to the roof and through a broken window in the locked door believes he sees Levine "borne aloft on a pair of magnificent black wings" (*Barrel* 56). A feather, presumably from the wings, drifts down; and "Manischevitz gasped as it turned white, but it was only snowing" (*Barrel* 56). The feather seems suggestive of the Holy Ghost descending on Christ at his baptism, and since Malamud is not above mixing Jewish and Christian lore, as he does most notably in *The Assistant* and *The Fixer*, the Holy Ghost is likely what he had in mind.

When the tailor returns to his flat, Fanny is healed and is energetically cleaning the place. Manischevitz says, "A wonderful thing Fanny. Believe me, there are Jews everywhere" (*Barrel* 56). Manischevitz' faith in the possibility of human divinity and in Levine's black magic transforms all three characters in this story. Malamud suggests that anyone might be an angel, particularly the low man on the social totem pole. Here two outsiders, two minorities, a Jew and a Black, are united by suffering and faith. The story is a testament to the possibility of human communion, but it is the only time in Malamud's fiction that Jews and Blacks achieve this communion. In the story "Black is My Favorite Color" and in the novel *The Tenants* Malamud presents a much bleaker view.

The Magic Barrel is Malamud's finest collection of short stories and it is a crucial book to any understanding of Malamud's hero. These stories contain Malamud's major preoccupations: the hero in love, the hero as his brother's keeper, and the hero learning to have faith in someone or profiting from someone's faith in him. These stories do speak of the primacy of human communion. And because the Nazi Holocaust is featured in seven of the twelve stories, Malamud underlines how urgent it is that people treat each other decently. Bessie Lieb and others mourn the lives already lost in Hitler's ovens. Malamud's theme of human mercy and sympathy becomes a life and death matter when seen in the shadow of Nazi inhumanity. The portrait of the hero in this collection is redrawn slightly in Seymour Levin of *A New Life*. Like Henry Levin/Freeman of "The Lady of the Lake," Seymour Levin seeks to escape a disappointing past, though not primarily to escape his Jewishness. However, Sy Levin does find a new life in love.

THE UNEXPECTED ROUTE TO *A NEW LIFE*

In 1961 Bernard Malamud published his third novel, *A New Life*. The hero Seymour Levin is a thirty-year-old New Yorker who arrives in Easchester, a fictional town in the Northwest, and begins his college teaching career at Cascadia College. The qualities that marked the earlier Malamud heroes are even more pronounced in Levin. The book is dominated by Levin's search for a new life, by his desire to overcome a disappointing past, and ultimately by his commitment to the love of a woman. Like the other heroes Levin is displaced: he is an Easterner in the West, A Jew among Gentiles, a single person among the married, a liberal among conservatives, a bearded man among the beardless. He is a loner with no family or close friends. He sees himself as a loser: a reformed alcoholic and a man unlucky in love. His movement toward a new life of connections and commitments in part results from his guilt over his sad past. As with most Malamud heroes, Levin's course in love does not run smooth, but at the conclusion of the novel Malamud leaves Levin with the promise of a richer life in love. Levin learns to love and be loved, to be more of a *mensch*.

Though Levin is a typical Malamud hero, other qualities in the novel are not typical of Malamud's fiction. *A New Life* is a departure in setting and scope from *The Assistant* and *The Magic Barrel*. Though Levin is a Jew, Jewishness does not figure prominently in the novel, except as one of many measures of his isolation. The rural Western setting contrasts with the cramped urban setting Malamud often uses. And much of the novel is about Levin in academia, a milieu far removed from Bober's grocery. Critical reaction to these shifts has been mixed. Some critics felt Malamud abandoned the magic and warmth of a rich world for a less interesting environment. Steven Marcus complained that in *A New Life* Malamud dealt with college life in Cascadia by "attempting to register the banal actualities rather flatly most of the time, without transfiguring them in his magical distorting mirror" (185). Others saw the shift in setting and subject as positive. John Hollander wrote that the novel can be seen as Malamud's attempt "to break out of a limited, almost regional area of performance" (139).

Malamud uses the academic setting to deal with politics for the first time. The novel, set in the early fifties, touches on the issues of those conservative years: the Red scare, censorship, and right wing reaction to the policies of the Roosevelt era. To Mark Shechner, "It is significant that the start of the Kennedy era in 1961 saw the publication of *A New Life*, in which Malamud announced his readiness to cast off stodginess and to mount a critique of intellectual and political reaction . . ." ("Jewish Writers" 208).

However, the novel is about more than Levin the college teacher with political concerns: it is also a novel about love and sex. The fate of Levin the teacher is linked to Levin the lover because he falls for Pauline Gilley, his boss's wife. Critical sentiment over the success of the two Levins, the two aspects of the novel, has been quite mixed. As Sheldon Hershinow notes: "We feel for Levin the man but find Levin the professor rather dull" (61).

Malamud said that *A New Life* was "the simple act of writing a novel out of my experience. The 'academic novel,' as such, simply doesn't interest me" (Field and Field 10). Part of the experience to which Malamud refers is his years spent as an instructor at Oregon State University. Louis D. Rubin agrees that *A New Life* is not primarily an academic novel, "not man as teacher, but teacher as man" (512).

In addition to the academic setting, nature and the woods figure prominently in the novel. Levin the city boy sets out to commune with nature, armed with binoculars and a copy of *Western Birds, Trees and Flowers*. At times he seems a comical sight, wearing a fedora and carrying an umbrella under his arm. In the novel nature and sex are closely tied together. It is in the woods that Levin first makes love with Pauline Gilley. Jessamyn West finds the pastoral element integral to the novel and to Levin's character: "his awakening to nature is as much a part of his new life as his awakening to love" (4). Charles Alva Hoyt, who sees Malamud as a Romantic writer, notes the novel's similarities to *Lady Chatterley's Lover*: the sex in the woods; the sterile husband Gilley like the crippled Chatterley; and the "cry against the machine age" in each novel, here Levin's battle against the values of a science and technology college (181).

Several important characteristics link Levin to other Malamud heroes. Typically, Levin carries the weighty baggage of a grim and tragic past with him into his search for a new life. His family life and love life have been a series of sorrows. He has had long bouts of alcoholism. All this tragedy and failure has formed his image of himself as a loser. In addition, like most of Malamud's heroes, Levin is displaced. He is at odds with his new environment and so his image of himself as a loner and a lonely man is aggravated. His often extreme fastidiousness reflects how tenuous his hold on his new life is. Yet, as is characteristic of the Malamud hero, Levin is a late-bloomer and still has a chance in life. In fact, all of Levin's sad experiences help catapult him into the new life he eventually finds.

First, one of the most distinctive markings of Malamud's heroes is their history of suffering. Levin's past is presented as one of the most grim and gloomy in all of Malamud. As he tells Pauline:

> The emotion of my youth was humiliation. That wasn't only because we were poor. My father was continuously a thief. Always thieving, always caught, he finally died in p r i s o n . My mother went crazy and killed herself. One night I came home and found her sitting on the kitchen floor looking at a bloody bread knife (*Life* 200).

He then goes on to relate his disappointments in love and his life as a drunk. For two years he drank and wasted away to about one hundred and ten pounds, till he woke up in someone's dirty cellar and saw the sunlight shining on his shoes. As he tells Pauline, "Then I thought, Levin, if you were dead there would be no light on your shoes in this cellar. I came to believe what I had often wanted to, that life is holy. I then became a man of principle" (*Life* 210).

After giving up drinking he went through a long period of depression. When he lifted himself out of the funk he sought a new life in a new career as a teacher. Malamud chose to give Levin this horrible past in order to intensify Levin's search for a new life, in order to underscore Levin's desperation.

But it is understandable that several critics have balked at the extreme nature of Levin's suffering. Frank Kermode says of Levin, "his necessary past is not authenticated. . ." (453). Leslie Fiedler finds it hard to believe in Levin the drunkard ("Malamud's Travesty Western" 216). And Stanley Edgar Hyman, who in general is very fond of this novel, argues: "Levin's past, when it is finally confessed to Pauline, seems unnecessarily melodramatic. . ." (35).

It is worth noting the similarities in the suffering pasts of three Malamud heroes of the early novels, Roy Hobbs, Frank Alpine and Seymour Levin. All three spent years wandering, being destitute; both Frank and Levin turned to drink. And in each of these three early novels Malamud relies on very brief descriptions of these sad periods in his heroes' lives; he does not depict them in much detail. Perhaps Malamud does cheat a little and inflate the sorrows of these young men without really showing the suffering. But he is not obligated to show every moment in his characters' lives; and, in general, these descriptions of the heroes' hard times are not so far-fetched. The descriptions serve Malamud's purpose: they explain why these young men are so frantic to find love and so ready to take chances.

Nevertheless, the particular complaint that it is hard to see Levin as a drunkard is valid. Though his alcoholism is mentioned several times in the novel, most notably in the opening sentence, and much is made early in the novel of his declining a cocktail at the Gilleys', Levin still does not seem to crave alcohol. He goes out to get beers with Sadek, the Syrian student who is also a boarder at Mrs. Beaty's, but Levin does not seem inclined to drink too much. Later at the Bullock's party he has several of George's powerful martinis but shows no great desire to get drunk. And when he and Pauline split up for a time, he "hid a brown bottle under the bed, then slept with it" (_Life_ 255). But again Malamud does not choose to depict Levin drunk. While Levin as a drunkard with a tragic past seems possible, Malamud does not make Levin's alcoholism convincing enough. It is a weakness in the characterization of Levin.

In general, Levin's suffering has formed his self image. Like many other Malamud heroes, Levin sees himself as a loser. For one thing, he has been unlucky in love. Like many other Malamud protagonists, Levin has had few women, and he says they were "the wrong kind. One or two made hash of me" (_Life_ 200). Of the first three encounters with women depicted in the course of the novel, only one results in sexual intercourse, and that encounter leaves Levin feeling guilty because the girl is a student. He feels she is too young for him and realizes their relationship goes against college rules. Though he gets much fulfillment from his relationship with Pauline, it is unlucky that she is married to Gerald Gilley. Levin is also a loser in his career. He is picked for his position only because Pauline liked his photo; it reminded her of a Jewish boy she used to know. He does not even realize he has been hired by a technical college which puts little emphasis on the liberal arts until he arrives in Cascadia to start teaching. And later in the novel he loses his bid for the chairmanship of the department when his campaign inevitably stirs up trouble.

Like many Malamud heroes, Levin is a displaced person and has a hard time fitting in. As a New Yorker, he engenders suspicion among the Westerners. They suspect that he feels superior and they distrust his liberal notions. When Gilley realizes Levin will not support him for the chairmanship of the department, he accuses Levin of being "an outsider looking in" (*Life* 288), an Easterner with a superior air. Levin does not know much about the sports popular in Cascadia: fishing, hunting, and golf. He even appears more dressed up than the other teachers like Gilley who favor sports clothes.

Levin is a loner, though not by choice. His parents are dead. When he starts his new career as a college teacher he tries hard to make friends, especially with Bucket and Fabricant. But Fabricant is too aloof and Bucket, too busy.

Levin has one quality that is new to the Malamud hero: he is very fastidious. He is organized, methodical, neatly dressed. Gilley comments on how shipshape Levin keeps his office when he warns Levin that Pauline is not so neat: Gilley adds, "I know how finicky you are about order and punctuality . . ." (*Life* 354). Levin's rage for order is especially noticeable in his yard work at Mrs. Beaty's. He rakes up leaves as they fall and is particularly wacky about the walnuts: "In bed, for hours he heard the nuts socking the wet earth in the dark. At dawn he quickly gathered them up, not at peace till all the walnuts were in and drying, and the tree was bare" (_Life_ 106). Levin's compulsions seem born of his fears of losing ground in his new life.

And like many of Malamud's heroes, Levin is a late-bloomer, late to come to his career, late to come to love. The sense that he is slightly out of step contributes to his charm and helps to explain his wilder side -- his love life and his campaign for the chairmanship.

Critics have looked for clues to Levin's character in his name. Ruth Wisse notes that "Lev," as Pauline calls Levin, means "love" in Hebrew (82). Tony Tanner notices Malamud's fondness for the name Levin in _A New Life_, "The Lady of the Lake," and "Angel Levine" ("Bernard Malamud and the New Life" 158). And several critics including Siegel ("Victims in Motion" 136) and Goodheart (104) associate Levin with the famous Levin of Tolstoy's _Anna Karenina_, who also tries to find communion with nature in a novel where the main action centers around an affair between Vronsky and Anna, like Pauline, a married woman with children. The epigraph for the novel from James Joyce's _Ulysses_ is also a source for Levin's name: "Lo, levin leaping lightens in eye-blink Ireland's westward welkin." "Levin" is an archaic word for "lightning"; "welkin," for "sky." So Levin is the lightning in westward Cascadia, perhaps also the lightening, the leavening.

The largest share of the novel is devoted to Levin the teacher. Unfortunately much of the description of academic life, while accurate and believable, is uninteresting. Several critics have noticed that while Malamud's attitude toward the academic life at Cascadia seems satiric, the extent of the detail and the literalness of the detail makes the novel, as Donald Malcolm said, "an unwitting tribute to much of what he [Malamud] sets out to deprecate" (105). Sheldon Norman Grebstein notes that the satire in *A New Life* "finally collapses under the weight of too much academic detail and too much debate . . ." (31). And Jonathan Baumbach has complained: "Where the novel goes dead, I feel, is in the literalness of its realism -- the scenes of academic 'life' (the internal politics of the Cascadia English Department) have the quality of transcription rather than vision" ("Malamud's Heroes" 98). Tony Tanner states: "I think *A New Life* is less successful than Malamud's other novels precisely because he strains to maintain uninterrupted continuity of realistic detail" ("Bernard Malamud and the New Life" 159).

The monotony of the academic detail contributes to the fact that Levin the teacher is not an entirely sympathetic figure. It is difficult to see why life at the college matters. But circumstances also conspire against him. He never completely recovers from the shock that Cascadia College is not a liberal arts institution, and the practical, technical bent of the school does much to undo Levin. Few of his students have any interest in literature, and department policy does little to encourage them. The freshman classes are dominated by *The Elements*, a dry grammar text written by Chairman Fairchild, a ludicrous figure whose dying words of wisdom to Levin: "The mys-mystery-of the in-fin--in-fin--in-fin . . . . In-fin-i-tive. Have-you con-sidered-its possi-bil-i-ties? To be-" (*Life* 304). The "bonehead" courses use *The Elements* and a workbook; and the regular freshmen are given a dull reader called *Science in Technology*. The department is directed to teach with the major objective of getting the students to pass the departmental grammar exam each term.

So even though Levin comes to teaching with a love of literature and an appreciation of the holiness of life, he feels he is defying authority if he lets any extraneous ideas creep into his lectures. And his students seem chiefly interested in getting good grades: when they dislike Levin or are doing poorly in his class, Gilley allows them to transfer to another instructor.

The two students described in the greatest detail are Nadalee Hammerstad and Albert O. Birdless, and Levin's relationship with each of them becomes unpleasant. At first Nadalee is eager for a sexual relationship with Levin, but he feels he is taking advantage of his role as her teacher. After their weekend at Nadalee's aunt's motel on the coast, Levin shrinks from Nadalee. And at the end of the term when she presses for a "B," a grade it turns out she earned but Levin's poor skills in computing denied her, it seems apparent that she was hoping for a good grade when she made herself available to Levin. The second student, Albert Birdless, is a nineteen-year-old who reminds Levin of a tugboat and whose eyes are "blue unsmiling marbles" (*Life* 169). Birdless, a "D" student at best, turns in an excellent paper ironically entitled "Build Your Own House and Like It" (*Life* 169). Levin realizes the theme on doing your own work is plagiarized and sets out to prove it. Birdless denies that he cribbed the paper and Levin is unable to find any source. Birdless begins to look bad: his eyes "were soiled with worry, and his face had taken on a yellowish cast. Levin felt bad: he had created a victim" (*Life* 174). Levin also feels guilty because he cheated once himself on a college exam. Levin decides to let Albert's grade stand, but Gilley gets the boy transferred to Avis Fliss's class. Nadalee and Albert O. even have names that suggest they have nothing to offer, and the experiences with both of them alienate Levin from his students and cause him sorrow and remorse.

For a person drawn to teaching by his ideals, his passions, Levin is curiously withdrawn from his students in general. Some of his students sleep through his classes but Levin learns to accept it. When Levin keeps his required office hours he seems to hope no one will visit him. When office hours end, Levin hides behind a closed door. In Levin's defense, though, it must be said that much of the chit-chat and socializing that goes on in the department among those who are more personable than Levin is not especially intellectual anyway. *Consumer Reports* ratings and sports are the chief topics of conversation among the teachers. When they congregate in the coffee room they hear Fairchild hold forth on "creeping socialism" and "the tyranny of the New Deal" (*Life* 100). Only Bucket and a few others spend any extra time with students. Bullock tutors the athletes but gets paid for it by the athletic department.

In spite of his commitment to teaching, or to the idea of teaching anyway, his career seems doomed from the start. Gilley warns: "What we don't want around here are troublemakers" (*Life* 37). And when they first meet Levin, both Gilley and Professor Fairchild feel compelled to discuss the case of Leo Duffy with Levin, as an implicit warning. Leo was a troublemaker, a liberal, and an "Easterner" from Chicago: he was hounded from the university as a "fellow-traveling radical" (*Life* 46). Levin inherits Duffy's office and his fate. Levin clashes with the establishment at Cascadia College over many of the same issues as Duffy, though his clashes are more subdued at first; and Levin, like Duffy, is really dismissed from the school because of an affair with Pauline Gilley. In addition to the Duffy resemblance, Fairchild sees in Levin an image of his own Papa -- "an incurable drunkard" (*Life* 50). So at the start of his new life out West, Levin is weighted down not only by the disappointments of his own past but also by the failures of those he resembles.

In spite of his shortcomings, Levin has a real respect for literature and ideas. The reader hopes Levin will succeed in his new career as college teacher. He does make an effort to fight the censorship of the Hemingway story "Ten Indians," and he suggests that the department scrap Fairchild's

Elements. And three quarters of the way into the book he changes toward his students. This change occurs after his affair with Pauline, while they are separated. The love he has shared with her has made him warmer toward others. He had allowed his disappointments in his students' work "to sour him against them." (*Life* 273). But suddenly he realizes: "Still they were human and possible" (*Life* 274).

Just as he is renewed as a teacher he has a thought: "It only takes one good man to make the world a little better" (*Life* 275). Unfortunately this noble, if banal, thought leads him to a second thought which causes him no end of trouble: "Holy smoke, Levin thought, suppose I were chairman" (*Life* 275).

It is in the race for the chairmanship that Levin becomes most unattractive. Though his aim at first appears worthwhile, his means are suspect. The first indication that Levin is not above professional intrigues comes when he happens upon George Bullock's memo to the football coach, listing teachers that athletes should avoid as "lukewarm if not downright unsympathetic to athletes" (*Life* 276). Later in the day Levin sneaks back into Bullock's office, takes the list to the library to be photostated and returns it to Bullock's desk.

By the time Levin withdraws his support for C. D. Fabricant for the chairmanship and announces his own candidacy, he is becoming more and more corrupt. He tells Fabricant he will not support him when C. D. admits he stopped the defense of Leo Duffy because Gilley showed him a picture of Leo and Pauline nude at the beach. Levin, while curiously not denying that proof of an affair between Leo and Pauline should be grounds for a dismissal, finds the evidence of the picture described to him quite circumstantial. Levin says to Fabricant, "I want you to know I like you personally but it's the principle involved" (*Life* 298). This talk of principle has an ironic ring because Levin himself has had an affair with Pauline. Levin then tells Fabricant he will run for the chairmanship himself.

During Levin's brief campaign he breaks into Gilley's office and Avis' office and threatens each of them with a kind of blackmail. He breaks into Gilley's office to get Duffy's folder and the photo of Pauline and Duffy. The idea of the picture aroused Levin's "prurience" (*Life* 299) and likely his jealous curiosity; but Duffy's folder is empty. Then when Gerald Gilley realizes Levin will not support him for the chairmanship and their cold war escalates, Levin threatens Gilley that he will tell everyone about George's "shit-list" and about George's extra income as a tutor of his own students, the outstanding athletes (*Life* 309). Then Levin does pass the list around but cuts off George's signature.

When Levin starts campaigning actively he creates "a terrible discord" (*Life* 318). His next act of espionage occurs when he sniffs Avis' orange blossom perfume in his office, realizes she has been snooping on him, and returns the favor. He finds her notebook detailing his activities, a letter from Pauline to Levin copied in Avis' hand, and two letters from Duffy to Avis. The first Duffy letter suggests an affair: "Dear Avis -- I am most grateful for last night, Yours, Leo" (*Life* 321). This opportunity for revenge is especially sweet for Levin since Avis was the first one to tell Levin of the Pauline-Duffy affair. So Levin confronts Avis and threatens to reveal his findings. He wants her to keep Pauline's letter to herself.

This snooping Levin has bothered at least one critic. Paul Pickrel claims: "Levin's tendency to rummage through other people's drawers and to make blackmailing use of what he finds seems to strike neither him nor his creator as morally reprehensible, but it is not easy to square with Levin's presumed moral awareness" (120). But Levin does feel guilty when he snoops in Gilley's office and he thinks of himself as a thief like his father. He realizes, "The nature of evil: one wrong door opened untold others" (*Life* 299). And Sidney Richman has noted "the role of Cascadia in eliciting the corruption in Levin" (81). Though it may not be justification for his own behavior, Levin is certainly surrounded by some unattractive people. Gilley spied on Pauline and Duffy and then secretly taped her confession of an affair with Levin. George Bullock and Avis Fliss readily betray their colleagues: George's list effects a boycott of worthwhile instructors, and Avis' spying includes spying on anyone associated with Levin.

Most importantly, the notion of Levin's moral development as zigzag is in keeping with the course of most of the Malamud heroes. Their search for a new life is not smooth. They are their own worst enemies. They give in to their vices rather readily. Frank Alpine continues to steal, Roy Hobbs accepts a bribe, and Seymour Levin sinks to these departmental intrigues. But these lapses serve two purposes. They redirect the hero's attention to what is really of value to Malamud. Levin does his spying and blackmailing when he is separated from Pauline; and it is Levin's love for Pauline that will make a new life possible, not his drive to be department chairman. I do not believe Malamud sees the chairmanship as a worthwhile goal for Levin. And a second purpose is served when Levin's guilt over his failings, like the guilt of Roy and Frank, in part provides the motivation for a new life on new terms at the end of the novel.

Levin's relationship with Pauline is not only the basis for Levin's new life, it gives the book most of its life as well. It is curious that the affair is the most memorable portion of the book though it takes up relatively few pages. Their affair does not begin until page 198 and by page 251 they separate until

Pauline reappears on Levin's doorstep in the last pages of the book. The fact that the book noticeably picks up speed when Levin and Pauline have their first encounter in the woods is one measure of the failings of much of the academic detail. Though many of the college scenes are entertaining and the types like Gilley and Fairchild are certainly believable, too much of the book is devoted to the academic material that Malamud does not seem to care for himself.

It is when Malamud writes of Levin in love that both Levin and Malamud come to life. The first two hundred pages of the novel are bearable in part because Malamud fits in three brief romantic forays for Levin. The first is the most humorous. Levin and his fellow boarder at Mrs. Beaty's, Sadek, a Syrian graduate student majoring in sanitary bacteriology, set out to roam the streets of Easchester. Sadek woos a waitress in a bar, but he gets arrested for "pissing against a wall" (*Life* 78). Levin takes advantage of Sadek's misfortune, which was caused by Sadek's fear of contacting germs in the tavern toilet. Levin and Laverne, the waitress, take a cab out to her brother-in-law's farm. As they begin to make love on a horse's blanket he tells her, "Your breasts . . . smell like hay." And she responds, "I always wash well" (*Life* 81). Alas, too soon, Sadek appears fresh from jail, snatches most of their clothes, and leaves in a waiting cab. The unlucky couple hike back to town, Laverne wearing Levin's pants. When they arrive at Laverne's home, Levin suggests they meet again; but Laverne is not interested: "Don't think those whiskers on your face hide the fact that you ain't a man" (*Life* 85).

While the unconsummated sex may suggest something ludicrous in Levin, it more significantly reflects Malamud's attitude toward sex. Sex is not easily come by for the Malamud hero, and Malamud seems to frown on sex without love, or the possibility of love. Just as Levin was approaching Laverne he "considered falling in love with her, but gave up the idea" (*Life* 81). Half a page later Sadek appears. Still, the scene is so farcical that it detracts from the seriousness of Levin's problems.

The next encounter is with Avis Fliss, fellow instructor at the college. Avis visits Levin in his office on a Saturday night. After some preliminaries, including the reading of poetry, Levin fetches a blanket from her office and she begins to undress. But of course, in typical Malamud style, they are interrupted. Gilley knocks at the door. When Levin and Avis resume she takes off her brassiere and "her breasts, handsome under clothes, hung like water-filled balloons from her chest" (*Life* 133). Levin shivers but is prepared to go on, thinking "Still for a starving man --" (*Life* 133). But when he touches her left breast she stops him: "Not that one, it hurts" (*Life* 133). She, like Memo Paris of *The Natural*, has sick breasts. Avis has a benign fibroma, and her "good" breast has a scar from the surgery to remove an earlier tumor. Levin is turned off and draws on his pants, saying: "When we have a better place, when you feel better . . . I don't want to hurt you" (*Life* 134). Avis leaves in a huff.

The third encounter is the one with Nadalee Hammerstad, Levin's student. Nadalee shows her favor for Levin by nuzzling "her hard little breast against Levin's lonely elbow" (*Life* 136), as he is evaluating her themes in his office. Days of turmoil follow for Levin; he fantasizes, rationalizes, and takes cold showers. "He argued with himself: I have evil thoughts, expense to my spirit; they represent my basest self" (*Life* 139). The degree of this guilt, especially even before their weekend together, seems a bit extreme; but Levin feels he should not take advantage of the fact that the girl is a student. Then after a chance encounter in the book store on Nadalee's twentieth birthday, Levin calls her and asks her to go for a walk. She soon reveals that she wants "real companionship" (*Life* 142) and promptly arranges a scheme for a weekend at her aunt's motel on the coast.

Though Nadalee eagerly awaits Levin, he has a hard time getting to their rendezvous. He is frightened by the mountains and his twenty mile per hour crawl angers other drivers. His car overheats and he is pushed to a garage for a "reverse flush" (*Life* 146). When he is again on his way he is run off the road by a log truck carrying "the largest, most terrifying hunk of wood Levin had ever seen; it looked like a threat to humanity" (*Life* 147). These phallic logs dog his whole trip, a not so subtle insult to his manhood. Finally a farmer with a tractor pulls Levin out of the ditch and then tries to get Levin to extract a tooth, a Freudian image of castration. Levin's next impediment is a mule in the road. Levin tries to woo the mule out of the road with a Life Saver; but when he retreats in defeat to his car and lays his head on the wheel, the sound of the horn budges the mule. When Levin is on the road again he fears he is lost and stops someone who gives him the wrong directions. Levin thinks of himself, "It served him right for his evil intentions" (*Life* 151). But Levin gets a whiff of the ocean and realizes he is headed in the right direction. He arrives at the motel where he is greeted by Nadalee in a sheer nightie.

The extent of Levin's difficulties in reaching Nadalee seem a kind of pre-pentance for an ill-gotten lay. His ridiculous struggle makes any gratification he does get seem anti-climactic. After the weekend Levin is plagued with guilt and fear. He feels "no genuine affection for Nadalee" (*Life* 155), and he is afraid she will leak news of the affair, as she eventually does.

The incidents with the three women taken together form a progression. The first encounter is interrupted through no real fault of Levin; the second encounter is interrupted by Levin; and though the Nadalee affair does result in sex, Levin is left the worse for it. These encounters serve as interludes before the feature length relationship with Pauline, and the disappointments highlight the value of the affair with Pauline in spite of its complications.

Several things are noteworthy in Levin's dealings with all these women. First, their breasts figure prominently. They become such a preoccupation that the novel takes on a "Goldilocks and the Three Bears" quality: These breasts smell like hay; these breasts are too large, too sick; these breasts are too small. Nadalee's breasts are just right, but they are forbidden. Much is made of Pauline's small breasts, especially in Levin's mind, since to him "her poor chest" reminds him of "the American prairie" (*Life* 17). The size of women's feet is a second common preoccupation in Malamud's fiction. Nadalee's small feet, "her childlike ballet-slippered feet" (*Life* 140) attract Levin but cause him guilt, reminding him how young she is. Pauline's big feet bother Levin: "He was irritated by her long empty shoes on the floor" (*Life* 18). These feet and breasts remind Levin of the women's weaknesses and vulnerabilities.

It is also interesting that Levin is not especially handsome: Avis even tells him, "For a person who isn't handsome, Seymour, you act as though you were" (*Life* 129). Yet the women in the novel are very attracted to him and when he shows the slightest interest, attempts the most minimal wooing, the women begin to make arrangements. They take charge: Laverne gets Levin to the barn and gets the blanket positioned, Avis suggests the office and sends Levin for the blanket, and Nadalee plans the whole weekend with Levin. Later Pauline takes charge much of the time. Sometimes the discussion of logistics is strikingly unromantic and gives the first three encounters in particular all the charm of deals struck over used cars. When sex begins, it seems fast, mechanical, and without preliminaries.

But the relationship with Pauline does produce more romance, love, and sex, and does result in the biggest changes in Levin. It is with Pauline that

Levin learns to give and accept love, to take chances, and in the end, to take on responsibilities. Pauline, in her own flawed way, has her place in the long line of Malamud teachers that includes Iris Lemon, Morris Bober, and Pinye Salzman. She has a warm heart and she has the courage to act on love.

Levin is aware of Pauline and interested in her from the very start. He is drawn to her, always noticing her features, her clothing. And she is drawn to him. When she first meets him she asks, " 'Have you any pictures of your family in your wallet? Or perhaps a sweetheart?' She laughed a little" (*Life* 5).

Two incidents that occur during Levin's first visit to the Gilley's are often cited as proof that Levin is a *schlemiel*: Pauline drops some hot tuna casserole on Levin and then the Gilley's little boy Erik urinates on him. But there is another way to view these incidents: Pauline and Erik are marking off their territory, branding Levin for domestic duty. Pauline manages to get Levin into her husband's pants after the hot tuna baptism. And when Erik, hysterical over Levin's storytelling, urinates on Levin, Pauline gets Levin to wear Gilley's underwear, "a pair of Gerald's French-back shorts" (*Life* 13). She insists on the underwear, to the point of tears. What all this suggests is Pauline's early attraction to Levin; it does not make Levin a *schlemiel*.

During his first evening with the Gilleys, Levin slips easily into domesticity. When Gilley is putting Erik to bed, Pauline sits crocheting, and Levin peruses the book shelf. Pauline begins by listing Gerald's accomplishments, but implicit in her comments is a dissatisfaction, a disappointment in Gerald. She says, "If Gerald were among people who were doing literary research and writing, I think he would too" (*Life* 15). While she shows Levin Gilley's *PMLA* article and his photos, she seems to be trying to convince herself of Gilley's worth. Then she shows Levin a picture of her bearded Papa, "A wonderful man --

very affectionate and maturely generous" (*Life* 16). Pauline has warm thoughts of the bearded. But her husband Gilley suggests that Levin shave his beard, saying, "This is a sort of beardless town" (*Life* 23).

As Levin and Pauline talk, Levin begins to find her attractive. Though he notes her faults, flat chest, big feet, "Levin thought her, despite her longness and lacks, an interesting-looking woman" (*Life* 17). She begins to ask Levin about himself and he reveals more than he intended. He tells her he is starting out in a new life: "Now that I can -- ah -- move again I hope to make better use of -- things" (*Life* 18).

When Gilley finally does come downstairs, after having fallen asleep in Erik's room, his aggressive affability seems an intrusion. He offers Levin a drink again, saying, "It'll relax you" (*Life* 20). Pauline and Levin are more comfortable with each other than either is with Gilley.

It gets late and Pauline insists that Levin spend the night. After he goes to sleep he hears Erik calling "papa" and tries to rouse himself (*Life* 24). "On the point of sleep he had the odd feeling he was being covered by a second blanket. Or maybe that was what she was doing to the children across the hall" (*Life* 24). So the conclusion of the novel, when Pauline and Levin drive off with the children, is suggested even in this first chapter.

During his early days in Easchester Levin makes two unannounced visits to the Gilleys'. The first time Gilley is out and Pauline answers the door dressed in "tight violet toreador pants" (*Life* 60). She has been painting chairs and when Levin sees how embarrassed and distracted she is, he leaves. On the second occasion, on the same day Levin has fallen on the wet sidewalk at school and cracked his head, he surprises the Gilleys in domestic disarray. The children are not in bed, the dishes are not done, and Pauline and Gerald are fighting. Through a partially opened kitchen door, Levin hears Gerald tell

Pauline that they must entertain more often and sees Pauline fling a butter dish at the kitchen clock. But during this visit Levin is again noticing Pauline and what she is wearing. She changes into a green wool dress: "Now, with the same apparatus, the green dress, her hair brushed, she seemed to glow. She knew how to use what she had, not a bad talent" (*Life* 126). As he is leaving he shows her his lump, his wound from the fall. "She touched the bump gently with cold fingers, Levin conscious she smelled like a flower garden" (*Life* 127). She offers to get him some ice. Pauline, unlike Levin, is not turned off by hurts or wounds. Once again Levin and Pauline are drawing each other out, drawing out the best in each other.

During the department potluck at the opening of the term Pauline cares for Levin, introduces him to people, sees that he gets enough to eat. When Fairchild formally presents Levin to the faculty and their families, Erik lets out a big "Hooray," again expressing his approval of Levin. "Levin quickly sat down. When his color diminished to cool he noticed that Pauline's face still retained an embarrassed glow" (*Life* 95). She is embarrassed by Erik's cheer, a verbal echo of her own feelings.

During the Christmas break Levin gets a dreadful cold and as a result falls "into sadness, an old kind; this lonely man in the dark of a dirty room" (*Life* 164). Just as his thoughts light on "the sad golden beauty of a fifth of whiskey" (*Life* 164), Pauline appears to try to nurse him back to health. She brings medicine, lemons, oranges, cookies, and her knitting; and she offers to read him Hardy's *The Woodlanders*, which depicts a woman nursing a sick man. He is cold to her, closing his eyes and waiting for her to leave; still he dreams of whiskey. But her visit does exert a healing influence on Levin. When she leaves, he goes out for a walk. The rain has stopped and suddenly, "His thirst was gone. . . . He was once more the improved Levin. . . . He regretted not having said a kind word to her; but he felt like a man entering a new life and entered" (*Life* 165). It is significant that thoughts of Pauline and a new life occur in a single sentence.

By the time the Bullocks have their cocktail party, Levin and Pauline are clearly interested in each other, and any affection Levin once felt for Gilley has diminished. Gilley has started transferring students, including Birdless, out of Levin's classes. Levin realizes, "This man is my enemy" (*Life* 178). The feelings between Pauline and Levin become more intense and more explicitly sexual. Both are loosened up by George's powerful martinis. When Levin sees Pauline he thinks: "She was attractive in a tight black dress. A small veil floating before her eyes from a wisp of a hat created a mystery where none had been before. Who was the masked lady?" (*Life* 182).

Later Levin seeks Pauline out in the garden, suitably enough. He is in an intense state: "Levin sighed at the stars and was at once unexpectedly emotional" and "the lights of the town below affected him as though he were listening to music" (*Life* 185). He is primed for some encounter; and when he smells smoke, he looks around and sees Pauline standing amid the fir trees. He apologizes for his rudeness when he was sick and she answers with a very direct question: "Don't you like me?" (*Life* 185). He protests that he does like her. When she asks him, "What do you do for sin, Mr. Levin?" (*Life* 186), he guffaws. Suddenly she mentions Gerald and her sick children. The thought of sin in the garden causes her guilt even before the fact. Pauline is a reluctant Eve, offering herself and then backing off.

Levin becomes more attracted to her, noticing that her figure is better than he realized. She complements him on his beard, "sensitive lips" and "kind eyes" (*Life* 188). Then he tells her, "Ah, but you're a lovely woman" (*Life* 188). When Gilley appears on the verandah above the patio, Levin and

Pauline are silent and still until he goes back into the house. Gilley is already the odd man out.

In these scenes Malamud makes it clear that Pauline and Levin are thinking of more than simple sexual diversion. Pauline asks Levin what he wants in life and he says, "Order, value, accomplishment, love." "Love last?" Pauline asks. "Love any time" (*Life* 189). She asks Levin if he is unhappy and if they are both misfits. Soon she is listing Gerald's good qualities, again in such a way that she is implicitly expressing her dissatisfaction. When Levin and Pauline briefly discuss Leo Duffy, she says that she admired Duffy. Levin says, "I have his office now" (*Life* 190). He will soon follow Duffy's tracks in an affair with Pauline.

Levin offers to take Pauline home because Gilley is sick and drunk. In the car Pauline tells Levin she knows him, "Who you really are" (*Life* 192). Then she tells him Gerald is sterile and the children are adopted. He says, "I don't want to hear about his personal troubles" (*Life* 192). But soon she is asleep with her head on Levin's shoulder.

When they get to her house, Levin fits quickly into the domestic scene as Pauline stretches out on the couch. To Levin, "The legs were exciting though the long black shoes were like stiff herrings aimed skyward. Her chest had the topography of an ironing board" (*Life* 193). Levin tries to pluck her hat off, but she holds on, saying, "Stop, it's my only defense" (*Life* 193). Soon she is asleep and Levin is tending to the children upstairs. He gets them to sleep and thinks, "The poor orphans" (*Life* 193); he bursts into tears. He is ready to care for them; and with his own parents dead, he quickly identifies with the fact that they are orphans.

Next, on a sunny day in the end of January Levin heads to the woods with his copy of *Western Birds, Trees, and Flowers*. Deep in the magical woods Levin comes upon a green clearing where he spots a red-headed woodpecker, a Seattle wren, a chickadee, and Pauline Gilley. "Her presence in the woods aroused a renewed momentary sadness, as if he had come too late to the right place, familiar situation of his dreams" (*Life* 197).

But soon they are making love. It is a perfect scene, the natural setting a sharp contrast to the scenes of Levin's previous troubles with women and to the terrain of the English Department. It is easy to see a man and a woman meeting by chance in the woods and making love, momentarily free of the pressures of social constraints. Levin marvels at his good fortune. "Lying on the coats, Pauline raised her hips and drew back her skirt, to Levin the most intimate and beautiful gesture ever made for him" (*Life* 199).

It rains and they huddle under Levin's umbrella under an old elm tree. Levin tries not to think of the future. Pauline tells him not to worry, "I mean if you have any regrets you're not bound to me" (*Life* 199). But in no time the connection between them deepens as Levin tells her his life story, all about his sad past. Pauline is moved to tears and promises not to interfere with his plans for a new life: "We shan't meet again" (*Life* 202).

During the next week Levin thinks of Pauline and mulls over the possibility of an affair. Though he fears a return of his old self, his old failures, he wonders what love with Pauline could bring them both: "Could he, with Pauline, be more than he was?" (*Life* 204). He then decides, "if I have her again I must keep romance apart from convenience. Love goes with freedom in my book" (*Life* 206). And, as if by magic, Pauline appears at his door.

During their affair Levin and Pauline mature, and the warmth and intimacy between them makes the affair seem a "holy adultery," as Stanley Edgar Hyman calls it (33). The intensity of their connection keeps the affair from being tawdry. Malamud presents Levin and Pauline as different from the other characters in the book, like Gilley, who is warm and ingratiating only in order to get ahead.

But because Pauline is married, because the town is so small, the affair quickly becomes complicated: "The forest had shrunk to a double bed" (*Life* 211). The sex between them starts out perfect, but in no time Levin is experiencing "a fiery pain in the ass" (*Life* 213) after intercourse. When this has happened several times, Levin consults a doctor who tells him it is "tinsion" (*Life* 214) and prescribes relaxants and anti-spasmodics. But Levin tears up the prescriptions. He at first thinks the complications of love with a married woman have caused the pain, but he then concludes, "Love ungiven had caused Levin's pain" (*Life* 215). Though he has doubts and misgivings, Levin falls in love -- the "human-woven mystery" (*Life* 217).

When he tells Pauline he loves her, she puts her hands over her ears, fearful of the consequences of love. But then she, too, admits love: "I love you, Lev" (*Life* 219). When they are in love, things become even more complicated and they feel more guilty. Levin feels he is betraying Gilley, interfering with another man's "rights" (*Life* 222). Pauline has increasing difficulty in getting out of the house, and "She looked sometimes as though it were all too much for her" (*Life* 234). Levin grows wild and desperate. He steals a picture of faculty members and their wives from a photo shop window and cuts out Pauline's picture.

Levin and Pauline begin to talk of a future together after a time of fulfillment in bed, but Mrs. Beaty catches Pauline leaving Levin's apartment and the affair becomes more difficult than ever. Levin moons over Pauline. Once, like Oliver Mellors in *Lady Chatterley's Lover*, he stands across from her house one night. A neighbor calls the police. Once he stares at her through his binoculars at a basketball game and overhears a student of his commenting on the bearded teacher who is "nuts about some dame" (*Life* 246).

Levin shaves his beard and he and Pauline meet in motels outside of town. She fears losing the children and her guilt takes a toll. Soon she is unable to have an orgasm and is tired of sex. "Now we have truly come to adultery, Levin thought" (*Life* 249). After a fourth frustrating time in a motel, Levin and Pauline oversleep and do not arrive back in town until the next morning. Levin worries whether Pauline has gotten in safely, but she does not let him know. He resolves not to see her till summer, and their separation begins.

But Levin is grief stricken. He debates the morality of the affair and decides one moment to give her up: "The strongest morality resists temptation; since he had not resisted he must renounce the continuance of the immoral" (*Life* 258). But he is still obsessed with Pauline: "Unable to resist the beauty of the spring night, love still tormenting despite all his exertions, he left his dreary room and walked in the direction of Pauline's house" (*Life* 259). He is interrupted by the sudden appearance of Avis Fliss, who gives Levin the details of the Duffy case and Pauline's relations with Duffy in hopes that Levin will support Gerald Gilley rather than C. D. Fabricant for chairman. Avis' gossip causes Levin to think of himself as a second Duffy, a failure, a man who chose badly; and he gradually gives up thoughts of Pauline, "Duffy, exposed by Avis, made fast the trembling quittance" (*Life* 266). Levin begins to write critical papers and becomes enmeshed in the race for the chairmanship.

During their month of separation both Pauline and Levin try to bury their love, Levin with more success. He pours his energies into the campaign, with some results. In one of the funnier academic scenes in the novel, Meredith Schultz offers support for Levin from an adjoining stall in the men's room:

"You have more friends than you know" (*Life* 319). But Levin's chances still look slim and a victory would not seem to be a significant step toward a new life anyway because Levin's character sinks to its lowest level during the campaign and the department is no prize.

Still, when Pauline returns to haunt Levin's doorstep, in spite of the fact that he is "moved to see her" (*Life* 323), he avoids her for several mornings in a row. He runs from her instinctively and then mulls over their difficulties in bed and the Duffy affair. When he resolves to forget his Duffy obsession, he then tells himself the break with Pauline is best for her.

Pauline calls Levin, and Mrs. Beaty -- suddenly quite sympathetic to Pauline -- begs Levin to talk to her. He says, "I'm in an election. I have my future to think of" (*Life* 328). After Levin avoids Pauline two more times, Mrs. Beaty insists that he talk to Pauline one rainy morning as she and her two children wait outside under a tree.

Mrs. Beaty invites her in. When Levin and Pauline meet, he is unable to resurrect any feeling: "The depression . . . hung in him like a dead animal. Where's my love gone? He wanted to warn her something was wrong; instead he hid it" (*Life* 330). Levin has already described the serious depression he underwent in the past; he himself links his lack of feeling now to the earlier period. He tells Pauline, "I've been through it before. I know what it is" (*Life* 341). The fact that Levin sees himself as depressed, rather than simply out of love, suggests that his separation from Pauline has not been good for him. His depression is linked to his old self, his old lonely life.

Both Levin and Pauline explain they had split for the sake of the other. Pauline says that it was at Fairchild's funeral, suitably enough, that she realized she still loved Levin. So the death of one chairman leads to the certain loss of Levin's campaign for chairman. But Levin is not eager to embrace Pauline in his life until she tells him of Duffy's suicide. Levin, who always identifies Duffy with his old and worst self, who considers himself "the extension of Duffy's ghost" (*Life* 325), likely fears that his own death, or the death of his new self, is foretold in Duffy's. Suddenly, in fear, "Levin sprang to her and they desperately embraced" (*Life* 334).

Soon Levin engages in the most intense internal debate of the novel. He considers fleeing to freedom and considers his plans for his new life as a college teacher. But Malamud puts Levin's thoughts of choosing life at Cascadia College, rather than a life with Pauline, in pathetic terms: "Now that classes were over, he was moved by an oppressive desire to rush to Humanities Hall and teach all who would listen, the mysteries of the infinitive" (*Life* 335). The image suggests Levin slouching into Fairchild's simple-minded and rather senile path.

At the peak of his debate, Levin goes to a bar. For the first time in the novel there is a sense of a reformed alcoholic about to go on a binge. But in his despair he orders "Love" (*Life* 338) and flees, resolving to love Pauline. When he sees her, "More than once he told himself he was no longer in love with her" (*Life* 339), but Pauline plans to tell Gerald all, and Levin agrees. Pauline also suggests that she and Levin refrain from sex till they are married: "I want to come to you with a little innocence saved up" (*Life* 341). This abstinence is a strange touch in the novel, second only to the promise Gilley later extracts from Levin to give up college teaching. It would seem that if Levin and Pauline ever needed sex, they need it now. Malamud may be hinting that Pauline is in a depression of her own -- tired of sex and fearing frigidity, hoping to give sex some meaning. Or, more simply, she may still be feeling very guilty.

After Gilley learns the news, he confronts Levin at his room at Mrs. Beaty's. He tells Levin that Pauline picked him for the teaching job in an effort to replace Duffy. He begins to warn Levin of Pauline's shortcomings and then suggests a deal: "I'm willing to forgive and forget if you will resign and leave. I promise you good references" (*Life* 345). Later he offers a second deal in a note he sends Levin; he throws in one year of teaching for Levin at Cascadia College. Levin declines and Gilley spreads word of the affair and the marital break up. Levin gets no votes in the election and receives a dismissal "for good and sufficient cause of a moral nature" (*Life* 346) from President Labhart. "Levin put his fist through Duffy's window" (*Life* 346). Like Duffy, Levin is drummed out of the college as "a frustrated Union Square radical" (*Life* 346) and an adulterer.

Next Gilley tries to prevent the divorce by threatening Pauline that he will keep the children. When Levin hears this news he makes one feeble comment to Pauline: "Suppose I said I didn't want them?" But Pauline counters, "I don't think you would" (*Life* 349). So Levin sets out to ask Gilley for the children, but with misgivings about Pauline and the children: "He wanted to give Gilley back everything he had taken from him and more" (*Life* 350).

Gilley's response to Levin's plea for the children is a detailed, hilarious and misogynistic account of women, as Gilley says, "women as they really are and not as they pretend to be, or as they are when it's a question of going to bed with them" (*Life* 351). Gilley lists all Pauline's particular liabilities, from poky cooking to chronic constipation and irregular menstruation. He warns Levin of the childrens' colds, allergies, and doctor bills. Finally Gilley agrees to give up the children only on the condition that Levin promise to give up college teaching forever. Levin agrees to the terms after he learns they have no chance to win the children in court. Gilley not only has a tape of Pauline's confession of an affair with Levin, including her admission that she left the children unattended at times, but Gilley also has learned of Levin's affair with Nadalee.

This promise of Levin's to give up teaching college is a little far-fetched. Though it is easy to see that Gilley is desperate for some sort of revenge and does not really want the children himself, this particular request seems so arbitrary. And because the academic portion of the novel is so undermined by its absurd humor, it is hard to accept Gilley's request as one Levin would be honorbound to follow. However, Levin is depicted as a sincere man who would keep a pledge. But Levin agrees because Gilley leaves him no choice, and Gilley trusts him to keep the promise. "I'll take your word, you're a fanatical type" (_Life_ 360).

At the very conclusion of the novel, Levin is still in doubt. Though he has told Gerald Gilley he can take on the responsibility of a wife and two children, "Because I can, you son of a bitch" (_Life_ 360), he still fears the loss of freedom. He wonders if "The prison was really himself. . . . Unless the true prison was to stick it out chained to her ribs" (_Life_ 362). But again when he contemplates fleeing, he is haunted by the memory of his years "in stinking clothes" and "bug-infested room" (_Life_ 363), and he wanders to Pauline's house. He hears her playing the violin and recognizes the music. Her image in the window is a homey contrast to thoughts of his dreary past.

The next day Pauline tells Levin she is pregnant. She offers to get an abortion but Levin says, "I want the child" (_Life_ 265). So Levin, the two children, and pregnant Pauline set off for a new life in Levin's Hudson. Gilley, who has been photographing the cutting down of a maple tree on campus, and who has recently cut down a tree in his own yard, turns his camera and snaps a picture of the new family as they depart. Gilley, with his gadgets, tape recorders and cameras, is removed from nature and is a distortion of all that is natural. He is comical and ridiculous. Not life itself, but a photograph of life -- first of Duffy and Pauline in the nude, now of Levin and Pauline and the kids -- is what he ends up with. In contrast, Pauline brings Levin a new and natural life: "Her body smelled like fresh-baked bread, the bread of flowers" (*Life* 366). As Levin and Pauline leave Cascadia they have the promise of a new life and an actual new life in the child they are expecting.

Though the endings of Malamud's works often result in rather contradictory critical interpretations, none has been more variously interpreted than the ending of *A New Life*. Some insist the ending is bleak. To Leslie Fiedler, Levin is a "schoolmarm" who ends up "marrying Madame Bovary" ("Malamud's Travesty Western" 214). Granville Hicks claims the conclusion "holds little promise of happiness" ("Hard Road to the Good Life" 20). For Theodore Solotaroff, Levin's success "is qualified to the bone" ("The Old Life and the New" 244). For Ihab Hassan, in the conclusion there is "drudgery, the spiritual blunting, implicit in human acceptance" ("The Hopes of Man" 5). And to Samuel Weiss, "Malamud's hero is true to the Dostoievskian cult of suffering and martyrdom. The candle of morality burns in Levin's crucial decision, but its light is cold and abstract in his consciousness and leaves his deeper motivations in the dark" (99).

Still other critics like Louis D. Rubin see Levin departing "not so much in defeat as in the realization of his commitment to life" (513). For Robert Ducharme "the banishment is a liberation from a false paradise into involvement and responsibility in the larger world of men and affairs" (23).

I hold with those who favor the hopeful reading, for several reasons. First, Levin's alternatives to a life with Pauline are rather bleak: a return to his life as a drunkard, a stultifying career at Cascadia College, or a rerun of Duffy's clash with the school and subsequent suicide. And no one in the novel offers the promise of real warmth and communication that Pauline offers. Levin's other relations with women have been dismal. He tells himself as he contemplates a life with Pauline, "She loves me still, I have never been so loved" (*Life* 338). And second, when Levin has been with Pauline he has been at his best. She has drawn him out, awakened him to a life of the senses, of beauty. With her "He thought of his unhappy years as though they had endured only minutes, black birds long ago dissolved in night" (*Life* 217). With her Levin is most warm, most alive. Without her he is often withdrawn, self-serving and scheming, as in his campaign for the chairmanship. While Levin, from the opening pages of the book, is depicted as a person with many ideals, sensitivities and concerns, Pauline seems able to draw these qualities out.

Those who see Levin's fate as gloomy or ironic are rankled by two things. First, they see his departure from the university as a defeat. But Malamud presents Cascadia College as alternately a hotbed of political infighting and a haven for mediocrity. Levin's departure from the school is a liberation and a departure from the worst of his old self. Second, critics are bothered by Pauline's pursuit of Levin in the final pages of the novel. After all, Pauline makes all the crucial decisions and Levin agrees, at times reluctantly. But her pursuit is in the great Malamud tradition of Susskind chasing Fidelman, Iris Lemon seeking out Roy Hobbs, and Salzman arranging the fate of Leo Finkle. Pauline pushes Levin into a larger commitment, into a more meaningful life.

The fact that Levin has some qualms as he rather abruptly departs with wife and child to be, plus two toddlers, contributes to his believability, but it does not necessarily mean he has made the wrong choice. Only a few days pass between Pauline's return to Levin's life and their departure in the

Hudson. Anyone not frightened and confused by such a sudden and radical change in his life would be out of touch.

In general Levin is one of the most fully drawn of Malamud's *mensch*-heroes and his fate is characteristic. He starts out with intense feelings but little direction. He believes he will find a new life in teaching but is disappointed in many ways. Like Roy Hobbs, Levin has the promise of a new life in the private world of love, not in the public world. Malamud is most concerned with people's responsibilities to a few other people. In this private world people exert some rather strong claims on each other; Pauline and Malamud require a good deal of Levin. But by accepting responsibility and choosing love, Levin finds his new life.

In *A New Life* Malamud further formulates the values of the *mensch*-hero. Love is foremost, even if that love is adultery in the eyes of others. The hero may have to leave a society which does not share his values. He is propelled into his new life partly out of guilts and fears that he will return to his old, baser self. As with Frank Alpine, whose robbery of Morris Bober and rape of Helen Bober eventually lead to his becoming a new person and devoting his life to the Bobers, Levin finds love by way of an affair with a married woman.

Levin is in many ways more ordinary than either Frank Alpine or Roy Hobbs. He lacks Roy's mythic proportions as a baseball hero. His love for Pauline is less idealized than Frank's love for Helen. Levin loves Pauline as she is; he is aware of her lacks. And because Malamud gets into Levin in greater detail than any hero so far, Levin's internal debates and doubts are striking. His struggles are commonplace and quite compelling at the same time.

In the hero Levin, Malamud has moved closer to the natural, human person. While it takes courage for Levin to drive off with Pauline and the children, the life suggested at the conclusion is in many ways an ordinary life. But Malamud places great value on his hero learning to deal humanely with others, learning to love, learning to be committed to someone.

IDIOTS FIRST: SHARED SUFFERING ON A SINKING SHIP

Idiots First, Malamud's second collection of short stories, was published in 1963. Again Malamud exhibits his usual preoccupations in these stories: his heroes search for meaning, for communion, for connection in a world that is hostile to their needs. Malamud is concerned with love, here often failed or disappointing love between men and women. Yet love is still man's greatest hope. For Malamud, "The kelson of creation is love," as Oskar Gassner quotes from Whitman in "The German Refugee," the concluding story (*Idiots* 211). The theme of these stories is the brotherhood of man, yet this brotherhood is often betrayed by characters who harbor feelings of superiority they may even be unaware of. Still, in some of these stories the characters do move toward self-knowledge, though this knowledge is usually accompanied by a painful loss.

Taken together these stories are an extension of the themes Malamud set forth in *The Magic Barrel*. But in spite of many hilarious details in this second volume, these stories are generally more grim. The pressures of poverty, poor health, cultural conflicts, an uncaring or hostile God, and especially Hitler's extermination of the Jews, exact a tremendous toll on these people. They are worn thin by fortune; like Schwartz in "The Jewbird," their scant feathers offer little protection from the elements.

This feeling of a world laden with hostile elements is underlined by the epigraph for *Idiots First*: "Women and children first. Old Saying." This is presumably said on occasions such as the sinking of the Titanic. Malamud suggests that idiots, like the thirty-nine-year-old Isaac in the title story "Idiots First," are more vulnerable than women and children. Though several of the women and the one child in this volume are more sensitive and gentle than some of the men, at other times Malamud seems inclined to a view that women are tougher than men. In many ways Pauline is stronger than Levin in *A New Life*. And in the *Idiots First* stories women are often quite formidable: in "Still Life," one of the two Fidelman stories, Annamaria Oliovino is a tough, self-serving character; Mary Lou Miller, the ex-prostitute in "A Choice of Profession," also has a tough streak; Sura Tomashevsky in "The Cost of Living" is a nag; and the rabbi's wife in "Idiots First" fights tough when the rabbi is giving his new coat to Mendel. In his epigraph Malamud may be hinting that women, in particular, can often fend for themselves. Maurie Cohen of "The Jewbird" is the only child in the collection: he is good, kind, but not very bright. As James Thurber said: "The simplest things last longest, the microbe outlives the mastodon, and the female's gift of simple creativity happily lacks the ornaments and handicaps of male artifice, pretension, power, and balderdash" (2). Malamud's women are not always simpler than his men, but they are generally tougher.

Idiots First is a rich volume of stories and it was greeted with a great deal of acclaim when it first appeared. Theodore Solotaroff, Ihab Hassan, Robert Alter, and Irving Malin all had high praise for the collection. Most of them noticed that Malamud was dealing with new material as well as old. For Alter, stories like "Idiots First," "Black is My Favorite Color," and "Life is Better than Death" "all happily demonstrate that Malamud is beginning to do new and interesting things with his trapped protagonists" ("Out of the Trap" 89). Solotaroff also favored the stories with new material and treatments like "The Maid's Shoes" and "Black is My Favorite Color," he said:

> However, the change one most notices in *Idiots First* is not
> a matter of new settings and subjects but an opening up and
> outward of Malamud himself, his new taking of stock and
> initiative. Almost all of the stories follow the familiar design
> of two characters bound in a relationship that becomes
> obsessive, creating new possibilities of feeling to be either
> mastered or betrayed and lead to a new lease on life or a
> diminished type of survival. . . Malamud manages to
> communicate "the language of the heart" with new
> delicacy, . . . and to free the moral interest from an overly
> fatalistic or mournful moralism ("Showing us 'what it means
> human' " 12).

Other critics like Nat Hentoff and Herbert Leibowitz notice that there is
something grim in these stories. Leibowitz says, Malamud's "human solidarity
inclines him to a Whitmanesque faith in the radical goodness of creature man,
but the evidence of his senses, his moral experience, and of modern history
seems to evade his faith" (22). Nat Hentoff sees the characters in *Idiots First*
as experiencing "small hope and little love," and concludes: "Malamud, in
sum, does cut through the impotence and aloneness which are   variously
common among his contemporaries of all kinds, but he is also a much angrier
writer than appears to be understood, especially by himself" (328).

Though the four Italian stories in *Idiots First* have proved popular over the
years, Hassan liked these stories least. For Hassan "Still Life" and "Naked
Nude," in particular, "seemed a bit slick in their bizarreness" ("Hopes of Man"
5). These two Fidelman stories will be discussed in detail in a later chapter on
Pictures of Fidelman.

The stories in *Idiots First* can be divided into four categories: two stories
most clearly linked to early Malamud, three stories dealing with cultures in
conflict, three stories with false teachers or spokesmen, and two stories with
true teachers.

In both "Idiots First" and "The Cost of Living," the two stories closest to his early work, Malamud presents older heroes oppressed by poverty and a hostile environment, fighting an inevitable, destructive fate. Both men are reminiscent of Morris Bober in *The Assistant*. Mendel in "Idiots First" gains a small measure of success but is near death; Sam Tomaschevsky in "The Cost of Living" loses entirely, his tiny grocery a victim of a national chain store.

"Idiots First" is one of the finest stories in the volume; and as it is the first story and the title story, it sets the tone for what follows. Mendel is a standard older Malamud hero. His whole life has been struggle. As he says: "I was poor. I suffered from my health. When I worked I worked too hard. When I didn't work was worse. My wife died a young woman" (*Idiots* 14). Now at a time in his life when he seems least equipped for the fight, Mendel struggles to raise the money to send his thirty-nine-year-old idiot son to an eighty-one-year-old uncle in California. The name Mendel suggests the famous Gregor Mendel, the pioneer in botany and genetics. Malamud's use of the name may be ironic because here Mendel has an idiot son. All of this Mendel's experience is grim. His clothing is "embittered" (*Idiots* 3), the night is "cold and bleak" (*Idiots* 4), and at one point he and Isaac "huddled behind a telephone, both freezing" (*Idiots* 9).

What is most striking in the story is how hostile a world poor, old Mendel must deal with. As he attempts to raise the thirty-five dollars, people, as well as the weather, are antagonistic. A pawnbroker offers little for Mendel's gold watch, and when he learns of Mendel's plan to send Isaac to California says only, "It's a free country" (*Idiots* 5). When Mendel and Isaac call on the philanthropist Fishbein, he is unmoved: "Private contributions I don't make -- only to institutions. This is my fixed policy" (*Idiots* 8). When they go to call on a rabbi, first the sexton discourages them; then the rabbi's wife tries to turn them away. Only the rabbi, "an old skinny man with bent shoulders and a wisp of a white beard" (*Idiots* 11), offers any help.

The rabbi says at first, "God will give you" (*Idiots* 11). But when Mendel answers, "In the grave" (*Idiots* 11), the rabbi, perhaps in silent agreement that God cannot be counted on, hurries off and fetches Mendel a new fur-lined caftan. Because the coat is valuable the rabbi's wife starts shrieking; but the rabbi says, "Who can go among poor people, tell me, in a new coat?" (*Idiots* 12). In an hilarious scene the wife and Mendel wrestle for the coat. When Mendel yanks the coat from her hands, the rabbi yells "Run" (*Idiots* 12) and falls to the floor in an apparent heart attack. Two things in particular are noteworthy in the encounter with the rabbi: the rabbi does not insist on prayer; and he offers a coat for Mendel to pawn, the coat itself a symbol of warmth and comfort.

But Mendel's most significant struggle occurs with Ginsburg, his omnipresent antagonist. Ginsburg is one of the most suggestive and symbolic minor characters in all of Malamud. And he must be understood symbolically because on a literal level he makes little sense: ticket collectors do not pursue prospective ticket buyers. Solotaroff calls Ginsburg "the Spirit of Death" ("Showing us 'what it means human' " 5), and Ben Siegel calls him "the Angel of Death" ("Through a Glass Darkly" 133). He is certainly associated with death, most particularly Mendel's death. He tells Mendel, "You shoulda been dead already at midnight" (*Idiots* 13).

But Malamud intends Ginsburg to represent more than merely the Angel of Death, God's emissary: Ginsburg is God and a rather horrific God at that. Many details in the story suggest this interpretation. First, he is omnipresent. Mendel describes Ginsburg to Isaac as a kind of bogey man lurking everywhere: " 'That's the one, with the black whiskers. Don't talk to him or go with him if he asks you . . . Young people he don't bother so much' Mendel said in afterthought" (*Idiots* 4). When Mendel is walking in the street he is always glancing about furtively, seemingly expecting Ginsburg. Twice Mendel and Isaac are frightened by figures who are not identified but appear to be Ginsburg. When they sit on a park bench under a dead tree a stranger approaches and says "Gut yuntif" (*Idiots* 9), or "good holiday." A policeman beats the bushes looking for the man and he has vanished; but Mendel and Isaac hurry out of the park. Then they go to a cafeteria and are frightened by "a heavyset man eating soup with kasha. After one look at him they left in haste" (*Idiots* 9). Later, after the rabbi has given Mendel the coat, "Mendel and Isaac ran through the streets . . . After them noiselessly ran Ginsburg" (*Idiots* 12). He is everywhere they turn.

A second reason for associating Ginsburg with God is the parallel in the Mendel and Isaac relationship with the Biblical Abraham and Isaac story. The angel of God commanded that Abraham sacrifice Isaac (Genesis 22:2). Though Mendel's death is imminent in "Idiots First," it is Isaac's fate, the preservation of his life, that is of greatest concern to Mendel. In the final scene, Ginsburg, appearing as a uniformed ticket collector, at first refuses to allow Isaac to get to the train, citing the time, "Already past twelve" (*Idiots* 13) and claiming the gate is already closed. As God spared Abraham's Isaac, Ginsburg relents and allows Isaac passage to the California bound train. Abraham is permitted to sacrifice a ram and in this final scene in "Idiots First" Isaac is described as mewling and yelping (*Idiots* 14), or making animal noises.

Finally Ginsburg's own words link him most closely to God. Ginsburg says his responsibility is "To create conditions. To make happen what happens. I ain't in the anthropomorphic business" (*Idiots* 13). Though man often envisions an anthropomorphic God, Ginsburg warns that God is not made in man's image; presumably he is without human pity and sympathy. For Ginsburg, "The law is the law . . . The cosmic universal law, goddamit, the one I got to follow myself" (*Idiots* 13). Mendel protests Ginsburg's cruelty and calls him "You dog you," the word a reverse of God, asking Ginsburg "You bastard, don't you understand what it means human?" (*Idiots* 14). Ginsburg, angry and laughing at the same time, says to Mendel: "You pipsqueak nothing. I'll freeze you to pieces" (*Idiots* 14). Mendel feels "an unbearable cold icy dagger invading his body, all his parts shriveling" (*Idiots* 14) and is certain he is dying. So Ginsburg also has the supernatural power to inflict harm.

When Mendel and Ginsburg are wrestling Mendel sees his own terror reflected in the ticket collector's eyes, "But he saw that Ginsburg, staring at himself in Mendel's eyes, saw mirrored in them the extent of his own awful wrath. He beheld a shimmering, starry, blinding light that produced darkness" (*Idiots* 15). One meaning of the word "wrath" is "divine retribution." So Ginsburg or God is moved to mercy by the horror of his own reflection and he loosens his grip on Mendel and lets Isaac pass. When Isaac passes through the gate there is some small measure of hope.

Ginsburg's characterization as God is crucial to understanding Mendel and the Malamud hero. The hero is in a hostile world. He is often a frail person with enemies like Ginsburg, Fishbein, and the rabbi's wife who are all "bulky" and insulated from his needs. For Mendel and the Malamud hero in general, any hope still lies in man, in the *mensch* in man, not in God. At his worst, God is man's enemy, the one who set up the difficult conditions of man's existence. The small victories in the story speak of human love. The rabbi kindly offers his new coat though the resultant hoopla appears to cost him his life; but the rabbi's love makes it possible for Mendel to buy Isaac's ticket. And Mendel's love for Isaac, his willingness to wrestle even with God for his son's fate, makes Isaac's journey possible. Though Mendel will soon die and though Isaac's salvation is at best temporary because Uncle Leo who will care for Isaac is eighty-one years old himself, the story still speaks to the primacy of selfless human love.

Malamud, a great admirer of Thomas Hardy, chose Hardy's *The Dynasts* as the subject of his master's thesis at Columbia University. Malamud's portrayals of God and of human suffering are quite close to Hardy's. In "Idiots First" and *God's Grace*, Malamud presents a hostile or indifferent God, as does Hardy in his novels and in many poems, including "Hap" and "The Blinded Bird." As Hardy says of the blind bird: "And all this indignity/with God's consent, on Thee" ("The Blinded Bird" 2-4). For both Hardy and Malamud, suffering is pervasive, unjust. But from the deepest gloom, the sweetest, most loving song is sung -- as Hardy says, "I stand and wonder how/So zestfully thou canst sing" (6-7). Mendel's love for Isaac, his struggle, is his sweet song.

Like Mendel, Sam Tomashevsky is an older Malamud hero struggling with financial worries in a world that is hostile to his needs. His story is clear and simple: after twenty years of "eroding toil" (*Idiots* 144) in his grocery, he is squeezed out of business by a national chain grocery offering bargain prices. Sam is much like Morris Bober of *The Assistant* and, in fact, "The Cost of Living" was first published in 1950.

In this story Malamud again paints a grim world. Sam is not alone in his despair: he is haunted by the memory of Pellegrino, the Italian owner of a shoe-repair shop who has already been driven to peddling in the streets by a "streamlined shoe-repair shop" (*Idiots* 142). And the barber who owns the building that the new grocery store will lease does not want to drive Sam out of business; he wants to show pity. But he is pressed by financial concerns himself, has become absent minded since the death of his son in the war, "and sometimes when he walked one had the impression he was dragging something" (*Idiots* 145). So everyone suffers.

The one person in a position to help Sam is I. Kaufman, a former neighbor from their early days as merchants in Williamsburg. Sam wants Kaufman to invest in a shoe store in the barber's vacant store so that the new grocery will not move in. But Kaufman is haughty and when he inspects the vacant store says, "who do you think, if he is in his right mind, will open a shoe store in this stinky neighborhood?" (*Idiots* 148-49). Though Sam tries everything, bargain beer, new displays, fewer lights, his struggles are useless and he sells his store in auction and moves away.

Sam is one Malamud hero with small cause for hope. Even a tomato blushes at the suffering of Sam. He is driven to eating less, getting fewer hair cuts and even shaving less often to save on razor blades. His wife berates him. And though he is sensitive and likely generous, after years of "doling of credit to the impoverished by the poor" (*Idiots* 144), the world beats him down. And at the end he is alone in his misery. The barber and Sam's former customers avoid him, guilty for their part in Sam's fate.

Though poverty exerts its pressure in three other stories, "The Maid's Shoes," "Black is My Favorite Color," and "The Death of Me," failed communion caused in part by cultural and racial differences dominates these stories.

"The Maid's Shoes" has two main characters, Orlando Krantz, an American law professor living in Rome, and Rosa, his maid. Professor Krantz is a man of limited compassion and insight who feels superior to Rosa, his Italian maid. Like many Malamud protagonists, Krantz is displaced and somewhat alienated from his new environment. He is also alone in the story. His wife and daughter are vacationing in America. He resembles Carl of

"Behold the Key," though Krantz is older and more affluent. Like Carl, he speaks Italian but does not seem to communicate with the Italians. Krantz is described as sixty, nervous, with "a bit of a belly" -- "a somewhat odd-looking man" (*Idiots* 155). He has a creepy, repressed side, unusual for a main character in a Malamud story. He is very disturbed by the split in the seam of Rosa's threadbare black dress and he notices her white underwear shining through. He is a bit like Seymour Levin: imperfection in a woman turns him off. He has previously rejected a young maid because of the way her aunt "played up certain qualities of the girl" (*Idiots* 154). Krantz also snoops in Rosa's room and opens her chest of drawers. He is always watching Rosa working. It is fitting that he is a legal scholar because he investigates, interrogates and judges Rosa. Though he once allows her to use his tub in the big bathroom and often lends her his hot water bottle to press against her ailing liver, "they almost never shared speech" (*Idiots* 159). Krantz is cold and aloof, believing employer-employee relations should be handled on "an objective level" (*Idiots* 160).

Rosa is Krantz' opposite. A poor, uneducated widow, she reads romance magazines and is desperate for any sort of communication. Like many Malamud characters aged by their rough lives, she looks older than her forty-five years. And like Bevilacqua in "Behold the Key," she lives by her wits, saving cigarette butts, old newspapers, and pencil stubs Krantz throws away. Rosa makes use of everything she saves. She is too poor even to offer a bribe to the portinaia for the maid's job and instead must promise a portion of her first paycheck. She wears the same worn dress every day and her shoes are six years old. She tells Krantz, as she tries to involve him in her troubles, "Your troubles hang on all your life but it doesn't take long to tell them" (*Idiots* 160).

Rosa's need for a new pair of shoes soon involves Krantz and her new lover in a comical, twisted way. Krantz first considers buying Rosa new shoes but decides to wait till his wife returns. Then Rosa insists on talking to Krantz and explains that a married, middle-aged tax bureau worker named Armando, who sometimes takes her to the movies in the afternoons, has offered to buy her a new pair of shoes. She tells Krantz that if she accepts the shoes, Armando may make demands. Krantz, in a bossy manner, advises her not to take the shoes and then decides to buy her shoes himself. Ironically, when Krantz presents his medium-heeled, practical shoes he gets demanding: "Tell your friend you must refuse his. And when you do, perhaps it would be advisable also to inform him that you intend to see him a little less frequently from now on" (*Idiots* 163). Krantz seems to derive vicarious pleasure from the promise of Rosa's sexual repression. But Rosa is overjoyed with the shoes and even attempts to kiss the professor's hand.

The next day, after giving Rosa permission to leave an hour early, Krantz discovers Rosa "wearing a pair of dressy black needlepoint pumps" (*Idiots* 64). He is furious, apparently feeling he has been tricked. He fires Rosa. But she shows up again in a week, conveniently on the first morning the heat has been turned on for the winter, and begs for her job back, claiming she had been given the pumps first but that she will give them back. This results in a comical situation: Krantz takes her back after she promises to return the needlepoint pumps, feeling "a certain sympathy for her" (*Idiots* 164). He is also relieved to see that the hole in her dress has been sewn.

Krantz does soften slightly toward Rosa after she returns. He notices how sad she is: "This is their nature, he thought; they have hard lives" (*Idiots* 165). "They" evidently refers to poor Italians. He allows her to live in, to drink some of his wine, and to eat some of his fruit. But when she tells him she is pregnant he is disgusted. At first he gives her money to go to a midwife, but instead she buys a present for her son. Then Krantz takes her to a doctor in his building, discovers she is frightened but not pregnant, and fires her. Armando appears; they wrap her few things in newspaper and depart. But she leaves the shoes Krantz gave her.

Though Rosa is not above some trickery, she is a sympathetic character, certainly more human than Krantz. Krantz could learn much about life and Italy from Rosa if he did not feel so superior. It is significant that Krantz is one of the few financially secure characters in Malamud's fiction and he is one of the least sympathetic. He feels insulated from Rosa and her troubles and wonders how to handle her; when he is moved by her he is condescending and patronizing. His morality consists solely of a simple-minded concern for propriety. The story suggests real human sympathy is rare, perhaps especially from people who could easily afford to give it. Rosa is closer to the Malamud *mensch* than Krantz is. Softened by her troubles, she longs for companionship of any kind. While she is not a person of strong character, her living on odds and ends, by her wits, links her to other Malamud characters like Susskind and Salzman. And while she is weak, she is linked to the *mensch*-hero by her willingness to live fully in spite of the difficult conditions of her life. Krantz is distanced from the usual Malamud hero because he never achieves much insight. He does not see how tied up he is.

Nat Lime in "Black is My Favorite Color" is another character who lacks insight. He is patronizing in his relationships with blacks and then wonders why they reject him. His naivete compounds the usual conflicts between blacks and Jews in America. Solotaroff admires the realism, the "actual world" of this story: "The point of this story of Negro-white relations is as open and overt as tomorrow's headlines" ("Showing us 'what it means human' " 5). For

Marc L. Ratner, "Nat's fault lies in a naive belief that his acts of kindness can counter centuries of degradation" (679). Both Solotaroff and Ratner seem engaged in typical liberal breast-beating. Malamud's story is more about people than about issues.

Several characteristics link Nat to other Malamud heroes. Though he is forty-four, he has never been married. After his mother dies, he lives alone and appears to have no close friends. He is displaced in that he is a Jew operating a liquor store in predominantly black Harlem. He is linked to the *mensch* in the Malamud hero in that he has a warm heart and longs for company. He tries to do what he thinks is right.

The story is told from Nat's point of view and he is an amusing, believable, and consistent narrator. This point of view also nicely reveals Nat's naivete, his limitations, and his lack of insight. On the one hand, he is sympathetic. He is genuinely moved by the poverty of his childhood friend Buster. He is sensitive. When Buster's father is beaten and arrested by cops Nat recalls: "I personally couldn't stand it, I was scared of the human race so I ran home . . ." (*Idiots* 21). Nat also cares deeply for Ornita Harris, a black woman he hopes to marry. And the story contains reverse of the situation in "The Maid's Shoes": here Nat, the employer, seeks out the black maid's company, but she hides in the john eating her boiled eggs. And in one final incident in particular, Nat is rejected quite gratuitously. He tries to help a blind man across the street; but the man says, "I can tell you're white" (*Idiots* 30), and a black woman rushes over and pushes Nat away.

On the other hand, Nat does not understand his own motivations in seeking out the company of blacks and he is unaware of ways in which he is likely to give offense. One reason he seeks out blacks is that he has been unsuccessful with whites. He has had few friends, male or female. He tries to be friends with Buster because "I had no others then, we were new in the neighborhood, from Manhattan" (*Idiots* 20). After he and Ornita Harris first make love, Nat falls in love for the first time, "though I have liked one or two nice girls I used to go with when I was a boy" (*Idiots* 25). So his experiences with women have been quite limited. When he wants someone to invite him and Ornita over for supper he must resort to calling up an old friend from the Army and asking for an invitation. And when he seeks out the company of his maid Charity Sweetness, it is partly because she reminds him of his mother, "Mama had such eyes before she died" (*Idiots* 17).

But he offends blacks and often tries to buy their friendship. And the blacks in the story are easily offended. He appears to be motivated both by his loneliness and a vague sense of guilt he feels over the condition of blacks. This guilt could result in part from the fact that though he has made a living selling liquor in Harlem he has no black friends. As a child he buys candy and movie tickets for Buster until Buster says, "Take your Jew movies and your Jew candy and shove them up your Jew ass" (*Idiots* 22). Nat learns little: "I thought to myself how was I to know he didn't like the movies. When I was a man I thought, you can't force it" (*Idiots* 22-23). He never learns that people sometimes resent a handout. As an adult, he absurdly tries to fend off black thugs by telling them he owns a liquor store in Harlem and gives "discounts to certain customers" (*Idiots* 28). He even ingratiates himself to Ornita by offering her discounts on liquor for eight months before he asks her out.

And finally, though Nat claims "there's only one human color and that's the color of blood" (*Idiots* 18), his own comments betray him. Lime is "a white caustic solid," and Malamud may have used Nat's last name to suggest how white Nat is. And he is quite preoccupied with race. He notices his maid's "frizzy hair" (*Idiots* 17) and Ornita's "lips a little thick and nose a little broad"

(*Idiots* 24). Ornita is "dark but not the most dark" (*Idiots* 24). Nat prefers to be white himself: but "If I wasn't white my first choice would be black" (*Idiots* 18-19). He is very concerned about people he knows seeing him and Ornita together so he takes her to the liberal Village and later offers to move to San Francisco "where nobody knows us" (*Idiots* 26). And in one weird detail Nat reveals how he first came to see himself as a lover of races, a person with "an eye for color": "once in the jungle in New Guinea in the Second War, I got the idea when I shot at a running Jap and missed him, that I had some kind of talent . . ." (*Idiots* 19). So his friendship for blacks or "Japs" is born of his own inadequacies; he is a poor shot. But he neglects the fact that a person cannot love people who do not want the love.

Still Nat Lime is linked to the Malamud *mensch*-hero in that he has the capacity for love and is driven to find human communion. But he differs from most Malamud heroes in that he, like Orlando Krantz, does not change significantly or even get to understand himself. Nat does achieve some closeness with Ornita, but the pressures of a racially divided society and Nat's naivete drive Ornita away. As she says, "I got trouble enough of my own" (*Idiots* 30). Presumably she does not want to take care of Nat. And she may have a more realistic view of how hard their life together would be in a destructive world full of extreme racial hostility.

The third story of failed communion aggravated by cultural differences is "The Death of Me." Here Marcus, an old Jew who owns a clothing store, hires two assistants: Josip Bruzak, "a heavy, beery, perspiring Pole" (*Idiots* 57), as his presser; and Emilo Vizo, "a thin, dry, pigeon-chested Sicilian" (*Idiots* 58), as his tailor. The story has the feel of a fairy tale or allegory. At one point Marcus is described as looking like "an old hermit, if not a saint" (*Idiots* 65). And when Marcus considers dismissing his warring assistants, he realizes he would have "to pay a fortune in gold" (*Idiots* 64) to replace them, an image suggestive of many fairy tales. But this is a perverse fairy tale with two wicked helpers who destroy the good merchant.

Marcus is a true Malamud *mensch*. Tall and "because of his illness, quite thin" (*Idiots* 64-65), he has "benevolent hands" (*Idiots* 57). Because Marcus is sensitive and kind the world weighs heavily on him: the news in Josip's sad letters "wrung his heart" (*Idiots* 59), and when he hears of Emilio's wife leaving him for the fifth time, "Marcus offered the man his sympathy" (*Idiots* 60). When his workers start fighting every day, Marcus wastes away and his hair turns white. Their fighting drives out customers, but more importantly it breaks Marcus' heart. He tries to teach them love. Near the end of the story Marcus offers Emilio and Josip a "homily" about how his father cautioned Marcus and his poor starving brothers and sisters: "Children we are poor people and strangers wherever we go, let us at least live in peace, or if not --" (*Idiots* 65). The assistants are moved to tears but resume fighting as soon as Marcus goes out.

In one way the story is a study of the effects of suffering on different people. Marcus has become more sensitive to others because he has suffered himself, but Josip and Emilio seem hardened by their suffering. They are both loners. Josip has a tubercular wife and sick son in Poland. He cries over his wife's letters, "oily tears smearing his cheeks and chin so that it looked as though he had been sprayed with something to kill flies" (*Idiots* 59). But Marcus suspects Josip could have brought his wife and son over earlier, before they were so sick, "but for some reason he preferred to weep over them where they were" (*Idiots* 60). Josip is likely false and sentimental. And Emilio whispers constantly to himself, "moaning softly though he never wept" (*Idiots* 60). Five times his wife has run out on him. Marcus suspects the whispering drove her crazy--- "at night when they were in bed and he was whispering about her in the dark . . ." (*Idiots* 60).

Though Marcus tries to bring out the humane side of Josip and Emilio, he fails. Even when he has a partition built between them they are still determined to destroy each other. Instead their hatred kills Marcus, breaking his heart. "Although the old Jew's eyes were glazed as he crumpled, the assassins could plainly read in them, What did I tell you? You see?" (*Idiots* 67). The reason for the intense hatred between "the Pole" and "the Sicilian" is never completely explained, also like in a fairy tale, though it seems to be compounded of lack of sympathy and immigrant rivalry. They cannot stand each other's tears and whispers.

Three other selections have characters who are in some way false teachers or advisers: "A Choice of Profession," "Life is Better Than Death," and the scene from a play "Suppose a Wedding." All these stories also involve romantic relations between men and women. And in each story a major character offers friendship or support, but he turns out to be self-serving.

Cronin in "A Choice of Profession" has much in common with S. Levin of *A New Life*. He is starting out a new life as a college teacher in a Western town, here in Northern California. Like Levin, he is disappointed in teaching, finding it "a bore" (*Idiots* 69). And both Cronin and Levin have problems with women and liquor.

Cronin's character is an unusual mix. While he has some of the makings of the Malamud *mensch*, he is also petty, judgmental obsessive and neurotic, like Krantz in "The Maid's Shoes." His unhappy, unpleasant side is accounted for, in part, by his recent divorce: "Cronin, after discovering that his wife has been two-timing him with a friend, suffered months of crisis" (*Idiots* 69). His nasty side exhibits itself in his relationship with a twenty-five-year-old student,

Mary Lou Miller. After finding himself attracted to her "deep-breasted figure" and "fairly heavy but shapely legs" (*Idiots* 70), he looks up her records, snooping like Levin and Krantz, discovers her age, and asks her out. Because he finds her "a bit boring" (*Idiots* 71) he is reassured, believing he will not get too involved.

When they go out, he starts the evening off by trying to make her someone she is not: "Do you mind if I call you Mary Louise?" (*Idiots* 73). But she tells him the name in her birth certificate is simply Mary Lou. She feels that Cronin puts a lot into his teaching, and believing him to be sensitive and sympathetic, she confides in him. She was once a prostitute, set up by her "prick" of a husband (*Idiots* 75).

Again Malamud exhibits his genius for pairs of characters. Cronin is from a conservative background. He grew up in Evanston, Illinois, where his grandfather was an evangelical minister. And on the basis of his experiences with his wife, Cronin distrusts women. He wants women to be neat, faithful, inexperienced, unworldly; but he becomes attracted to a former whore. Mary Lou is Cronin's nightmare come true. Even her "light hair in a bun" (*Idiots* 70) is loose. He dislikes her rouge and nail polish. She gulps down three drinks in a flash when they have their first date. She chain smokes. She makes him uneasy. Her use of the word "prick" irritates him. And her confession leaves him feeling "let down by Mary Lou" (*Idiots* 78).

But after their first date, after a month of thinking obsessively about Mary Lou, wondering "Could he have guessed from the way she performed in bed that she had been a professional?" (*Idiots* 78), he feels lonely and asks her out again. They go for a drive to a lake and she goes swimming in the nude. She invites him in, suggesting "You could keep your shorts on and later get dry in the sun" (*Idiots* 81). He declines. As in the rest of the story, she reveals all and he hides. Later she reveals that her brother raped her when she was thirteen. Cronin translates this into "You committed incest?" (*Idiots* 82). He tells her he does not want to hear any more and drives her home. When she says she trusted him he says, "Well, don't trust me" (*Idiots* 82). She drops his class.

When Cronin sees Mary Lou walking with his friend George Getz, the art teacher, he becomes both obsessive and petty. The idea of them in bed together is "frightening" to Cronin (*Idiots* 82); he recalls his ex-wife Marge and his previous jealousy. He waits for hours for Mary Lou and George to come out of the art building; and later, in echoes of S. Levin, he waits for five and a half hours under a tree across from Mary Lou's apartment till George leaves. He decides to tell George, "a family man" (*Idiots* 84), about Mary Lou's past. Cronin rationalized that George, as her teacher, has a right to know -- a poor excuse for his cruelty. George says Mary Lou is not a student but his model, but admits he "almost" took her to bed (*Idiots* 85). A few nights later Mary Lou appears at Cronin's apartment and demands to know what he told George that has made him cool to her.

Cronin is a teacher who appears to be understanding; he has "sensitive eyes" (*Idiots* 70) and at first Mary Lou listens to him in class, "as if she were expecting a message or had got it" (*Idiots* 70-71). She feels she can trust him. But he betrays her and her confidence. He is also a false teacher in that he appears to enjoy teaching but really does not.

Yet, in spite of his shortcomings, Cronin has some sympathetic qualities that link him to the Malamud *mensch*. He has had some rough times: "He, though he sometimes felt forty, was twenty-nine" (*Idiots* 71). He can be sensitive: he realizes teaching can be "giving oneself to others, a way of being he hadn't achieved in marriage" (*Idiots* 70). Though he is quite calculating about Mary Lou at first, he does soon realize "he had been appraising her superficially" and begins to develop "a sincere interest" in her (*Idiots* 72). And after her confession of her life as a prostitute he felt "not unsympathetic to the girl" (*Idiots* 77).

But what links him most clearly to many other Malamud heroes is that he finally learns something from his mistakes. At the end of the story, after Mary Lou tells him she has made peace with herself and her life, he tells her he has not made peace. She is no longer interested in him and leaves. "Afterwards he thought, She has learned something from her experience that I haven't learned from mine" (*Idiots* 87). Cronin's treatment of Mary Lou likely contributed to the ulcers she is developing at the end of the story. But he wisely gives up teaching and she writes him a card saying that she hopes to teach someday. She has already taught Cronin something worthwhile about himself. Mary Lou has begun her new life, but Cronin will have to try again.

A second story with a false teacher or adviser is "Life is Better Than Death." As in "A Choice of Profession," a woman confides in a man who appears wise and understanding but who lets her down.

A thirty-year-old widow named Etta Oliva meets a widower, Cesare Montaldo, as she leaves her husband's graveside in a cemetery in Rome. Cesare engages her in conversation and tells her of his wife who "was hurrying to meet a lover and was killed in a minute by a taxi in the Piazza Bologna" (*Idiots* 91). As it is raining Etta offers to share her umbrella and Cesare invites her to a bar.

Etta is "stricken by his story" (*Idiots* 91) and moved by "his sad serious expression" (*Idiots* 92). She relates the story of how she prayed for her husband's death, jealous because he loved her eighteen-year-old cousin Laura. The girl had come to live with them, and they hoped to save her rent and buy a T.V. so they could watch a popular quiz program at home. Instead, she finds Armando and Laura in bed together and they send the girl off; but the husband misses Laura and sets out to bring her back. Etta prays for his death and he falls out of the truck he is riding in and is killed. Etta, of course, feels very guilty. But Cesare listens to the story and offers his advice: "Prayers have little relevance to the situation" (*Idiots* 94), a view often expressed in Malamud.

Cesare gets Etta's address from a friend at the electric company. When he visits her he claims he has found her place by accident. He begins advising her to enjoy life, reminding her she is young and "There are certain advantages to self belief" (*Idiots* 96). He claims that he has given enough to the dead: "Where there's life there's life" (*Idiots* 96), not a very insightful observation. But he does point out that both he and Etta were betrayed, "They died and we suffer" and "Spiritually and physically, there's no love in death" (*Idiots* 97).

A month later Cesare visits Etta again and they go for a walk. Cesare becomes excited and begs Etta to take up her life. He wisely observes, "We mourn them because we hate them. Let's have the dignity to face facts" (*Idiots* 98). And he notes that if Armando were alive he would be back in Laura's bed.

Suddenly Etta begins to desire Cesare: "Overnight her body became a torch" (*Idiots* 99). They have an affair and she hopes for marriage. But Cesare says love is more important and adds, "They both knew how marriage destroyed love" (*Idiots* 100). He sounds like an idealist, but when he discovers she is pregnant he says, "Let's not regret human life" (*Idiots* 100) and promptly disappears.

The story hinges on several ironies. Etta is self-deluded and fails to see her mourning as a form of revenge; yet she has real warmth and feeling and is moved by Cesare's story. Cesare sees clearly, both his own feelings and the feelings of others; but though he appears sensitive and sympathetic, he is manipulative and false. Still, he speaks the truth to Etta. But when a new life, Etta's child, is on the way, Cesare runs.

Though Etta, like other Malamud protagonists, has taken the necessary leap into a new life in her affair with Cesare, the pregnancy makes her feel like "an adulteress, and she never returned to the cemetery to stand again at Armando's grave" (*Idiots* 100). So Etta has won half a victory: she is free from Armando's grave but not from her guilt over her adultery.

"Suppose a Wedding," the scene from a play, also deals with a teacher or adviser who is false. Maurice Feuer, "a retired sick Jewish actor" (*Idiots* 171) tries to influence Adele, his daughter, in her choice of a husband. Feuer expounds on many Malamud themes such as the value of suffering and the significance of tragedy in reminding people that they are human; but these themes are undercut in Feuer's mouth because he is selfish and egocentric. As in "Life is Better Than Death," the words are true, the spokesman false.

In the first half of the scene Feuer tries to scare off Leon Singer, Adele's fiance, the sporting goods store owner, by grilling him on the books he reads, the meaning of tragedy, and his philosophy of life. This discussion takes place as they play gin rummy. Leon is waiting for Adele to get home from work so he can surprise her and take her to a Chinese restaurant, but Adele has promised to go out for a walk with her neighbor Ben Glickman, a poor struggling writer whom Maurice prefers to Leon.

Leon Singer is a decent young man, but limited. Like other characters in Malamud's fiction who go to college, he learns little from it. He belongs to the Book Find Club, reads *The New York Times*, and quotes Aristotle's definition of tragedy; but he appears shallow. When he returns, after an argument with Feuer, to take Adele out, he is insistent in a way that offends her. He pressures her to go out with him by reminding her that they have planned to spend a week together in the country in September. But Florence Feuer, Adele's mother, approves of Leon and believes he will provide Adele a comfortable, secure life -- a life she and Feuer have not had.

Ben Glickman appears only briefly at the end of the scene, but what Feuer and Adele say about him suggests he is a sensitive fellow. Adele says, "he's gone through a lot" and "I like him, he's interesting. I like to talk to him" (*Idiots* 191). When he appears at the door he is a gentle sight, holding "a small bouquet of daffodils" and asking "Am I too early?" (*Idiots* 193).

Marc. L. Ratner claims, "The trite melodrama of a daughter's choice of husbands is less than secondary to the parrying, wounding and surrender to one another of Feuer and his wife as they review their sad history" (682). When the Feuers rehash their stormy marriage, full of separations and affairs, it is the most intense part of the scene. And their accusations underscore the theme: Who is the better person; who has the stronger claim? Florence or Maurice Feuer? Leon or Ben? Though Maurice Feuer sounds almost like Morris Bober when he speaks of suffering and tragedy, he is a self-serving person. Florence correctly identifies Feuer's reason for wanting Adele to marry Ben Glickman: "It's because you see yourself in him, that's who you see" (*Idiots* 183).

But Maurice Feuer is linked to the Malamud hero in that he moves toward self-knowledge at the end of the scene. He realizes, "I am not a good man" (*Idiots* 187). He accepts some blame for the failures of his marriage, Florence is willing to share the blame, and there is at least temporary reconciliation.

The two remaining stories "The Jewbird" and "The German Refugee" are close to the heart of Malamud's fiction: they are lessons in the necessity of human sympathy and brotherhood. Both are refugee stories and both have characters who are true teachers, spokesmen for Malamud's values.

The hero of "The Jewbird" is Schwartz, a delightful talking bird, a "dovening" "old radical," who looks like "a dissipated crow" (*Idiots* 101, 103). He is a fugitive from "anti-Semeets" (*Idiots* 102), and in the true Malamudian fashion of the attraction of opposites he flies in the window of an apartment belonging to Harry Cohen, a coarse, mean seller of frozen foods, a Jew, but a type of anti-Semite himself. Like a number of Malamud heroes, Schwartz has incredible staying power. He remains in the apartment or in his cage on the balcony despite Cohen's threats and harassment, even after Cohen brings home a cat. Schwartz refuses to be evicted till he is tossed out, half dead, after a confrontation with Cohen. His presence in the apartment seems perverse, unless, as Malamud suggests, the bird is on a mission to humanize Cohen and to care for the son Maurie.

Schwartz is close to the Malamud *mensch*. He is skinny, frail and bedraggled, unlike Cohen who is "a heavy man with hairy chest and beefy shorts" (*Idiots* 102). Schwartz is displaced: "I'm flying but I'm also running" (*Idiots* 102). But most important, his suffering has made him sensitive to others. He befriends Cohen's ten-year-old son Maurie, "a nice kid, but not overly bright" (*Idiots* 102). He teaches Maurie his school work and listens to him practice his "screechy violin" (*Idiots* 106). Like a number of Malamud teachers such as Pinye Salzman in "The Magic Barrel," Schwartz has some ability to elicit sympathy in others. As Salzman teaches Leo Finkle to have sympathy, to offer food, Schwartz comes begging for food. After Schwartz asks twice for "a piece of herring with a crust of bread" (*Idiots* 102), Cohen's wife Edie gets him a jar of herring and some rye bread. Though Cohen encourages Schwartz to be migratory and "hit the flyways" (*Idiots* 110) and tries to substitute dry corn and watery cat food for Schwartz' herring, both Edie and Maurie are kind to the bird.

There is some question of who Schwartz really is: a ghost, a dybbuk, or an old Jew metamorphosed into a bird. Schwartz says he is no dybbuk but later adds, "Does God tell us everything?" (*Idiots* 104). Schwartz is closely associated with Cohen's ailing mother because he appears when the family returns suddenly from their vacation in Kingston in order to tend to Cohen's mother. And Cohen makes his final attack on the bird the day after his mother dies and Maurie makes a zero on a test in arithmetic. The way Cohen treats Schwartz may be in some part a test which will decide the mother's fate; a similar situation occurs in a later story "The Silver Crown." In any case, when Cohen throws the bird out, he has made of Schwartz a scapebird.

The story speaks of a basic Malamud theme, the validity of one human's claim on another, or even a bird's claim. Those in need have a right to food, shelter, and care. And the needy can often teach the comfortable. Cohen, who appears to have all he needs, begrudges Schwartz his crust of bread and herring. Solotaroff sees Cohen's hostility as "the anti-Semitic hostility the assimilated Jew bears toward the immigrant generation" ("Showing us 'what it means human' " 12). Ironically, in this story the bird speaks for the truly human and humane point of view.

Still, Cohen's hatred for Schwartz has a completely irrational element. Schwartz asks him, "What did I do to you?" (*Idiots* 110). Finally Cohen grabs the bird out of his cage and "He whirled the bird around and around his head" (*Idiots* 112). Schwartz at least manages to grab Cohen's nose, making it bloody and swollen. One critic, Neil Rudin has noted:

> This curious finish closely parallels the ancient Orthodox Jewish custom of waving a bird above the head on the eve of Day of Atonement as a sacrifice, thus seeking to transfer

> one's sins to the poor bird prior to seeking forgiveness and
> atonement for the transgressions of the past year. Even
> Cohen's punching the bird is part of the tradition, which is
> called *shlogin kappores*, literally meaning to punch or beat
> atonements (14).

Rudin claims this act may initiate Cohen's atonement. I agree that Malamud seems to allude to this ritual, but I find the allusion ironic because Cohen feels no remorse whatsoever. Instead he stands waiting to beat Schwartz up with a broom should the poor bird dare to return.

Schwartz' death, like the death of Marcus in "The Death of Me" from a broken heart, comes because man can be persistently, irrationally hateful. As Marcus was unable to teach his assistants love, the Jewbird is unable to teach the frozen foods salesman. But as Rudin has pointed out, there is some measure of hope at the end of the story because Maurie, who finds the dead bird when the winter's snow melts, weeps. He has learned compassion from Schwartz.

The final story "The German Refugee" concerns a sensitive young man teaching a middle-aged, Jewish-German refugee to speak English. Both Martin Goldberg, the tutor, and Oskar Gassner, the refugee, are linked to other Malamud heroes. And both are true teachers, moved by thoughts of the brotherhood of man. But Gassner who struggles with English so he can give a speech on Whitman's *Brudermensch*, his humanity, must learn his own lesson.

The story hinges on the close friendship that develops between the young tutor and his older pupil who has great difficulty mastering English. Oskar, a critic and journalist, is offered a job as lecturer at the Institute for Public Studies, in New York. He is due to begin lecturing in the fall, but the long, muggy summer is spent grappling with English. Oskar is a sensitive man who cannot even bear to listen to the news on the radio. He feels deeply the loss of language and longs to communicate what is in his heart. The narrator Martin Goldberg is Oskar's third tutor. For the first half of the story Oskar is in a deep depression over his failure to make progress. At one point he tries to speak but in despair "lifted a hand, and let it drop like a dead duck" (*Idiots* 196). First he threatens suicide if he cannot prepare his lecture. Then he recounts a suicide attempt during his first week in the United States. Soon Goldberg worries that Oskar will try again, and once when he knocks on Oskar's apartment door and gets no answer he fears Oskar has killed himself and searches for pills or a gun. Martin Goldberg is a dedicated, sensitive young teacher. He is only twenty, "a skinny, life hungry kid" (*Idiots* 195). But he becomes so involved with Oskar that he catches Oskar's depression: "What's more, I was sometimes afraid I was myself becoming melancholy, a new talent, call it, of taking less pleasure in my little pleasures" (*Idiots* 207). He neglects his other students, his livelihood, in order to devote himself to Oskar. Finally he works a kind of rebirth on Oskar, almost accidentally. Goldberg goes to the library to see if he can begin to write the lecture on the German poets who were influenced by Whitman. He shows Oskar his notes about Walt Whitman's love of death; but "Then he [Oskar] said, no, it wasn't the love of death they had got from Whitman -- that ran through German poetry -- but it was most of all his feeling for *Brudermensch*, his humanity" (*Idiots* 209). Goldberg feels he has failed, but Oskar is inspired by writing a letter explaining all to Goldberg and finds he is writing his lecture. Oskar thanks Goldberg "for much, alzo including your faith in me" (*Idiots* 209). So, as often happens in Malamud's fiction, one man's faith in another brings about a new life. Oskar's lecture goes well and Goldberg realizes "what's meant when somebody is called 'another man' " (*Idiots* 210). Suitably enough the catalyst for this change is Whitman's *Song of Myself*.

But two days after the lecture Goldberg goes to Oskar's apartment and finds a crowd gathered around the dead refugee. Oskar Gassner has taken his life by gas. He has left everything to Goldberg. When the young tutor finally reads through Oskar's correspondence, he discovers a letter from Oskar's mother-in-law describing how his wife converted to Judaism after Oskar left and how the Nazis later took her away and shot her. Earlier in the story Oskar had told Goldberg that though he had been married for twenty-seven unhappy years, he had left his gentile wife in Germany. He felt she was "ambivalent about their Jewish friends and relatives, though outwardly she seemed not a prejudiced person" (*Idiots* 208). He did not really want her to come to America so she did not come. When Oskar received the news of her death he killed himself, likely realizing he had betrayed the humanity of his own wife. He had not understood the person she was or the love she felt for him. Though this conclusion is somewhat convenient and rigged, the portrait of Oskar as an agonized immigrant is compelling.

This story emphasizes the importance of love, particularly in the friendship between Oskar and Goldberg. They bring out the *mensch* in each other. But the pressures of a destructive world are overwhelming and have the final say.

This very fine volume of stories helps to further define the Malamud hero. The hero is often a person with limited means who must stand up against the forces of poverty, death, and man's cruelty and hatred. Malamud again emphasizes the often molding value of suffering and struggle. But the collection, with several widows and widowers and three stories that end in death, suggests the hero's struggle may be doomed. And several of the main characters in these stories are isolated from others, locked in prisons of their own making. In general, a number of these heroes are more limited and culpable than the earlier heroes, perhaps truer to life. Malamud continues to move toward a more natural and flawed hero.

THE FIXER: GREAT HOPES PINNED ON ONE SMALL MAN

Malamud's fourth novel *The Fixer* was published in 1966. Its hero Yakov Bok is a natural successor to the earlier heroes. He is a most ordinary man, flawed and weak, who is placed in extraordinary circumstances which shape him into the Malamud *mensch*. He is made the scapegoat for Russian anti-Semitism, accused of the ritual blood murder of a twelve-year-old Russian boy Zhenia Golov. He is said to have stabbed the boy in order to draw out his blood for use in baking matzos. Through more than two years of cruel imprisonment, beatings, and even poisoning, Bok endures. In Yakov Bok, Malamud has created a hero who at first seems the most small and vulnerable of the heroes in the novels, but who finds himself able to stand up to a whole nation.

The Fixer was generally well received when it first appeared. In 1967 it was awarded both the Pulitzer Prize and the National Book Award. Partly because of the political and historical content of the book, it engendered a great deal of interest and a wider audience for Malamud. It was made into a film starring Alan Bates as Yakov Bok. The novel also was published at the right time, the late sixties, when its theme of a simple man against a corrupt state was eagerly received.

Those who praised the novel did so in glowing terms. Granville Hicks said, it "is one of the finest novels of the postwar period" ("One Man to Stand for Six Million" 31). Elizabeth Hardwick found it a great book, "a work of moral imagination" (208). And Robert Alter found it "Malamud's most powerful novel":

> In his recent book he gives new imaginative weight to his conception of Jewishness by adding the crucially important dimension of history, and in so doing he manages to transform his recurrent symbol into the stuff of an urgent, tautly controlled novel that firmly engages the emotions and the intellect as well ("Malamud as a Jewish Writer" 76).

In general those who did fault the novel found the detailed and brutal depiction of Bok's prison life offensive, excessive, or even boring. Whitney Balliett, claiming "Human misery does not catalogue well," said, "Bok suffers unendurably in prison, but we are no longer affected after the first fifty pages" (235). Josh Greenfield said Malamud "makes Yakov physically suffer far beyond the point of meaningful purpose" (10). And for Edmond Fuller, Malamud "piles atrocity upon atrocity so relentlessly as to fall under the law of diminishing returns" (12).

Malamud's handling of Yakov Bok can be examined in terms of several issues: first the characteristics that link him to the earlier heroes, then the particular nature of Bok's personality and his suffering, and finally Bok as he appears at the conclusion of the novel, en route to his trial.

Bok fits the model of the Malamud hero quite closely, particularly as the hero appears in the first three novels. He is alone, childless, and separated from his wife. He is displaced: his move to Kiev, where he lives in an area forbidden to Jews, is motivated by his search for a new and more prosperous life. Bok is in part responsible for the troubles he runs into. And, finally, he does find a new life, though not in the terms he expected.

The degree to which Bok conforms to the model of the Malamud hero is particularly interesting when one considers the sources for the novel. Malamud has emphasized the fact that *The Fixer* is "an imaginative piece of work" (Frankel 39). But he has also acknowledged some historical cases which influenced him. He started out with the idea of the plight of the Negroes in America, began to think of the Dreyfus case, and then settled largely on the Mendel Beiliss case. Beiliss was a Jew arrested for the ritual blood murder of a Russian boy in Kiev in 1911. Malamud said, "To his [Beiliss'] trials in prison I added something of Dreyfus's and Vanzetti's, shaping the whole to suggest the affliction of the Jews under Hitler" (Frankel 39).

By an odd coincidence, a book on the Beiliss case appeared within a month of *The Fixer* titled *Blood Accusation: The Strange History of the Beiliss Case* by Maurice Samuel. Though the Beiliss case, a worldwide cause celebre in its time, had faded from public memory in the wake of WWI, the Russian Revolution, and then later the slaughter of six million Jews under Hitler, the appearance of these two books renewed interest in Beiliss. The books were often reviewed together and compared, though as most critics noted, Samuel focused on the politics of the case and Malamud focused on the accused man.

Malamud used many details from the Beiliss case in *The Fixer*, but what is most significant is the ways Malamud departs from Beiliss and alters him to make Bok more closely fit the usual Malamud hero. These alterations suggest that Malamud had a firm model of his hero consciously in mind.

As with the heroes of the earlier novels whose parents are either negligent or dead, Bok is an orphan. As Bok says, "I was practically born an orphan -- my mother dead ten minutes later" (*Fixer* 6). His father was killed when Bok was only a year old: "two drunken soldiers shot the first three Jews in their path, his father had been the second" (*Fixer* 4). But Beiliss had a close family. His father was a respected Chassid who, in fact, first got Beiliss the job in the brickworks (Samuel 56).

Bok is thirty when the novel opens, close in age to Levin, Alpine and Hobbs. Malamud often seems to favor heroes of this age because it suits his image of someone getting a slightly late start but still being young enough to find a new life. Because of his hard times Bok is also linked to a number of Malamud characters: "He looked young but felt old . . ." (*Fixer* 9). But Mendel Beiliss was older, thirty-nine when his trial began (Samuel 55).

Bok is a loner. When he rides out of the shtetl he passes the market: "Though the market was his usual hangout, the fixer waved to no one and no one waved to him" (*Fixer* 16). Bok has only two cronies besides Shmuel, his father-in-law: as Bok leaves, "The first had shrugged, the other wordlessly embraced him, and that was that" (*Fixer* 16). But Beiliss was a popular respected man in his community. He was even on good terms with the Orthodox parish priest (Samuel 59). In fact, his reputation as a good man helped to save him: his neighbors were reluctant to libel him.

One of the reasons Bok leaves the shtetl to find a new life in Kiev is that his wife has left him. She ran off with a stranger, as Bok says, "-- a goy I'm positive" (*Fixer* 7). After five and a half years of marriage they were childless and Bok, blaming her, had begun to refuse to sleep with her and to stay away from home. But Mendel Beiliss had a wife and five children. In fact, when Beiliss was first arrested his oldest son was arrested with him and then released (Samuel 55, 61). But with the exception of Pauline's children in *A New Life*, Malamud does not deal with young children in any of his novels. Children would tie Malamud's hero down; he would be more settled, less singular.

Bok is a much more displaced person than was Beiliss. Bok sets out for Kiev. When he arrives he first lives in the Jewish quarter of the Podol district. But the Jewish quarter "swarmed and smelled" and "Its worldly goods was spiritual goods; all that was lacking was prosperity" (*Fixer* 32). So Bok ventures out into an area forbidden to Jews, looking for work. He rescues a drunken man named Nikolai Maximovitch Lebedev who has fallen down with his face in the snow. Lebedev first offers Bok a job restoring an empty flat, and then later he offers Bok a job as overseer of his brick factory. Soon Bok is living on the site of the brick works, in an area forbidden to Jews; and his employer Lebedev is a member of the Black Hundreds, a monarchist, reactionary, and anti-Semitic organization. Bok must hide his identity as a Jew and gives Lebedev a false name, Yakov Ivanovitch Dogogushev, with the ironic and revealing initials Y.I.D. Bok's Russian is self-taught and people recognize his strange accent. He tells the anti-Semitic boatman who ferries him across the Dnieper that he is Latvian. And later Proshko, the thieving foreman at the brickworks, asks Bok, "why is it you talk Russian like a Turk?" (*Fixer* 58). Though Beiliss also spoke Russian poorly, he was not a displaced person like Bok. He was a dispatcher of a brickworks who had lived outside the Pale, or Jewish settlement, for fifteen years. He was known to be a Jew and yet lived openly on the premises of the brickworks, in a non-Jewish section of town. In fact, the factory was owned by the Zaitevs, a prominent Jewish family. The elder Zaitev, who died in 1907, was a sugar magnate and was friends with Beiliss' father. Beiliss' position appeared relatively secure prior to his arrest; he and his family were intentionally spared during the pogrom of 1905 (Samuel 56-59). So Malamud chose to make Bok more isolated, more of an outsider in a completely Gentile world than was Beiliss. William Kennedy, who reviewed both the Malamud book and the Samuel book, briefly noted two of the changes from Beiliss to Bok: Bok's separation from his wife and his failure to obtain permission to live in a restricted area. Kennedy said, "Such changes seem purposeful, designed to heighten the alien quality, the absolute emptiness and aloneness of Bok's life" ("The Frightening Beiliss Case" 19).

Malamud also departs from the Beiliss case by making Bok more culpable than Beiliss was. Bok contributed to an appearance of guilt by giving a false name, concealing his identity as a Jew, and living in a forbidden area without obtaining legal permission. Malamud also introduces some circumstantial evidence against Bok. Bok does chase boys out of the brickyard. He later rescues an old Orthodox Jew who is being attacked by young boys. Bok brings the man to his room and nurses him: as a result, Passover matzos and a bloody rag are found in Bok's apartment and used as evidence against him. Though the case against Bok is very flimsy indeed, the case against Beiliss was altogether ludicrous. It was a hodge-podge of scurrilous and contradictory evidence so unconvincing that even some officials who wanted to further the cause of anti-Semitism in Russia felt that the case should be dropped because it would fail (Samuel 90-91). Though the Beiliss jury was hand-picked by the prosecution and composed mostly of uneducated and likely anti-Semitic peasants, they found Beiliss innocent. They did, however, agree to the second charge, that a ritual blood murder had been committed by someone (Samuel 248). But Bok is not quite the absolute victim that Beiliss was. Malamud chose to make him, like the other heroes in the novels, in part responsible for his fate.

Malamud also introduces a sexual element into the case against Bok, another departure from the Beiliss case. Lebedev's daughter Zina, "a young woman with a crippled leg" (*Fixer* 33), becomes interested in Bok and invites him to dinner and later to her room. Like Raisl, Bok's wife, Zina speaks of love; but Bok says, "I can't say I love you" (*Fixer* 50). He undresses but when he sees her washing herself at the basin and realizes she is menstruating he says, "But you are unclean!" (*Fixer* 52). Though she assures him it's "the safest time" (*Fixer* 53), he dresses and leaves. She later writes to him at the brickworks and invites him to call on her again at home, but he never answers the letter. She retaliates by testifying to the Investigating Magistrate Bibikov that Bok undressed and attempted to assault her, adding "I saw he was cut in the manner of Jewish males. I could not help seeing" (*Fixer* 91). Bibikov finds the letter Zina sent to Bok and realizes that Bok's version of the incident is true. But in keeping with the pattern of the Malamud hero, Bok has difficulties with women and his attempted affair is unconsummated.

All these alterations from the Beiliss case serve to make Bok a most typical Malamud hero. Malamud also departed from the Beiliss case in other ways, generally to present a more streamlined and dramatic tale. The boy Beiliss was accused of murdering, Andrei Yushchinsky, was really murdered by the mother of a friend, aided by three accomplices (Samuel 41). In Malamud's novel the boy Zhenia Golov is murdered by his own mother Marfa and her blinded lover. And though a number of the investigating officials in the Beiliss case were honest and paid for it by being transferred from the case or even arrested on phony charges, none paid for their honesty with their lives as does Bibikov in *The Fixer*, whom Bok discovers hanging in a neighboring cell. In fact, several of Beiliss' persecutors ended up being shot by the Bolsheviks for miscarriages of justice prior to the revolution. Generally Malamud presents Bok realistically and sympathetically, as more than a symbol of suffering man. Whereas Beiliss' victimization was so arbitrary and sudden, Bok's character and difficult lot in life help to explain why he would become a scapegoat. The particular nature of Bok's personality and his suffering is depicted in great detail. Never before had Malamud focused so singlemindedly, so closely on his hero. Since the largest part of the book is taken up with Bok's solitary confinement, his thoughts are the sole subject of many of the pages.

The picture that emerges throughout the novel is of a sensitive, intelligent and quite resourceful man. Again many details suggest other Malamud heroes. Bok has had a bitter and disappointing life. Much of the early section of the book is taken up with Bok cursing his fate, but he has still retained a gentle and sensitive quality that emerges in his dealings with Shmuel. Perhaps because people sense Bok's humanity, he is at times able to draw out the best in others. While he is distrustful and suspicious of women, two women in the book are drawn to him. Like most Jews in Malamud's fiction, Bok is not a strict observer of the law. But ironically he becomes a symbolic Jew. And finally, more than in any other book, in *The Fixer* Malamud deals most directly with the effects of suffering on his hero. The significance and the symbolic nature of suffering is shown here: Bok is a scapegoat, a symbol of the Jewish people, and a figure of Christ.

First, Bok's disappointments are legion. At thirty he is still sad and bitter about his lonely childhood. He does not have the "heart" to visit his parents' graves before he leaves the shtetl: "The past was a wound in his head" (*Fixer* 14). Then he averts his eyes from the orphanage when he passes it on his way out of town. He is most bitter about being abandoned by his wife Raisl and his bitterness wounds Shmuel. Shmuel says, "Nobody has to be a Prophet to know you're blaming me for my daughter Raisl" (*Fixer* 5). Though Bok wishes "a black cholera on her!" (*Fixer* 8) for leaving him, he also says he "might have waited the legal ten, but she danced off with some dirty stranger, so I've had my fill, thanks" (*Fixer* 11). So if they were still childless after ten years, he might have left her. He thinks, "Yet if she had been faithful he would have stayed. Then better she hadn't been" (*Fixer* 19).

In the early pages of the novel the degree of Bok's bitterness seems extreme. When Bok and Shmuel have a late glass of tea together, Shmuel kindly offers him a half of a lump of sugar from his caftan pocket. Bok declines, but when he thinks of the tea, "It tasted bitter and he blamed existence" (_Fixer_ 5). Bok's troubles have even shaped his appearance: "Yakov, in loose clothes and peaked hat, was an elongated nervous man with large ears, stained hard hands, a broad back and tormented face, lightened a bit by gray eyes and brownish hair. . . . His nervousness showed in his movements" (_Fixer_ 9). Bok thinks of the shtetl as a prison: "It moulders and the Jews moulder in it. Here we're all prisoners" (_Fixer_ 11). Later when Bok's more grave troubles begin he will look back with fondness on many features of shtetl life.

His personal disappointments are aggravated by his poverty. In fact, one difficulty in his marriage was that Raisl thought they should leave Russia: "Let's sell everything and leave while we can" (_Fixer_ 211). But Bok believed they needed to save for a few years in order to have enough money to leave. He does also admit, "I was in no hurry to run to another country. . . . In other words, in those days to make me move, somebody had to push" (_Fixer_ 211). This inertia is typical of Malamud characters like Schwartz in "The Jewbird," Kessler in "The Mourners," or the Bobers in _The Assistant_, who remain in situations which appear hopeless or even threatening. Here the poverty of the shtetl is pervasive and Bok, as an odd job man, is often paid, "If I'm lucky, a dish of noodles" (_Fixer_ 7). When he moves to Kiev and the Jewish section of the Podol district, "The wages were soup" (_Fixer_ 32). When rubles do flow in Bok's direction they come from Lebedev and appear cursed.

But in spite of all the hostility Bok expresses toward shtetl life, Raisl, and God early in the novel, Bok's gentle side is also evident. As with most of Malamud's heroes, the seeds of the _mensch_ Bok will later become have been there all along. In the opening pages he speaks fondly to the cow he has left for Shmuel: "Goodbye, Dvoira," he said, "and lots of luck." "Give what you

got left to Shmuel, also a poor man" (*Fixer* 10). Bok admits some of the blame
for the failure of his marriage, especially because he would not follow Raisl's
advice and leave the shtetl: "It's true," said Yakov, "it was my fault" (*Fixer*
11). And when Shmuel, who has been accompanying Bok to the edge of town,
embraces Bok and trudges back to the synagogue, "Yakov felt a pang for
having forgotten to slip him a ruble or two" (*Fixer* 18).

Bok's sensitive side is also expressed in his love of books. He is
self-educated: "What little I know I learned on my own -- some history and
geography, a little science, arithmetic, and a book or two of Spinoza's. Not
much but better than nothing" (*Fixer* 6-7). He loves his books a great deal and
when he leaves the shtetl all he takes with him are his books and his tools.
Later he describes how he read constantly, more all the time, as his marriage
failed:

> I picked up books here and there, a few I stole, and read by
> the lamp. Many times after I read I slept on the kitchen
> bench. When I was reading Spinoza I stayed up night after
> night. I was by now excited by ideas and I tried to collect a
> few of my own. It was the beginning of a different Yakov
> (*Fixer* 212).

This genuine love of learning, especially in those with little formal
education, is always a good sign in a Malamud character. Like Sobel in the
story "The First Seven Years," Bok loves learning for its own sake. One of the
things Bok hopes for when he sets out for Kiev is "Even some education if I
can get it, and I don't mean workmen studying Torah after hours" (*Fixer* 12).

Associated with Bok's intelligence is his wry humor. When he complains
about his work as a fixer in the shtetl he says, "In this shtetl everything is
falling apart -- who bothers with leaks in his roof if he's peeking through the
cracks to spy on God?" (*Fixer* 7). And after he has been in prison almost two

years he, at times, maintains a wry, if black, view. Though Bok is astonished and incredulous when the warden announces that Bok will receive a visit from his wife Raisl, "Please, not now," said Yakov wearily. "Some other time" (*Fixer* 283). The warden evidently feels Bok is being a wise guy and says, "That'll do" (*Fixer* 283).

Bok's personality is revealed in his relationships with others, his father-in-law, his wife, and those officials and guards he meets in prison. Bok's capacity for connection, for love, is most tested in his relationships with Shmuel and Raisl. Both father and daughter serve as true teachers in the Malamud tradition: they are thin, worn, and sad *luftmenshen* like Susskind in "The Last Mohican" and Salzman in "The Magic Barrel"; and they offer Bok wisdom and love.

Shmuel is a surrogate father to Bok, as was Morris Bober to Frank Alpine in *The Assistant*. Even though Bok is bitter after Raisl leaves him, he remains close to his father-in-law. But Bok feels that he is more enlightened and educated than Shmuel who believes in God. Shmuel offers much good advice that Bok ignores. He cautions Bok against going to Kiev: "It's a dangerous city full of churches and anti-Semites" (*Fixer* 11). He warns that it will be difficult to get a residence certificate in Kiev and asks Bok, "Why should you walk straight into the hands of the Black Hundreds, may they hang by their tongues" (*Fixer* 12). All Shmuel's warnings about the dangers of Kiev prove prophetic.

Even the horse Shmuel gives Bok in exchange for the cow is the image of Shmuel himself, "a naked looking animal with spindly legs, a brown body and large stupid eyes, who got along very well with Shmuel" (*Fixer* 9). "Like an old Jew he looks, thought the fixer" (*Fixer* 27). Though Bok believes his father-in-law is superstitious and curses the old nag who is spooked and reluctant to head for Kiev, it later seems Bok would have been wiser to have heeded both Shmuel and the horse. When Bok moves into the impoverished Podol district, Aaron Latke, who rents Bok a room, echoes Shmuel's cautionary words: "For God's sake, patience" (*Fixer* 33).

Shmuel also lectures Bok on the importance of charity. When Bok says he did not consult a rabbi about his childless marriage to Raisl because "All in all he's an ignorant man" (*Fixer* 6), Shmuel answers, "Charity you were always short of" (*Fixer* 6). Later Bok says, "I have no charity to give" (*Fixer* 7). But Shmuel answers, "Charity you can give even when you haven't got. I don't mean money. I meant for my daughter" (*Fixer* 7). As Bok and Shmuel drive through town they are met by a *scnhorrer* in rags who asks for "a two-kopek piece for a Sabbath blessing? Charity saves from death" (*Fixer* 14). But Bok rejects the beggar, even when Shmuel asks to borrow money to give the man. Then Shmuel cautions Bok to be gentle and patient with the horse and to spare the switch. But after Shmuel gets out of the wagon Bok "belabored the beast with the birch rod until he drew blood," and later "beat the beast with his fist" and "kicked the beast with his heels" (*Fixer* 18, 24). When Bok gets to Kiev he sees a crowd of beggars outside the Lavra catacombs and though he stares at one who reads from the gospels, he gives them nothing.

Though Shmuel has little, in true charity he is willing to give away what little he has. In the opening sections of the novel Bok is put to a test by Shmuel, the horse, and the beggars; and Bok fails. But almost two years later when Shmuel visits Bok in prison, Bok has changed. Though he is still bitter on the subjects of his past and of God, he has softened to Shmuel. While Bok says God is "an invention," he feels sorry to hurt Shmuel who is a believer: "I'm sorry I'm making you feel bad on your expensive time, Shmuel, but take my word for it, it's not easy to be a free-thinker in this terrible cell. I say this without pride or joy" (*Fixer* 258). Shmuel has spent forty rubles, the biggest profit he has ever made, to bribe the guard Zhitnyak for a visit to Bok's cell.

Shmuel continues to caution Bok to remember God, to repent; and in spite of their differences there is a touching degree of warmth between them as they talk through the peephole of Bok's cell. Bok at first worries that Shmuel is a prisoner, too, and then warns, "Run Shmuel . . . get out while you can or they'll shoot you in cold blood and call it a Jewish conspiracy" (*Fixer* 256). In a pitiful gesture Shmuel tries to pass a pickle to Bok through the spyhole, but the guard grabs it. When Shmuel is told to leave, he runs off to tell the Jewish community about the plight of Yakov Bok.

So though Bok's suffering does not soften him to God, it softens him to Shmuel, to man. Later when Bok is near suicide he realizes his death might provoke a pogrom and he decides to endure: "if I must suffer let it be for something. Let it be for Shmuel" (*Fixer* 273).

Raisl serves a function similar to that of her father Shmuel. Bok's relationship to her is seen mostly through Bok's eyes, as he recalls their years together. Early in the book he curses her. But after he has been in prison over a year, he begins to soften toward her. He remembers her as "a pretty girl, intelligent and dissatisfied, with even then a sad face" (*Fixer* 209). He reminisces about their courtship. Like Pauline and Levin in *A New Life*, Raisl and Bok first make love in the woods: "One day in the woods we became man and wife" (*Fixer* 210). Afterwards she felt guilty and he asked her to marry him. But he proposed rather matter-of-factly and did not mention love: " 'Who talks of love in the shtetl?' I asked her. 'What are we, millionaires?' I didn't say so but it's a word that makes me nervous. What does a man like me know about love?" (*Fixer* 211). Here Bok associated money with love, as he associated money with charity in his talk with Shmuel. But he did say love to Raisl and she agreed to marry him.

After nearly six years of marriage Raisl became frantic that they were still childless. Bok recalls, "She blamed it on her sins. Maybe on my sins" (*Fixer* 212). She continued to beg him to leave the shtetl so their luck would change. She began to stay in taverns and then she left him. He cursed her. But prison changes him: "But now I look at it like this: She had tied herself to the wrong future" (*Fixer* 213).

By the time Raisl visits Bok he has been so worn by his two years of imprisonment that "After a while all he thought of was death" (*Fixer* 268). He contemplates suicide at one time and even decides, "I'll provoke them to kill me" (*Fixer* 268). He is in chains all day and is subjected to continual body searches. Released from his cell for his visit with Raisl, Bok can barely walk: "the prisoner limped slowly, stopping often to recover his breath" (*Fixer* 282).

When he sees Raisl he notices she is worn and thin but she "looked otherwise the same, surprising how young though he knew she was thirty, and not bad as a woman" (*Fixer* 284). He is at first moved to see her, but soon his bitterness returns: "You stinking whore, what did *you* do to me?" (*Fixer* 285). She reminds him that the failure of their marriage was not just her fault: "Did you love me? Did I love you?" (*Fixer* 285). And she also reminds him that when she married him he was "affectionate," "and when a person is lonely its easy to lean toward a tender word. Also I think you loved me although you found it hard to say so" (*Fixer* 285). Like Zina Lebedev, Raisl was drawn to the warm side of Bok. And as Shmuel speaks of charity, his daughter Raisl speaks of love.

At the beginning of Raisl's visit Bok is so bitter that all his memory of her is poisoned. He says, "Then you got me in the woods that day" (*Fixer* 285), as though her love for him was a trick, a trap. When he again mentions her infidelity she reminds him, "Because I slept with you before we were married you were convinced I was sleeping with the world. I slept with no one but you until you stopped sleeping with me" (_Fixer_ 286). When Raisl asks Bok to forgive her and tells him, "I came to cry" (_Fixer_ 287), "He felt as he watched her, the weight of the blood in his heart" (_Fixer_ 288). Seeing her so moved Bok is moved and shows a gentle side of himself: "I can't blame you more than I blame myself. . . . I'm sorry. I'm also sorry I stopped sleeping with you" (_Fixer_ 288).

Most importantly, he admits that his suffering has changed him: "I've suffered in this prison and I'm not the same man I once was. What more can I say, Raisl? If I had my life to live over, you'd have less to cry about, so stop crying" (_Fixer_ 288). Even when she tells him she has an eighteen-month-old son by another man, he agrees to write a note claiming the boy is his and instructs her: "Show it to the rabbi's father, the old melamed. He knows my handwriting and he's a kinder man than his son" (_Fixer_ 291). As Raisl leaves, "Yakov," she wept, "come home" (_Fixer_ 292).

Early in his relationships with both Shmuel and Raisl, Bok showed some capacity for warmth and communion. They both sensed that he was a decent man. But in typical Malamudian fashion, Bok grows, however unevenly, in his capacity to both give and receive love. And Shmuel and Raisl, who feel deeply for Bok, instigate his movement toward the Malamud _mensch_, toward a man who thinks of more than himself. They teach the language of the heart. As Bok says of Shmuel when he learns of his death: "He was a good man, he tried to educate me" (_Fixer_ 304). And Bok's subtle change toward both Raisl and Shmuel is one of the most concrete measures of his change as a human being during his long imprisonment.

Other characters in the novel function in capacities somewhat like Raisl and Shmuel. They are teachers or surrogate fathers for Bok. The most significant of these figures are Bibikov the Investigating Magistrate and Kogin the prison guard, who grow in their affection for Bok and pay for it with their lives.

Bibikov, "Investigating Magistrate for Cases of Extraordinary Importance," is assigned the task of formulating the charges against Bok and issuing an indictment. Though he is a government official, Bibikov is a humane man, a liberal, educated in the works of Spinoza and Marx. He may even be a revolutionary. Bibikov is loosely modeled on a figure in the Beiliss case, Krasovsky, "the Sherlock Holmes of Russia," who was assigned the task of investigating Beiliss and immediately became convinced of his innocence. Krasovsky was dismissed from the case, but he returned to Kiev as a private investigator and uncovered much of the evidence pointing to the true murderers (Samuel 41).

Bibikov functions in three capacities in his relationship to Bok: he is an educator, a kindly protector-father, and finally a fellow victim. As an educator, Bibikov prods Bok to think of larger things, of history, of Russia, of the world. In their first conversation, Bibikov asks Bok about Spinoza: "I ask because Spinoza is among my favorite philosophers and I am interested in his effect on others" (*Fixer* 76). Bok relates Spinoza's philosophy largely in terms of personal freedom: "That's in your thought, your honor, if your thought is in God" (*Fixer* 77). But Bibikov is interested in "historical necessity" and how man can be "politically free" (*Fixer* 77-78). Bok fears that talk of politics might be a trap. But Bibikov notes that Spinoza thought "a free man in society had a positive interest in promoting the happiness and intellectual emancipation of his neighbors" (*Fixer* 78). He asks Bok how changes can be made except through politics and adds, "You must read and reflect further" (*Fixer* 79). Even after this first meeting, though Bok is unsure how much to trust Bibikov, he is drawn to the man. Bibikov tells Bok: "Whatever happens you must have fortitude . . . It's a touchy thing . . . I depend on the law. The law will protect you" (*Fixer* 80). When Bibikov leaves, "The fixer felt at once a sense of intense loss" (*Fixer* 80).

The second time Bibikov interviews Bok, the magistrate slips into the role of a kindly protector or a father figure. He is concerned about Bok's asthma: "I ask because my son has asthma" (*Fixer* 89). He kindly tells Bok, "I'm glad it's cleared up" (*Fixer* 89). Soon he assures Bok that he believes Bok's version of the incident with Zinaida Nikolevna. And by the time the investigators return to the scene of the murder and interview Marfa Golov, it is clear to Bok that Grubeshov, the Prosecuting Attorney, and Colonel Bodyansky, the officer who arrested Bok, are determined to frame him -- that his only hope is Bibikov. When the guards point a gun at Bok, Bibikov says, "Put that foolish gun away" (*Fixer* 125).

After Bok has been in prison three months he receives his next and last visit from Bibikov. Bok is now in solitary confinement in Kiev Prison. Bibikov visits him at close to midnight and insists on being alone with Bok. He calls Bok "My friend" and says he will send Bok a new pair of shoes (*Fixer* 165-66). He informs Bok of the pressure to indict and convict him of ritual murder, despite the overwhelming evidence of Bok's innocence. Bibikov tells Bok that the murder was likely committed by Marfa Golov's gang of criminals and her blinded lover. He promises to get Bok an excellent lawyer when the indictment is finally issued; "But at present no lawyer can do as much for you as I. . ." (*Fixer* 175). He promises to do all he can to protect the fixer, and he sees his service to Bok as a service to his country's future:

There is so much to be done that demands the full capacities
of our hearts and souls, but, truly, where shall we begin?
Perhaps I will begin with you? Keep in mind, Yakov
Shepovitch, that if your life is without value, so is mine. If
the law does not protect you, it will not, in the end, protect
me. Therefore I dare not fail you, and that is what causes
me anxiety -- that I must not fail you (*Fixer* 176).

Bibikov's concern for Bok gives Bok some hope. When Bibikov leaves,
Bok tries to seize Bibikov's hand "to press to his lips" (*Fixer* 176). The
devotion of Bibikov to Bok suggests other pairs of characters in Malamud's
fiction, especially Morris and Frank in *The Assistant*. Like Morris, Bibikov acts
in a generous and humane way, though he has little to gain and much to lose.
Morris' lesson to Frank is the lesson of love and devotion. Bibikov offers Bok
friendship as well as political enlightenment. At the end of *The Assistant* Frank
continues in Morris' tradition, working in the store to support Helen and Ida.
At the end of *The Fixer* Bok stands firm in the cause of human freedom; he
becomes a political man like Bibikov, and like Bibikov he is ready to give his
life for the cause.

The transformation of Bibikov from father and teacher to fellow victim is
gradual. The confident, dapper man of the early pages is turned into a nervous
fellow who knocks over a glass of water and whose hands tremble. Soon his
face is "drawn and grim" (*Fixer* 96). By the time he visits Bok in Kiev Prison
Bibikov wears a "wilted yellow straw hat" and "a crumpled linen suit," "his
pallid face contrasting with his dark short beard" (*Fixer* 163-64). He is more
nervous and he says "there are signs of gastric disturbances" (*Fixer* 164). He
fears, justifiably, that his carriage was followed to the prison. He is so
enmeshed in Bok's cause that he cautions Bok not to repeat anything; "I ask
this for our mutual protection" (*Fixer* 171).

Shortly after Bibikov leaves Bok's cell, Bok hears another prisoner being locked into the next cell. Bok does not realize this other prisoner, pounding on the wall with his shoe, is Bibikov. Hearing the shouting and pounding, "Yakov pounded back with his shoe. . . . it sounded to the fixer as though someone was trying to tell him a heartbreaking tale, and he wanted with all his heart to hear and then tell his own. . . ." (*Fixer* 176). Earlier in the night Bibikov had promised Bok new shoes, hardly realizing he would soon be using his own shoe in an attempt to send a coded message to Bok. After more than a week of pounding and moaning, the other prisoner, Bibikov, "stopped beating the wall, and neither of them shouted to the other" (*Fixer* 178). Then one night Bok is awakened by a distant moaning and footsteps in the corridor. The next morning Bok's guard leaves the cell unlocked and Bok eventually sneaks down the corridor, hoping to escape, only to find Bibikov hanged in the adjoining cell. "He was staring down where his pince-nez lay smashed on the floor under his small dangling feet" (*Fixer* 180). Bok is certain Bibikov was murdered and in a dream or vision Bibikov appears and cautions, "I fear they will kill you, too" (*Fixer* 181). Soon they do try to poison Bok. The authorities may have murdered Bibikov because they could not afford to have him work against them or admit to imprisoning him. If he committed suicide, he felt he had no choice.

The scene of Bibikov and Bok pounding on the walls and shouting, Bok unaware of the fellow prisoner's identity, are among the most heartbreaking scenes in *The Fixer*. Two men suffering unendurably are prevented the comfort of sharing their suffering. And when Bok sees the hanged Bibikov, all hope is gone. If the law will not protect Bibikov, a Gentile, a man of education and means with training in the law, how can it protect Bok, the lowly Jew? In fact,

Bibikov's death is more shocking than what happens to Bok: it is more abrupt, precipitous, and unexpected.

Another man to give his life for Bok is the guard Kogin. He and Zhitnyak are the first two guards at Kiev Prison. Zhitnyak gives Bok a birch broom, a needle and thread, and a copy of the New Testament: he also accepts Shmuel's bribe to visit Bok and is later caught and arrested. But Kogin, who at first shows little sympathy for Bok, softens most to Bok as a result of his own troubles.

In Malamud's fiction most thin and worried looking people are sympathetic and "Kogin, the night guard, was a tall man with a gaunt face and watery eyes, worn with worry" (*Fixer* 190). At first Kogin keeps a journal of Bok's night-time ravings, but by Bok's second winter in prison Kogin changes. He tells Bok his own family troubles. He has a wayward daughter and a thieving son who killed an old man during a robbery -- echoes of Minogue and son in *The Assistant*. The son is sentenced to twenty years of forced labor in Siberia. Kogin offers Bok a cigarette as he tells his tale and confesses to Bok that he is aware of Bok's "misfortunes": "I try not to think of you there in chains all day long. The nerves can take just so much, and already I have all the worry I can stand" (*Fixer* 271). When he learns that Bok no longer has the gospels to read, he quotes: "But he who endures to the end will be saved" (*Fixer* 272). Later Kogin tells Bok of the death of the thieving son: "He has drowned himself in a river in Irkutsk on the way to Novorosiik" (*Fixer* 276).

By the time Bok is to go to his trial, Kogin is quite sympathetic to him. He urges Bok to eat his breakfast, "Eat anyway, it'll be a long day in court" (*Fixer* 320). Then when the deputy warden reads a telegram from the Tsar insisting Bok be searched and Bok is returned to his cell, the deputy warden orders Bok to take off all his clothes, including his undershirt. Bok flings the undershirt into the face of the deputy warden, who then draws his revolver to shoot Bok. But Kogin intervenes: "I've listened to this man night after night, I know his sorrows. Enough is enough, and anyway it's time for his trial to begin" (*Fixer* 326). Kogin places his revolver against the deputy warden's neck and then shoots at the ceiling: but the deputy warden shoots Kogin in the head.

The incidents with both Bibikov and Kogin suggest Malamud's theme of men molded by suffering, their own suffering and the suffering of others. And the Malamud hero is often able to draw out the best in some other people. In fact, in *The Fixer* only the warden and the deputy warden are unmoved by the suffering of Bok. The detective who accompanies Bok to the Plossky Courthouse to hear the indictment buys the fixer an apple from a street vendor. Even the guard Berezhinsky says, "Well, good luck, and no hard feelings" (*Fixer* 322), as Bok heads for his trial. And the counterfeiter and spy Gronfein, who is planted in Bok's cell during the early days in Kiev Prison and who tricks Bok into writing letters to Shmuel and Aaron Latke, which Gronfein then turns over to the Warden, later has an attack of guilt over betraying Bok. Shmuel tells Bok during his visit, "A counterfeiter by the name of Gronfein got sick from his nerves and went around saying that Yakov Bok was in Kiev Prison for killing a Russian child. He saw him there" (*Fixer* 255). And the Prosecuting Attorney Grubeshov is affected by Bok's struggles. Grubeshov begins to look older; he coughs and trembles when he reads Bok his indictment. He asks Bok if he suffers from "a chill"; and then he says, "Have you been ill? . . . A pity . . ." (*Fixer* 220). The pressures of Bok's case weigh on Grubeshov heavily and he feels personally persecuted by the Jews, a neat projection of his own guilt: "I personally consider myself under the power of the Jews; under the power of Jewish thought, under the power of the Jewish press" (*Fixer* 226). So Bok's suffering deeply affects others even as it changes Bok. Grubeshov is moved by suffering, as was Gruber in "The Mourners."

The particularly brutal nature of the depiction of Bok's imprisonment, the searches, the poisoning, and the chains, raise the most interesting critical issues of the novel. In artistic terms, how much suffering is too much suffering? Is the extent of the detail self-defeating?

Those critics who find Bok's suffering too brutal or too detailed have that reaction for two reasons: first, the very nature of Bok's imprisonment results in a novel with little action and a plot which advances through repetitions and slight variation, rather than through evolving situations; and second, human suffering is difficult, unpleasant to read about. A number of critics including Dan Jacobson ("The Old Country" 307), Mordecai Marcus (89), and Robert Scholes ("Malamud's Latest Novel" 108) have found the narrowing of subject to Bok in prison too restrictive.

But I feel that enough happens in *The Fixer*. Malamud is most interested in what happens inside Bok, in how Bok becomes a new man. In depicting Bok's suffering in such detail, Malamud delineates the hero and how he changes in the course of his suffering in prison. In fact, many of Malamud's heroes are locked into restrictive settings, stores, offices, prisons. Sometimes Malamud even chooses to write about writers who are not writing or painters who are not painting, restricting himself still further. But it is the inner life of a person that is Malamud's true subject. And as Malamud has said of *The Fixer* in particular, "I was very much interested in the idea of prison as a source of the self's freedom . . ." (Stern 54).

The most interesting argument that *The Fixer* is too brutal is made by Malamud's fellow novelist Philip Roth. He finds Alpine's fate in the grocery of *The Assistant* grim enough, but:

> Yakov Bok, the helpless, innocent Russian-Jewish handyman of _The Fixer_, is arrested and imprisoned, in something far worse even than a dungeon of a grocery store. In fact, I know of no serious author whose novels have chronicled physical brutality and fleshly mortification in such detail and at such length, and who likewise have taken a single defenseless innocent and constructed almost an entire book out of the relentless violations suffered by that character at the hands of cruel and perverse captors, other than Malamud, the Marquis de Sade, and the pseudonymous author of _The Story of O_ ("Imagining Jews" 235).

Roth sees Malamud as writing about good Jews and bad goys. _The Fixer_, he says,

> is at its center a relentless work of violent pornography in which the pure and innocent Jew, whose queasiness at the sight of blood is at the outset almost maidenly, is ravished by the sadistic goyim, "men," a knowledgeable ghost informs him, "who [are] without morality" ("Imagining Jews" 236).

But Roth is oversimplifying the novel. First, not all the goyim are bad. Bibikov is practically a saint and even the prison guards show mercy at times. And not all the Jews are good: the spy Gronfein is Jewish; and as the lawyer Ostrovsky tells Bok, many Jews are too afraid to help Bok. Roth's charge that the fictional depiction of Bok's imprisonment is excessive hardly holds up in the face of history. One need only pick up a current report from Amnesty International to read of prisoners who often suffer in conditions far worse than Bok's. And in the novel Ostrovsky points out to Bok that Dreyfus "went through the same thing with the script in French" (_Fixer_ 306). But most importantly, Bok's trials pale in comparison to the suffering of six million Jews under Hitler. Malamud has said he had the Holocaust in mind. As Granville Hicks noted of _The Fixer_, "Six million was a figure, but one man was a man.

... We the readers could be made to feel for this one man what we could not possibly feel for six million" ("On Man to Stand for Six Million" 31). And Bok's suffering is not artistically excessive or gratuitous because it makes the reader feel for Bok, the man.

And in part directly because of the extensive detail, Bok's suffering takes on a symbolic significance. First he is a symbolic sufferer, the scapegoat. Then he is the symbolic Jew: he suffers because he is a Jew and he suffers for the Jewish people. And finally, he is a figure of the suffering Christ, who suffers for us all.

His role as scapegoat or sacrificial victim is underlined by his name. Naomi Ben-Asher pointed out, "In Yiddish a 'bok' is a dumbell, an innocent; in the original Slavik 'bok' is the word for goat -- obviously a scapegoat" (14). In addition, as Robert Ducharme pointed out, Bok's middle name is Shepsovitch, or son of sheep (48). As Bok thinks of himself, "he was the accidental choice for the sacrifice" (*Fixer* 155). And the images of blood which pervade the book, even if they often suggest the blood of the boy Yakov Bok is accused of murdering, intensify the suggestion of a scapegoat, or ritual sacrifice. And the historically regular pogroms against Jews in Russia were perverse, bloody ritual sacrifices.

Though early in the novel Bok is not interested in seeing himself as a Jew, he comes to identify more closely with the Jews. He believes he suffers because he is a Jew. In prison he realizes, "Being born a Jew meant being vulnerable to history, including its worst errors" (*Fixer* 155). Even the pages of the Old Testament in Hebrew which the deputy warden throws into Bok's cell are "covered with muddy brown stains that looked like dry blood" (*Fixer* 237). These pages are stained with the suffering of the Jewish people. During Bok's second winter in prison he decides against suicide because "What have

I learned if a single Jew dies because I did? Suffering I can gladly live without, I hate the taste of it, but if I must suffer let it be for something. Let it be for Shmuel" (_Fixer_ 273). And Bok thinks, "He's half a Jew himself, yet enough of one to protect them" (_Fixer_ 274). As Bok approaches his trial he thinks, "So for a Jew it was the same wherever he went, he carried a remembered pack on his back--a condition of servitude, diminished opportunity, vulnerability" (_Fixer_ 315).

In addition to being a scapegoat and Jew, Bok becomes a figure of Christ. Several critics have noted some of these Christ parallels. James Mellard sees the plot of _The Fixer_ as coinciding with the period of Christ's ministry: at thirty Bok leaves home for three years of service and eventual trial (72). Robert Ducharme notes that Kiev was called "the Jerusalem of Russia" and was situated on three hills, that Bok's encounter with Lebedev parallels Christ as the Good Samaritan, and that Bok's arrest and interrogation parallels Christ's (24-25). Ducharme also sees the nails in Bok's shoes and the chaining of Bok's hands and feet as suggesting the crucifixion (27). John F. Desmond adds that a fixer is in part a carpenter; that Bok's coat is sheepskin; and that Bok, like Christ, is an innocent victim betrayed by his own, here Gronfein, and subjected to public mockery (107).

In addition to these parallels between Bok and Christ, Bok openly identifies with Christ. After Zhitnyak sneaks in a New Testament for Bok to read, Bok becomes fascinated with the story of Jesus. He enjoys Christ's teachings and miracles, but he most closely identifies with Christ's suffering: "Jesus cried out help to God but God gave no help. There was a man crying out in anguish in the dark, but God was on the other side of his mountain" (_Fixer_ 232). But unlike Christ who said his kingdom was not this world, Bok becomes more and more rooted in his moment in history, in his here and now.

And most importantly, as John F. Desmond noted, it is "the humane-ness of Christ" that interests Bok and Malamud (109).

In spite of the rich symbolic nature of Bok's suffering some critics, like the reviewer in *The Times Literary Supplement,* says of the novel, "It makes a virtue out of suffering. . ." (286). But this conclusion is not justified. Bok is subjected to years of solitary confinement in a freezing or sweltering cell, fed watery and bugridden soup, and chained to the wall; but he never glories in his suffering. He curses his fate. He laments his wasted youth. As he tells the Tsar in his vision, "what suffering has taught me is the uselessness of suffering" (*Fixer* 333). Bok is hardly a self-flagellating saint. And as Donald Fanger points out, Malamud's attitude to suffering is not the attitude of Dostoyevsky or Tolstoy whose characters come to accept their guilt; "Malamud's hero comes to accept instead his human responsibility: to create responsibility" (289).

And Bok suffers because God, if he exists at all, has turned his back on man. If Bok can make something of his suffering, it is to his personal credit: he will not necessarily be rewarded for his suffering in this life or in any other. The image of God suggested in *The Fixer* is consistent with the image of God in other fiction by Malamud. Bok's view is very close to Malamud's own: Bok and Malamud are moved by the history of the Jewish people and the life of Christ; they like the stories in the Bible. But they wonder, where is God in the midst of man's suffering?

It is significant that Bok's anger seems more often directed at an unjust God than at the Russians who have imprisoned him. In fact, Bok thinks, "The rod of God's anger against the fixer is Nicholas II, the Russian Tsar. He punishes the suffering servant for being godless" (*Fixer* 240-41). In the beginning of the novel Bok tells Shmuel of God: "He's with us until the Cossacks come galloping, then he is elsewhere. He's in the outhouse, that's where he is" (_Fixer_ 12). In the early days of his imprisonment Bok does wonder if God is "punishing him for his unbelief" (_Fixer_ 153). But as his imprisonment wears on he decides God "had no pity for men. . . . pity was a surprise to God" (_Fixer_ 207). He recalls a Psalm in which God helps men to pursue enemies, "but when he looked at God all he saw was a loud Ha Ha" (_Fixer_ 209). Later when Bok reads the Old Testament history of the Jews he decides that God is "the huffing-puffing God who tries to sound, maybe out of envy, like a human being" (_Fixer_ 239). Bok thinks, "human experience baffles God. . . . Has he ever suffered? How much, after all, has he experienced? God envies the Jews: it's a rich life. Maybe he would like to be human, it's possible, nobody knows" (_Fixer_ 240). When Shmuel visits Bok in prison Bok says of God: "I blame him for not existing, or if he does it is on the moon or stars but not here. The thing is not to believe or the waiting becomes unbearable" (_Fixer_ 256-57). Bok adds that if God exists, he should show a sign.

Bok's attitude to God is important because it contributes to his becoming a new man at the end of the novel. The theme here is similar to the theme of the story "Idiots First": if God is unjust, all the more reason for man to be just and good instead. Man can take God's place by standing in the cause of what is decent and humane. When Bok decides he will suffer for Shmuel, for the Jews, Bok thinks of himself, "He will protect them to the extent that he can. This is his covenant with himself. If God's not a man he has to be. Therefore he must endure to the trial and let them confirm his innocence by their lies" (_Fixer_ 274). As he approaches his trial he fasts, "For God's world" (_Fixer_ 321), though he admits to Kogin that he does not believe in God. As Josephine Zadovsky Knopp has said of Bok's conversion at the end of _The Fixer_, it is not a conversion to theology but it "centers on standards of morality, on his attitude and behavior toward his fellow man" (_The Trial of Judaism_

124). She notes, "his moral conversion, the evolution into <u>mentsh</u> has been completed" (124).

The conclusion of the novel, with Bok en route to his trial, now a newly political man having a vision of shooting the Tsar, has raised several critical questions. For Giles Gunn, "Yakov Bok becomes too quickly an apostle for freedom and liberation and thus loses his potentially beautiful and disarming specificity as a concrete, particular individual" (81-82). Malcolm Bradbury had a similar reaction, feeling the book becomes too much of "a parable about the politicalisation of modern man" (11). Iska Alter accepts Bok as a changed man but says, "Nevertheless the force of Yakov's apparently liberating violence is contained, diminished, and perhaps negated because it has occurred in a fantasy" (171). Some critics feel Malamud cheated by not showing Bok's trial: Josh Greenfield said, "the final effect is like that of a distended prelude, a long one act play with larger potentialities" (10). A number of critics like Philip Roth feel Bok is "doomed" as he heads for his trial (236). Others like Tony Tanner believe Bok will be acquitted. But as Tanner says, Malamud chooses not to show Bok acquitted: "Surely because that would shift the emphasis from the individual attitude to the social fact. It would diminish a parable of universal significance . . ." ("Bernard Malamud and His New Life" 167). V. S. Pritchett likes the ending and notes, "Success at this stage would be an insult" (10).

But the changes in Bok are not too sudden, nor is he reduced to a symbol at the conclusion. I find the conclusion somewhat affirmative but sprinkled with Malamud's usual measure of ambiguity.

Yakov Bok is himself throughout the novel. The changes in Bok are gradual and can be traced back to the questions he raises in his earliest

conversations with Shmuel. Bok is a thoughtful man and the fact that he is
radicalized by his imprisonment is appropriate and believable.

As to whether murder of the Tsar is watered down by the fact that it occurs
in a vision or hallucination, Malamud himself provides some clues. Malamud
was incorporating some of the facts of the Vanzetti case:

> Vanzetti went mad and was confined to Massachusetts
> General; I incorporated that into Yakov Bok. When I leave
> him he is at the next step to commitment. What has
> happened to Yakov and how he changes is the story. But
> what happens to Yakov after I leave him, I don't know. It's
> part of life. I want something the reader is uncertain about.
> It is this uncertainty that produces drama (Haskel 39).

But that Bok's final thoughts are sprinkled with visions does not diminish
their validity. He has hallucinations because he has suffered unendurably. He
must dream of shooting the Tsar because he is hardly given an opportunity to
actually confront the Tsar. And his new political commitment is a natural
outgrowth of his relationship to Bibikov and his interest in the writings of
Spinoza. The night before Bok's trial Bibikov appears to Bok in a vision and
reminds him, "the purpose of freedom is to create it for others" (*Fixer* 319).
Bok tells Bibikov, "Something in myself has changed. I'm not the same man
I was. I fear less and hate more" (*Fixer* 319). On the final page of the novel
Bok recalls Spinoza's words: "If the state acts in ways that are abhorrent to
human nature it's the lesser evil to destroy it" (*Fixer* 335).

The degree of optimism in the conclusion results from the changes inside
Bok and from the fact that for the first time Bok has some real hope. He will
at last have a trial, and as he journeys to the courthouse crowds line the
streets, five and six deep, including some Jews who appear to commiserate.
"Most of the Russian faces were impassive, though some showed hostility and
some loathing" (*Fixer* 329). The bomb which blows off the leg of the young

Cossack may even have been thrown by a revolutionary intending to free Bok. At least Bok finally knows his case is a public cause. He is no longer in solitary.

And this conclusion is in keeping with the conclusions of the early novels. There is some loss mixed with the hope of a new life, which for the Malamud hero will not be easy, as Frank Alpine learns in *The Assistant*. But *The Fixer* is a more political novel than any of the earlier works, certainly more than *The Natural*, *The Assistant*, or *A New Life*, where the political concerns are largely peripheral, or do not exist.

The fact that Malamud stops short of the trial serves to emphasize the importance of the personal inner life of Yakov Bok. As the bomb rocks the coach the fixer rides in, Yakov does not think of politics, but instead, "He felt an overwhelming hunger to be back home, to see Raisl and set things straight, to decide what to do" (*Fixer* 330). As usual, the hero is moved in the direction of the personal, not merely political, commitment.

Though Bok is created in the image of the earlier Malamud heroes, he also represents a change or enlargement in Malamud's focus. As William Kennedy said, Bok "spits in the face of fatalism and despair. With his spit he saves himself and others" ("The Frightening of Beiliss Case" 19). For the first time Malamud applies the values of the hero to the needs of mankind in general. A true *mensch* must be concerned with the values of universal human freedom or no life of value is possible for mankind. In this very fine novel, Malamud created one of his most moving heroes.

PICTURES OF FIDELMAN: THE HERO AS WOULD-BE ARTIST

In 1969 Malamud published *Pictures of Fidelman: An Exhibition*. The novel is composed of six chapters, three of which were previously published as short stories: "The Last Mohican" from *The Magic Barrel*, and "Naked Nude" and "Still Life" from *Idiots First*. As William Kennedy noted, Malamud took the early stories and "touched them up for verve and speed . . ." ("Malamud Finds Renewal in a Fidelman Collage" 23). Arthur Fidelman, the hero of the novel, is an American living in Italy, a would-be art historian, painter, forger, procurer, sculptor and glass blower. The chapters in the novel portray Fidelman in search of himself, in hopes of finding his life in his work. But as usual Malamud redirects his hero. Fidelman does not find fulfillment in work alone; he must learn to love.

Fidelman is tied closely to the early Malamud heroes and is something of a bridge to the later ones. Like all the early heroes, especially in the novels, Fidelman starts out to find a new life. He appears to be in his early thirties at the outset, and his search takes him to a new and alien environment. Besides being geographically displaced, Fidelman is someone not at ease with himself, someone always homeless. He is single and his parents are dead. In his search for a new life he finds suffering and descends into increasingly reduced circumstances. And like some Malamud characters such as Mitka in "Girl of My Dreams," Cronin in "A Choice of Profession," and Krantz in "The Maid's Shoes," Fidelman has a petty, obsessive side. He is neurotic, compulsive and stingy. Like many Malamud heroes, Fidelman is dogged by a full complement of teacher figures: here Susskind, Esmeralda, and Beppo. And finally like most of the early *mensch*-heroes, Fidelman does find a new life and become a new man.

Fidelman is also linked to the later Malamud heroes because he is so ordinary. He is no baseball star like Hobbs, no persevering near saint like Alpine or Bok, no idealistic liberal like Levin. Fidelman is more limited. He is not even much of an artist. Though the early heroes are certainly flawed and do contribute to their own troubles, Fidelman is more deeply flawed, and often less likeable. He has suffered less than Alpine and Bok, yet he has made less of his life. As Robert Ducharme noted, "Fidelman's fate, however, seems largely self-created; all his suffering appears to derive from his wrong choices and his blind and selfish behavior" (140-41). Fidelman's failure occurs not for want of opportunity, but for want of discipline or resolve. In that he is more completely responsible for his fate, Fidelman is tied to the later heroes like Lesser and Dubin.

Because of his many flaws, Fidelman has often been characterized as a *schlemiel*. But Malamud claimed this classification is not accurate: "Peter Schlemiel lost his shadow and suffered the consequences for all time. Not Fidelman. He does better. He escapes his worst fate" (Stern 59). Malamud also claimed that Robert Scholes had best explained "What I was up to in Fidelman" (Stern 59). Scholes said that Fidelman moves towards salvation in the six chapters of the novel, "six stations of the cross," a salvation Fidelman finds in the last chapter ("Portrait of the Artist as Escape-Goat" 32-34). While most of the novel, in fact, depicts the failures of new roles, and Fidelman does not grow more than other Malamud characters, Fidelman does move in a zigzag fashion toward maturity and self-knowledge.

Pictures of Fidelman was generally well received when it was first published. Most critics found the Italian setting for the struggling artist refreshing and comical. Theodore Solotaroff, commenting on some of the early stories, saw:

> a kind of burlesque of the author's formerly grave theme of self-redemption through suffering, love and discipline: with a noticeably more whimsical and gamey prose, Fidelman -- Malamud lays the moral schema around the rim of the story, leaving the center clear for the sudden, unpredictable improvisations of life itself ("Showing us what 'it means human' " (12).

Critics have differed on the questions of the novel's unity and the consistency of Fidelman's character from chapter to chapter. Tony Tanner found the novel "beautifully organized" and Fidelman, a recognizable Malamud hero (*City of Words* 339-40). Charles Stellar claimed the six episodes in the novel are unified by extended metaphors on the themes of art, sex, and Jewishness; and he believed that Fidelman emerges as a complete person (341). Other critics like Thomas Lask have felt that Fidelman is a different person from chapter to chapter (33).

Generally, however, there has been critical agreement that Malamud in his treatment of Fidelman is dealing with his usual theme of a person searching for a life of value. As Lily Edelman noted, "Malamud reverts again to his moving theme of man's tortuous journey from degradation to *menshlichkeit*" (48). For Edelman, Fidelman's struggling is "to become and to remain a *mensh*" (49). Christof Wegelin claimed that Fidelman "grows in self-knowledge and courage as he declines in respectability" (82). And Robert Lasson said that though *Pictures of Fidelman* is very funny, the characters "retain a stubborn, unshakable human dignity" (4).

As with so many Malamud endings, critics are divided over the conclusion of *Pictures of Fidelman*. Robert Scholes claims, "Fidelman's submission to Beppo symbolizes his acceptance of imperfection in existence" ("Portrait of the Artist as Escape-Goat" 34). Philip Roth scoffs at Malamud's insistence that Fidelman find love with Beppo ("Imagining Jews" 40-41). Iska Alter feels Fidelman at the conclusion learns "Life, after all, is better than art" (147). And for William Kennedy: "Life, in a half-baked way, wins, art loses, and though we are conditioned to revere life above art, Mr. Malamud makes the loss seem sad. Not quite a tragedy, but a painful waste: of Fidelman's time, of Fidelman" ("Malamud Finds Renewal in Fidelman Collage" 23).

While focusing on the characteristics that make Fidelman a Malamud *mensch*-hero, I will also address the issues of the novel's unity and Fidelman's unity as a character and the issue of where Malamud leaves Fidelman, in life and in art, at the end of the novel in order to determine just what sort of a hero he is. By dealing with the novel chapter by chapter it becomes clear that gaps in plot and chronology notwithstanding, *Pictures of Fidelman* is unified around the character of Fidelman. And, most importantly, this Fidelman who develops from chapter to chapter is a recognizable human being in the Malamud mold.

In the first chapter "Last Mohican," Fidelman, newly arrived in Rome, sets out on a new life as a Giotto scholar, smartly attired in new oxblood shoes and tweed suit purchased with money borrowed from his sister Bessie. But Fidelman quickly meets Susskind, the man who will serve as teacher-tormentor throughout the novel. Fidelman becomes aware of Susskind's glance while engaging in a reverie of self-satisfaction and self-congratulation: Fidelman contemplates the "pure feeling in his eyes," "the sensitivity of his long nostrils and often tremulous lips," and in general, "his dignified appearance" (*Pictures*

4). Susskind appears to Fidelman as a shadow self, a raggedy, weathered, ghost-like reflection of all Fidelman wants to avoid in others and himself. Both men are the same height but Susskind is oddly attired in knickers, woolen socks, and "small porous pointed shoes" (_Pictures_ 5). He greets Fidelman with a "Shalom" and a "I knew you were Jewish" (_Pictures_ 5-6). Fidelman is reluctant to be identified as a Jew and may associate his past disappointments with his Jewishness. In this respect he is very much like Freeman in "The Lady of the Lake." Susskind is a personification of Jewish suffering and want: he is an eternal wandering refugee like Malamud's Jewbird. Susskind has flown even from Israel.

The intense struggle that develops between Fidelman and Susskind is standard Malamud fare. Fidelman identifies himself as an eternal student like Trofimov in Chekov's _The Cherry Orchard_, an optimistic idealist, superior to love. It takes the rest of the novel for Fidelman to learn the importance of love and responsibility. He does not want to be Susskind's pupil; he feels superior to the "shnorrer" Susskind. But Susskind insists on Fidelman's obligation to him, claiming Fidelman knows what responsibility means: "Then you are responsible. Because you are a man. Because you are a Jew, aren't you?" To which Fidelman replies, "Yes, goddam it . . ." (_Pictures_ 16).

Susskind is a _mensch_-teacher in the Malamud tradition. Like Angel Levine, Salzman the marriage broker in "The Magic Barrel," and Lifschitz the rabbi in "The Silver Crown," Susskind appears shady, ragged, suspect, but he does possess insight and a magical ability to live and travel on air. As he says, "I eat air" (_Pictures_ 15). His very thinness and poverty tend to mark him in Malamud's fiction as a wise and decent person who has suffered.

"Last Mohican," the title of this chapter, suggests several things about Susskind. First it echoes Cooper's _The Last of the Mohicans_ and suggests that

Susskind is the last of his breed, a Jewish Indian dealing from a wise and mythic ancient world. He is described "like a cigar store Indian about to burst into flight" (*Pictures* 8-9). "The Last Mohican" is often used as a general expression for the last one left, which suggests Susskind may be holding out for more humane treatment or a better handout. Most likely Malamud also had in mind the word "Mohican," also spelled "Mohegan" and meaning "wolf" in the Algonquin language. When Fidelman first sees him, Susskind is standing near a statue of "the heavy-dugged Etruscan wolf suckling the infants Romulus and Remus" (*Pictures* 5). Fidelman fears Susskind has come to sucker him, but he has really come to succor him.

Fidelman is leery of Susskind, in keeping with his character as presented in the first chapter. Fidelman is alone and a loner. Only once, after his briefcase is stolen, does he consider the need for some companionship. He is attracted to a prostitute, "a slender, unhappy-looking girl with bags under her eyes" (*Pictures* 26), but he fears for his health. Fidelman is in a precarious position himself. His new clothes are fragile armor, both a testament to his rejection of the past and to his hopes for a new life, but also a reminder of his past failures because the clothes were purchased with money borrowed from his sister Bessie. As he admits when quizzed by Susskind, he has no grant. And Fidelman either does not care about Bessie or resents her because he is in her debt, so he accumulates her unanswered letters. When he works he is "quickly and tightly organized" (*Pictures* 11). A pinched, self-centered quality in the early Fidelman may even be expressed in his precious Giotto chapter which Susskind steals and then burns page by page, lighting his candle, making something from nothing, light from darkness. Fidelman values the chapter for its form and order, but Susskind says, "The words were there but the spirit was missing" (*Pictures* 37). The secret of Giotto is feeling, likely the very quality Fidelman fails to appreciate. Like other Malamud heroes, Fidelman must learn from the past. A new life is not built alone; it must be built on acknowledged connections and indebtedness. Fidelman in his haughtiness misses the human and humane quality of life and art, in Bessie, Susskind, and Giotto. When he speaks to Susskind, Fidelman expresses a superior attitude on all subjects, from Giotto to human freedom. He is an eternal student who feels he has nothing to learn. And it is curious that when Fidelman discovers someone has been in his room, he examines his suit, his shirts, his suitcase, his passport, and his traveler's checks: he even reads ten pages of a book before he considers his briefcase and manuscript. Though the theft of the Giotto chapter sends Fidelman into despair, it seems the loss of direction rather than the loss of intellectual work that really concerns him. The chapter was his justification for borrowing money from Bessie, for coming to Italy.

Susskind's theft of the manuscript initiates changes in Fidelman that will continue throughout the novel. First Fidelman is furious and dreams of pursuing Susskind through the catacombs, threatening to clunk him over the head with "a seven-flamed candelabrum" (*Pictures* 22), which suggests a menorah. He wonders why a man he had been kind to would steal his "life work" (*Pictures* 30). He feels "somehow entangled with Susskind's personality" (*Pictures* 30). But when he sneaks into Susskind's apartment after having secretly followed him there the night before, the sight of Susskind's "black freezing cave," meager possessions, and bony goldfish somehow sustained in the icy place, changes Fidelman: "From the visit he never fully recovered" (*Pictures* 35). Fidelman goes home and dreams of Susskind lecturing on Tolstoy and the meaning of art -- to teach humanity, to communicate feeling. He pictures the Giotto fresco of the young Saint Francis giving his cloak to a poor old soldier and rushes out to give Susskind the suit he has been asking for. "Suit" and "skin" are interchangeable here. Susskind has asked Fidelman to give away his old suit, his old self. When Susskind thrusts the briefcase, sans chapter, at him, Fidelman is momentarily furious but soon has a "triumphant insight": "Susskind, come back," he shouted, half sobbing. "The suit is yours. All is forgiven" (*Pictures* 37). Susskind keeps running.

Some critics object to this ending. Robert Alter claims: "his [Fidelman's] sudden cry of moral recognition at the end of the story is not altogether credible and does not really compensate for the long chain of frustrations which precedes it" ("Out of the Trap" 89-90). But David Mesher has emphasized what Fidelman learns: "one who cannot act charitably and humanely in life cannot really appreciate, or has not sufficiently understood, great art, which has compassion at its root" (398). Mesher adds that just because Fidelman thinks Susskind is a "schnorrer" does not make it so; Susskind is really a peddler (399-400). For Philip Roth, " 'Last Mohican' is a tale of conscience tried and human sympathy unclotted . . ." ("Imagining Jews" 238).

The conclusion of this chapter is, in fact, believable and in keeping with other conclusions in Malamud's work. The move toward human connection is constant in Malamud's fiction. And the final insight is believable given Fidelman's character at this stage. After all, he never completely turns Susskind away: he gives him money, he offers him food. Though Fidelman wants to reject Susskind, he senses all along that he is obligated. And Fidelman's early feeling of superiority does not run that deep: he has girded up a new self in thin armor. He is an intellectual snob when the book opens, but he is ready to be deflated. His credentials rest on one thin chapter, a life's work. Susskind rattles Fidelman's small, safe world and draws him into the world of the poor, the wanderers, the refugees in flight.

In the second chapter "Still Life" Fidelman is still in Rome. He goes to rent a room in an apartment. His pittrice, his landlady, is Annamaria Oliovino, a gaunt, restless, tense woman dressed completely in black, distracted and "indifferent to him or his type" (*Pictures* 40). He later describes her body as smelling like "salted flowers" and "sweating flowers," and her breasts as "hard, piercing" (*Pictures* 44-51). Though he sees himself as "a plucked bird, greased, and ready for frying" (*Pictures* 41), he is drawn to Annamaria. Like many Malamud characters, he is now quickly entangled in relationships, even disastrous ones.

Fidelman does seem reduced and humbled at the outset of this chapter. He is still dependent on Bessie but now seems to have less money. He is now more open, less stuffy in his relations with others. But unfortunately this new openness makes him easy prey for Annamaria Oliovino, of the oily wine, who will soon turn him into a slave. When she sees he is vulnerable and trembling, she doubles the rent. Soon he is waiting on her, taking her out to lunch and dinner, giving her presents. After their sexual fiasco he cleans the house while she sleeps, serves her and then eats alone, leaves the studio while she works. All the while she calls him "Fatso" (*Pictures* 59).

While it might appear that the generosity Fidelman learned in the opening chapter is wasted on Annamaria who reacts only with scorn, they are really engaged in a battle of wills. Fidelman sees sex as "ultimate victory" (*Pictures* 59), and he hopes to earn the victory by swabbing the toilet and dusting. To say the least, it is a weird pursuit.

But the real route to Annamaria is through Fidelman's artwork. His *Virgin and Child*, Annamaria as virgin, wins her over the first time. She says, "You have seen my soul" (*Pictures* 55). He does not know at this point that she has thrown her child, conceived with Augusto her uncle, into the Tiber, fearing it was an idiot. But Fidelman's attempts at intercourse are interrupted four times: first to wait for Augusto, then for two real door bells and one imagined by Annamaria. When Fidelman, quite understandably, is prematurely spent, she calls him "Pig, beast, onanist" (*Pictures* 58). Later in the chapter they attend a party and she paints Fidelman as "A gigantic funereal phallus that resembled a broken-backed snake" (*Pictures* 63).

In one of the most memorable scenes in a Malamud work, Fidelman achieves victory. When Annamaria sees him dressed as a priest for a Rembrandtish self-portrait, she confesses all, begs forgiveness for her sins, and insists on a sexual penance. After some bartering over whether he should keep his cassock on, they settle for the biretta and "Pumping slowly, he nailed her to the cross" (*Pictures* 68). Though earlier in the chapter Annamaria has rejected a priest brought by Augusto to hear a confession, Fidelman as priest proves irresistible. The Jew in priestly garb nails the Roman penitent to the cross.

Philip Roth sees the conclusion as an idealizing of taboo and claims, "What would have been surprising is if Fidelman had disguised himself as Susskind, say, and found that working like an aphrodisiac, maybe even on a Jewish girl like Helen Bober" ("Imagining Jews" 239-40). For Roth, Malamud is again identifying Gentiles with sex and Jews with repression.

Fidelman does make some progress in this chapter. He is warmer, less smug. He tries to have a relationship with a woman, albeit a neurotic vampire like Annamaria, perhaps the least appealing woman in Malamud's fiction. And the ending of the chapter is more hilarious than sacrilegious. Though Annamaria paints crosses and Fidelman paints Stars of David, the chapter is not really about religion. The chapter is about sexual frustration; the sex comes as a relief to Fidelman. That Fidelman would be dressed as a priest does not seem especially odd. He is, after all, a painter in Rome, within sight of St. Peter's. And that Annamaria should desire him as a priest says more about her neurosis than about his. The story does not suggest, however, that Annamaria is rejecting Fidelman, the Jew. And I do not think Fidelman is rejecting his Jewish self in dressing up as a priest, though he may be rejecting his better self in fomenting the passion of a demented woman. Their intercourse clearly seems the end rather than the beginning of their relationship. It is not surprising that Annamaria is mentioned only once after this chapter, while the influence of Susskind lingers to the conclusion of the novel.

Though this chapter contains a series of frustrations with a dubious victory, the Fidelman that emerges is more likeable and substantial than the Fidelman of "Last Mohican." In the true fashion of the Malamud hero, he is softened by his hardships and frustrations, humanized by his mistakes.

The next chapter "Naked Nude" presents Fidelman in Milan, in greatly reduced and highly improbable circumstances. After an unsuccessful attempt at pickpocketing a Texan, Fidelman flees the carabinier only to end up as a prisoner in a hotel. Angelo, the homosexual padronne of the hotel for prostitutes, saves Fidelman from the law, puts him under hotel arrest, and makes him "maestro delle latrine" (*Pictures* 72). Angelo and Scarpio, his major-domo lover, keep Fidelman imprisoned and suggest he paint a copy of Titian's *Venus of Urbino* so they can switch it with the original and hold the original for insurance company ransom. In return Fidelman is to get his passport back plus $350, enough for a ticket home to America. Fidelman makes an excellent copy but falls in love with his work, and when he and Scarpio go to steal the original, Fidelman switches the paintings, knocks out Scarpio with the flashlight, and rows toward Switzerland, his own Venus in tow.

Several characteristics are significant about Fidelman in this third chapter. First, he has been considerably humbled since the first chapter. Now he is destitute: he has slipped into pickpocketing and forgery. He is physically abused by Angelo and threatened by both Angelo and Scarpio several times. He attempts suicide but is dragged back in the window by a prostitute's customer. He seems to blame his troubles on Susskind and draws him as "a long-coated figure loosely hanging from a gallows rope," while still referring to Susskind as "a friend" (*Pictures* 70). When Susskind stole the chapter, he did set Fidelman's fate in turbulent motion.

As Fidelman had blocks as an art critic, blocks as a painter and a lover, here he has blocks as a forger, or "copyist" as he refers to himself. At one point Angelo, who like everyone else in Malamud's Italy is an art lover, claims to have made a life study of Titian. He tries to inspire the blocked Fidelman by telling him that everybody desecrates and steals. With his "two chinned face molded in lard" (*Pictures* 70), Angelo is a false teacher, a corruptor. The one person who gives Fidelman some inspiration and affection is Teresa the chambermaid, but when Angelo discovers them having sex he fires Teresa and Fidelman does not attempt to intervene. In fact, he had been thinking of limericks during sex. The suffering, pitiful Fidelman still has a strangely detached air at times. When he falls in love with his painting it is only a copy and really, he believes, a reflection of himself: "The *Venus of Urbino*, c'est moi" (*Pictures* 89).

This chapter further develops Fidelman as a victim and a sufferer, but, unlike the suffering of most Malamud heroes, Fidelman's suffering is basically burlesque, especially in Fidelman's attempted escape in drag, clothes courtesy of the prostitutes, and in Scarpio's attempt to psychoanalyze Fidelman. At first the homosexual element in the story seems rather gratuitous, but it does foreshadow the homosexual affair between Fidelman and Beppo in the closing chapter. There is one strange revelation about Fidelman and women: in a dream he pictures Bessie at fourteen bathing; he considers painting her but sees himself as a boy, stealing fifty cents from her purse. The dream suggests guilt and anger over sex in general and over taking money from Bessie for his trip to Italy. The dream also reverses the relationship between men and whores: ordinarily men give whores money in exchange for sex. Fidelman steals the money.

In "A Pimp's Revenge" Fidelman becomes "F, ravaged Florentine" (*Pictures* 95), lending this chapter a Kafkaesque tone. Like Kafka's initialed protagonists, F struggles in a labyrinth, here Florence, to reach what becomes an impossible goal. F is still pursuing art, working on the same painting for five years. The painting is based on a photo of a ten-year-old F and his mother, shortly before her death. Bessie sent the photo years ago with her last check, perhaps hinting that he grow up. F is now a little past forty. While still immature and self-centered in many ways, he is beginning to understand himself. His preoccupation with the photo and the painting indicates how shaped and doomed he was by the loss of his mother. As is often the case when young children lose a parent, he feels guilt: he believes he mourned her inadequately and considers painting a Kaddish. He may even fear he caused the death somehow. And he is afraid of the painting: "The truth is I'm afraid to paint, like I might find out something about myself" (*Pictures* 116). In painting his mother he is "pretending" she did not die (*Pictures* 115).

F's Florence is like the rest of Italy in the novel, full of people scraping by, often illegally, each person with five or six others on his back. But all the Italians are also art lovers, historians, dealers, or agents, or they know dealers or agents. And all the Italians claim to know more about art than the uppity

Americans. The tourists are reducing the quality of art sold on streets like the Via Tornabuoni; they are just as happy with the machine made madonnas as with F's hand carved ones.

In this chapter F becomes closely involved with two Florentines, Esmeralda the eighteen-year-old prostitute and Lodovico her pimp, also a former art dealer. Both are teacher figures. Esmeralda, who loves F, has real insight into him and his work, but he does not listen to her or offer her respect or love. Lodovico is shrewd in his dealings with F. He is motivated by a destructive urge to get even with F for stealing Esmeralda, his livelihood.

F's relationship with Esmeralda is consistent with his relationships with other women. He admires them from a distance but he will use them if he gets the chance -- Bessie, Teresa, Esmeralda, and later Margherita. After sizing Esmeralda up on the street and being attracted to her youthful body, F goes up to his room to lock up his freshly earned lire before returning to offer Esmeralda a drawing in exchange for her services. He either suspects she will rob him or still worries about Susskind. New at whoring and embarrassed, Esmeralda apologizes for her performance in bed and then offers to live with F. Typically F fears for his health but lets her stay. "She fed him well. . . . made no complaints. . . . obliged in bed. . . generally made herself useful" (*Pictures* 118). Oddly, she sleeps on a borrowed cot in the kitchen where she exchanges her red chemise, which F thinks too red anyway, for her muslin nightgown. F is bothered by the fact that she does not bathe as often as he. All in all, she is more of a sexual maid than live-in love. And he offers her little affection, though when he gets her to return to whoring he promises to marry her.

She takes this second-class status humbly, till one day F tells her he does not feel like a man without art and she replies, "Personally, I think you have a lot to learn" (*Pictures* 124). He drones on about the mystery of art and Esmeralda says, "my idea of a mystery is why I am in love with you, though it's clear to me you don't see me for dirt" (*Pictures* 124). Esmeralda is like Susskind, only less abrasive in her message: F must learn to be a true, humane person first before he can understand anything. Esmeralda is also an insightful, though neglected, art critic. She notices how sad F looks in the painting with his mother: "To me it's as though you were trying to paint yourself into your mother's arms" (*Pictures* 122). In response F intellectualizes and her point is lost. She finally tears up his photo and thereby helps to end his artistic block: he can no longer depend on the photo. And later she orders him not to touch the finished painting *Prostitute and Procurer*. F never listens to Esmeralda though he should. Even her name suggests truth and beauty and Victor Hugo's Esmeralda and her hunchback; here F is the emotional, artistic hunchback. F is emotionally handicapped and he is an outcast in Florence.

Esmeralda also warns F about Lodovico. The worldly Lodovico is something of a serpent with his sneaky eyes and limp, yellow gloves. Lodovico, slippery talker, once links his pimping-supervision of Esmeralda to the basis of morality -- cooperation, and then adds, "After all, what did Jesus teach?" (*Pictures* 111). But Lodovico does nicely deflate F's artsy jargon in the tape recorded interview that ends so disastrously. And Lodovico does know a good painting when he sees one, though he cannot resist planting the idea of modifications in F's head when he sees the masterpiece completed. Lodovico is wise but fake. He likely got Pannero, the owner of the woodworking shop, to offer F less for the madonnas, because when F leaves the shop he remembers seeing the yellow gloves. Lodovico wants to squeeze Esmeralda back into prostitution.

The Fidelman of this chapter is slightly changed. He is neither as haughty as in the opening chapter nor as abject as in the second and third chapters. Still he is barely getting by; he is blocked in his work. But he does some painting and he has some companionship. He is beginning to realize that his artistic blocks are born partly of his fear of knowing himself or expressing himself in his work. Once again, as with Annamaria and Teresa, F is able to reveal women in his paintings. When he paints Esmeralda she says, "For me it's me" (_Pictures_ 143). He must have some talent as a painter because his _Prostitute and Procurer_ strikes everyone as a masterpiece. But when he talks about art he seems like a total phony. He copies the styles of famous painters or tries to "guess what's next" (_Pictures_ 96). As an artist, F seems mostly false.

As a man F is still somewhat pinched and stingy, qualities that Isa Kapp associates with Malamud's view of the artist (9). But F is opening up somewhat. He lets Esmeralda move in even if he does not bring himself to love her. And he is no longer Annamaria's "Fatso," but a skinny creature, like the _luftmensh_ Susskind. He is more hung up than harmful; his persistence in painting himself as a boy suggests that he is still "a boy with tight insides, on the verge of crying" (_Pictures_ 143).

F no longer sees himself as innocent. He says, after a discussion with Lodovico, "I'm at my most dishonest among dishonest men" (_Pictures_ 135). The words prove prophetic when F allows Esmeralda to return to whoring to support them and then becomes the pimp. His earlier hoity-toity condemnation of Lodovico's "nerve" now seems quite amusing:

> I'm not just referring to your coming up here and telling me what I ought to do vis-a-vis someone who happens to be here because she asked to be, but I mean actually living off the proceeds of a girl's body. All in all, it isn't much of a moral thing to do. . . (_Pictures_ 110).

Malamud saves the most humorous treatment in this chapter for F as a pimp, a treatment likely to keep up the reader's goodwill toward F. His dark glasses, velour hat, ankle length brown overcoat with a ratty collar, and white sneakers make F a funny sight. He also carries a slender cane with a concealed sword. While Esmeralda is at work he sketches obscene pictures or treats himself to cigarettes, espresso and pastry -- delights he was short of before Esmeralda. When Lodovico appears, demanding a commission, F offers him eight per cent to pimp so F can get more time for work. During this bargaining over the girl, F as pimp is less amusing.

But as is often the case in Malamud's fiction, the sin leads to the insight. F paints himself as a young procurer, Esmeralda as a young prostitute. The work makes him honest: "I am what I became from a young age" (*Pictures* 142). He has lived off Bessie for years and now he is living off Esmeralda. F is really still a child.

And as F is Fidelman, he must inevitably fail. Though he is wiser at the end of this chapter, he still fiddles with his masterpiece, destroying it. Lodovico and an art dealer friend laugh; Esmeralda screams and comes at F with a bread knife. F stabs himself and says, "This serves me right." "A moral act," agrees Lodovico (*Pictures* 147).

So far all the chapters have ended dramatically, with some insight or achievement. In the stabbing F is blaming himself more directly than when he kicked and burned his artwork earlier. The "pimp's revenge" in the story is not just Lodovico's; it is also F's revenge on himself. But though F achieves some insight, he is still like the crippled one-eyed eel an old fisherman gave him, a crippled phallus -- emotionally impotent. If he had been wiser he would have let Esmeralda make a good soup out of him too.

In "Pictures of the Artist," the fifth chapter, Malamud experiments with a new, more abstract style. William Kennedy sees this chapter as a successful collage: "The result is one of the most original stories to come along in years, the high point of the book, a delight, a gem" ("Malamud Finds Renewal in Fidelman Collage" 23). For me the chapter is too telegraphic, too fractured. And Fidelman's artistic pretensions seem reflected in the style of the writing itself. The chapter is thick with literary and religious allusions, and the style is dreamy and episodic. But the chapter does have some hilarious moments and it does continue the Susskind-Fidelman battle and the questioning of Fidelman's worth as an artist.

Fidelman is still desperate to be an artist, apparently undaunted by all his failures. He identifies himself with great painters, sculptors, writers and even saints. Inspired by Giotto who was said to be able to draw a perfect circle, Fidelman takes to "sculpting" square holes in the ground and charging the public for a viewing. Fidelman's justification for using dirt is that he cannot afford stone. He is a pretentious, delusional con artist. As Barbara Lefcowitz said, these holes are Malamud's joke: "Fidelman doesn't know his art from a hole in the ground" (119). As the chapter opens, "Fidelman pissing in muddy waters discovers water over his head" (*Pictures* 149). So maybe he is in over his head in art, though a hole in the ground beats a hole in the head. In one unbecoming remark Fidelman compares himself to Michelangelo: "However the pleasure in creation is not less than that felt by Michelangelo" (*Pictures* 151). Never was Fidelman more full of baloney. Art must be more than "pleasure in creation."

When Fidelman refuses to refund a poor young man the ten lire he needs for bread for his family, it is more than Susskind, guardian angel-tormentor can take. Fidelman first defends the fee and the exhibit to the young man by using art critic's hocus-pocus: "There is also a metaphysic in relation of up to down, and vice versa. . ." (*Pictures* 156). He sounds worse than in his earlier interview with Lodovico. Soon a stranger appears in a heavy cloak. His short bowed legs and Yiddish idiom suggest Susskind. After giving Fidelman a gold coin and then viewing the hole, Susskind throws his apple core in one hole. He says to Fidelman, "Form, if you will excuse my expression, is not what is the whole of Art" (*Pictures* 159). The worthy pun holds good advice. For Susskind "is a hole nothing" (*Pictures* 159).

The dark figure claims he is the youth who threw himself in the Bay of Naples for want of the ten lire for his babies' bread. He also says he is the devil. But he still sounds more like Susskind and he clunks Fidelman over the head with the shovel and buries him in one of the squares.

Soon Susskind appears as Christ delivering sermons. He insists on no paint or painting and in modified words of Christ to the fisherman tells Fidelman: "So give up your paints and brushes and follow me where I go. . ." (*Pictures* 163). But Fidelman, ever the slow learner, is soon back at work painting a likeness of the Master. Caught, Fidelman claims, "I am a changed man to my toe nails. . ." (*Pictures* 165). But at what Malamud describes as their Last Supper, Susskind predicts that Fidelman will betray him three more times.

Fidelman's painting is getting more empty and pretentious all the while, "red on red" and "white on white," "For the Resurrection, on Easter morning, he leaveth the canvas blank" (*Pictures* 167). Bernard Malamud himself in a remembrance of the painter Mark Rothko, relates that Rothko offered him some paintings, "one-tone flat maroons" and "almost solid blacks" (Waldman 15). Though Malamud and his wife Anne admired Rothko, they disliked these paintings and chose not to buy one. Fidelman mentions Rothko as an influence in the last chapter. In having Fidelman paint these monochromatic and blank canvases, Malamud seems to be criticizing the worst element in Abstract Expressionism.

Though Fidelman as an artist is disappointing, Susskind livens up the chapter as an hilarious Christ and an even better talking light bulb. In Malamud's version of the allegory of the cave, Fidelman spends years painting the walls and the roof of a huge cave under his sister Bessie's house. He labors in "a leafy loincloth" while Bessie is dying above him and does not even know where he is (*Pictures* 170). For Philip Roth this scene is "Malamud the folk comic at his best" ("Imagining Jews" 237). The bulb illuminates Fidelman to himself. He confesses, "The truth is I hate the past" (*Pictures* 172). Throughout the novel Fidelman has been dominated by guilt over the past. The light bulb, an electric burning bush, advises Fidelman to visit Bessie. The bulb will light the way but not accompany Fidelman. In a voice that is pure Susskind, "A bulb is a bulb. Light I got but not feet" (*Pictures* 174).

When Fidelman sees Bessie she reminisces about when their mother gave them apples and bread to eat. She cherishes the past but he says, "I don't like to remember those things anymore" (*Pictures* 174). Bessie dies in peace anyway, comforted by her brother's hello.

Like the prisoners in Plato's cave, Fidelman has had a distorted view of the world and of himself. He has given all for his paintings and cave drawings, but his attempt at art has left him is some holes in the ground and in his life. He has given all for nothing, in part because he lacked real talent. But his visit to Bessie represents progress. As Robert Scholes said, the visit prepares the way for his salvation in the sixth picture ("Portrait of the Artist as Escape-Goat" 34). And in this chapter Susskind continues his role as teacher of charity, connection, and indebtedness. His lessons may finally be taking hold in Fidelman.

In the final chapter "Glass Blower of Venice," Fidelman finds love and work in unexpected places. In his new modes of expression Fidelman moves closer to the Malamud *mensch*.

The sunny, historic Italy of the opening chapter is now a wintry Venice, palazzi standing in "slime-green algae" (*Pictures* 178). Fidelman as municipal garbage man fishes dead rats and lettuce leaves out of smelly canals. When the pavement of San Marco floods, Fidelman ferries people piggy-back across the plaza. He falls in love with one Venetian customer Margherita Fassoli, but in typical Fidelman fashion, he does so quickly and passionately at a distance. But when after a month of fantasizing he is up close and in bed, he is cool and critical. He notices her veins, splotches, stretch marks and feels disgusted: "She was forty if she was a day" (*Pictures* 187). Fidelman is past forty himself. The sex between them is flat and uninspired: Fidelman says, "I'll get there myself, it won't take but a few minutes. Just act affectionate" (*Pictures* 188). Fidelman, quick with an erection when he met Margherita in the street, is turned off by the real Margherita. But they do manage finally to satisfy each other. When Fidelman awakens to find an old woman reading in the chair by the window it seems a fitting end for the puncturing of Fidelman the romantic. The woman is Margherita's mother-in-law, deaf, dumb and dimwitted.

Fidelman begins to visit the Fassoli family and is soon involved with the husband Beppo. Beppo is an odd candidate for a Malamud *mensch*-teacher. He is a negligent husband and father of two sons, and he seems like a big baby when he is doted on by his mother. But Margherita considers him "wise about life" (*Pictures* 184), and Fidelman readily admires his good sense about art and life. Fidelman, ever preoccupied and guilty about his own sister and mother, may admire Beppo because he is respected by his wife and babied by his mother.

In this chapter the themes of love, sex, and art are once again intertwined. Beppo becomes the agent of a radical change in Fidelman's view of himself as an artist and as a man. First Beppo subtly woos Fidelman with a rose and then a bird he has blown in glass. When they take the boys, eight and ten, swimming Fidelman observes "their young asses flashing in the sunlight" and says, " 'Beautiful' . . . without innocence" (*Pictures* 191). Suddenly Malamud expects the reader to believe that Fidelman has been thinking of men and boys all along. When so much of the book deals with Fidelman and women, the expectation is unrealistic.

But when Fidelman confesses his failures in life and art to Beppo, the struggle for artistic and sexual dominance begins. Though Fidelman now calls himself an "ex-painter" he continues to think of himself as an artist. Fidelman shows Beppo his paintings and sculptures, again sounding like a trendy artist copying tricks he learned in *Art News*. Fidelman is full of jargon: "Note how the base colors, invading without being totally visible, infect the rose so that it's both present and you might say evanescing" (*Pictures* 195). He feels a sexual urge to paint Beppo while he is showing the pictures. But Beppo realizes the art is junk, vinylite toilet seat and all, and suggests, "Burn them all" (*Pictures* 197). Though Fidelman calls Beppo a "cruel fairy bastard" (*Pictures* 197), they are soon burning everything. Beppo wisely tells Fidelman, "Your painting will never pay back the part of your life you've given up for it" (*Pictures* 198).

After Beppo extinguishes Fidelman the artist, he comes along to sodomize Fidelman who is in bed with Margherita. The sex has a funny earthy quality, with mention of mentholated vaseline and piles; but the strange, strong medicine works and Fidelman finds love with Beppo. As Beppo instructs, "If you can't invent art, invent life" (*Pictures* 199).

Beppo also teaches Fidelman the art of blowing glass, which oddly excites
Fidelman sexually. For Fidelman the thought of changing male to female in
glass "helped you to understand the possibilities of life" (*Pictures* 201). But
Fidelman becomes compulsive about the glass and is soon repeating images
from Op Art and Jackson Pollock. Beppo cautions, "It's easy to see, half a
talent is worse than none" (*Pictures* 206). Once again Fidelman gives up art.

When he bumps into Margherita she begs him to leave Venice so that she
can have Beppo back, in part at least. First Fidelman creates a beautiful red
bowl and a "slightly hump-backed green horse for Beppo" (*Pictures* 208). "I
kept my finger in art, Fidelman wept when he was alone" (*Pictures* 208).
Beppo sells the horse and gives Fidelman the money. And finally Fidelman
returns to America where "he worked as a craftsman in glass and loved men
and women" (*Pictures* 208).

Two changes in Fidelman, from heterosexual to homosexual or bisexual
and from artist to craftsman, coming at the end of the novel, raise a few
issues. Philip Roth finds the homosexual element unconvincing: "That is a
dream of the way it works, and all of it neatly koshered with the superego and
other defense agencies, with that reassuring word 'love' " ("Imagining Jews"
240). Love does comes too fast on the heels of sex, but the bigger question is
whether a man in his forties, after a lifetime of involvement with women,
would so quickly and easily become homosexual. In defense of Malamud's
ending, it must be noted that Fidelman's relationships with women have been
unsuccessful. His affair with Margherita, casual as it seems, is "the first long
liaison of his life" (*Pictures* 191). The only woman Fidelman seems to think
much of is Annamaria, an artsy, witchy commandant. And the constant
references to Fidelman's sister and dead mother suggest a man arrested in an
earlier stage of life; he is often painting himself as a young boy. And since

Fidelman has given so little of himself to women in the novel, any conclusion where Fidelman finally discovered himself in the love of a woman would not simply have been too banal, it would have been improbable. Though love with a man is not necessarily more probable than love with a woman, the affair between Beppo and Fidelman suggests that diverse solutions are available to Malamud's hero. Malamud, the artist, does not want his hero to be reduced to merely conventional love. However, Malamud's invention here, his sudden use of homosexuality as a path to the new life, seems to work poorly on a literal level.

The move of Fidelman from artist to craftsman is justifiable. Throughout the novel Fidelman the artist is a disappointment, especially when he talks about his work. Fidelman is not strong enough to be an artist: he lacks the courage to be original and to be honest with himself. He has little insight into himself or life. But his isolation and selfishness are broken down throughout the novel, by Susskind and Beppo especially, so that he is ready to work with others and learn a craft: "But he worked for the first time in his life, instructed" (*Pictures* 203).

This novel expands the image of the Malamud hero by making him a failed artist. Malamud questions the toll that art takes on life, the selfishness it demands. But Fidelman pays his dues to bad art and so wastes much of his time. Though in the epigraph Fidelman suggests that perfection of both art and life matter, in the conclusion of the novel life and love are presented as more important than bad art. The more interesting question of what personal sacrifice great art really deserves is not raised.

Fidelman represents some other changes in the Malamud hero. While earlier heroes were small and even pitiful at times, Fidelman is often downright silly. His exploits are funnier, wilder, and more flamboyant than those of any hero before him. Fidelman also starts out with promise and opportunity and then loses most everything. The more typical movement of the Malamud hero is from less or nothing, through struggle and suffering, to more, even when the victory is an internal, personal one as with Yakov Bok.

But Malamud sticks to his basic themes in the treatment of Arthur Fidelman. The _mensch_-hero must suffer and learn. He must see himself as part of the human community, not above those he meets. He must accept the demands of those he knows and those he does not know. As always in Malamud's fiction, love is all important. When Beppo shows Fidelman love, Fidelman enters a new life.

The strength of the book is in its humor, its breadth and daring. Fidelman is an endearing hero. The reader can easily picture him as he learns to see himself in his pictures. But the weakness of the book is that Fidelman as an artist is such a disappointment that the whole debate about art seems silly. Malamud, perhaps sensing these weaknesses himself, continued the theme of the hero as artist in the next novel _The Tenants_. The novel is serious, even grim, in its treatment of the question of what price art or writing can extract from a person. And because Harry Lesser seems more talented than Fidelman, the question seems more worth asking.

THE TENANTS OR THE COLOR OF ART

In 1971 Bernard Malamud published his sixth novel, *The Tenants*. Again Malamud stuck to his usual themes in the treatment of the hero. The question of what it means to be a *mensch* is raised quite explicitly. And Harry Lesser has many of the basic markings of the Malamud hero: he is alienated, single, a loner; he is tenacious and immovable; and he has had an impoverished emotional life. Willie, a secondary hero and antagonist of Lesser, shares some of Lesser's characteristics; but he is seen mostly through Lesser's eyes and is something of a caricature of a black militant. The two men do share a passion for writing, and the questions of art and life raised in *Pictures in Fidelman* are raised again in *The Tenants*. The setting, a nearly deserted tenement in Manhattan, is the shattered contemporary world, full of destruction and violence. The major question raised in the novel is who has the right to speak for a human view in the midst of a decaying civilization.

But the novel is weakened by several serious flaws. First, the talky, abstract quality of the book makes it unreal and didactic. It is a book openly about issues, uncharacteristic of Malamud. A clue to this weakness comes in Malamud's own description of the inspiration for *The Tenants*: "Jews and blacks, the period of the troubles in New York, of the teacher's strike, the rise of black activism, the mix up of cause and effect. I thought I'd say a word" (Stern 61). For the first time in Malamud's fiction the reader senses that Malamud is starting from ideas and moving to characters. In Malamud's other books the ideas spring from the lives of very believable and sympathetic people. *The Tenants* is topical and does not strike the deep chords of most of Malamud's work. As Marie Syrkin said, it is "fashionable": "Regrettably he [Malamud] is stylish at the expense of his own style" (64).

Another major weakness is that in a great deal of the book too little happens. The subject of writers writing is difficult; Malamud tried it earlier in "The Girl of My Dreams" with mixed results. The setting of an abandoned tenement with Lesser refusing to be evicted and Willie squatting makes things even more static. Often Malamud's traps and prisons are his tools for revealing, testing, and molding his characters, especially in *The Assistant* and *The Fixer* where the narrowness focuses on worthwhile people. But here the trap is made to seem artificial and Lesser a less compelling character. He could leave his tenement, accept the landlord's $10,000, and finish his book elsewhere. As Syrkin says, "we are never adequately convinced that Lesser must stay in his freezing flat. . ." (64). His staying on is but another abstraction in the book.

In addition, one central issue of the novel, whether a writer can be a *mensch* at all, is raised but not dealt with adequately. A *mensch* moves toward commitment to other people; writing is a solitary business requiring some self-ishness. Pearl Bell claimed: "In Lesser's very absorption in the processes of his mind, Malamud is telling us, the writer has become less than a man, for the only value he derives from his commitment rests on words instead of people" (18). But I do not believe Malamud wishes to denigrate writing; generally writing is presented in the novel as a civilized alternative to barbarism. Still, the issue of the writer's life creates a muddled undercurrent in the book and is never resolved. The reader is left to guess whether Lesser has problems because he is Lesser or because he is a writer.

Any discussion of the Malamud hero as presented in _The Tenants_ is also hampered by the fact that both Lesser and Willie are such stereotypes. In general, Malamud's characters are marked by their believability, their humanity. They are quite sympathetic, even when they are acting badly. But Lesser and Willie are more like disembodied, warring points of view. As Syrkin said, "one wished that Willie were less a Black Panther caricature and Lesser not so much an amalgam of Jewish liberal impulses and confusions" (68). Early in the book Lesser and Willie are set up as opposites. Lesser is an educated, intellectual Jew, restrained, sexually repressed, and solitary. Willie is a self-educated, emotional black man, uninhibited, sexual, and social. They seem to exist more in relationship to each other as ideological opposites than as separate characters. However, their relationship is still the most real one in the book. Lesser's affair with Irene seems unreal, a by-product of the Willie-Lesser struggle. And as Melvin Maddocks noted: "The fact that Willie exists primarily as a problem to Harry's image of himself is both the most important point and the most important weakness to be noted in the novel" (134).

In spite of the fact that Lesser is abstract and remote, more the voice of the writer in the novel, it is still worthwhile to compare him to the model of the Malamud hero. First, his isolation is typical. He is practically an orphan. His mother died early in a street accident: "She had gone out for a bottle of Grade A milk and had not come back" (_Tenants_ 198). His brother was dead or missing in Korea, and Lesser became alienated from his father. He feels the uselessness of the deaths and finds solace in writing: "One thing about writing a book you keep death in its place; idea is to keep writing" (_Tenants_ 198). Lesser has never married or lived with a woman. Of the heroes in

Malamud's first five novels only Yakov Bok was married throughout the book, though his wife left him early on. As a rule Malamud prefers single heroes.

Typical of these heroes, Lesser is somewhat displaced, or one might say his neighborhood has been displaced. The building and the neighborhood have changed radically. The previous tenants have been replaced by vagrants, vandals, dope dealers and addicts, and graffiti artists. Lesser's insistence on remaining in this alien environment is typical of the Malamud hero. The Malamud hero has the ability to stay on forever in an impossible situation. Lesser has this same glued to the floor boards quality that keeps Frank Alpine in the grocery and allows Bok to endure his more tragic prison. As Kessler refuses to be evicted in the "The Mourners," Lesser refuses to leave even when the landlord Levenspiel ups the bribe to $10,000. The Malamud hero is often willful and obstinate even when it appears to be against his best interests.

Lesser has another quality sometimes found in the Malamud hero: he thinks cold but often acts warm. Though he resents Willie the intruder even before he meets him, throughout the first half of the book Lesser treats him very well. Though Lesser thinks rather abstractly of women, he treats Mary well and seems to love Irene for a time. And like Fidelman who mentally curses Susskind but ends up feeling in debt to him, Lesser is irresistibly drawn to relationships which he fears.

Though Lesser does have some warmth, the prognosis for him is still grim. He is so tied up in knots that he sees all of life as fodder for his novel. Each encounter with another person is measured by how much it will affect his writing. It takes a volatile Willie to draw Lesser out, but the relationship inevitably ends in violence as the races and writers vie for a place.

Still, the most believable note in the novel is Lesser as writer. Though Malamud claims racial issues inspired him, it is the life of the struggling writer, though slow going at times, that seems most realistic. Lesser has his writing rituals; he times himself and counts his pages. He fears for his manuscript and for the most part of the novel keeps a copy locked up at the bank.

Lesser's book is about Lazar Cohen, a thirty-five year old writer, who is stricken by anxiety over his inability to love. Cohen thinks he can teach himself to love by writing about love, and believes that in writing about love he may be able to love his present girl. But this house of mirrors' effect of a writer writing about a writer writing seems very artificial and trendy. Through most of the novel Lesser stews over the ending of his book. He wants to offer some love, some redemption, but as he tells Irene after the imagined double wedding of Lesser to Mary and Willie to Irene: "It's something I imagined, like an act of love, the end of my book, if I dared" (_Tenants_ 217).

Early in the novel the neat, orderly life of Lesser in his apartment is shown as surrounded by an encroaching jungle of chaos and despair, "-- huge mysterious trees . . . ferny underbrush, grasses sharp as razor blades, giant hairy thistles, dwarf palms. . ." (_Tenants_ 11-12). Lesser sees himself as a "Robinson Crusoe" in his top floor apartment (_Tenants_ 7). His solitude is interrupted by the clack of a typewriter heralding not Friday but Willie Spearmint, black writer. Lesser is wishing for "company in this unpeopled place" (_Tenants_ 27). But Willie is a strong man bent over an ancient L. C. Smith "resembling a miniature fortress" (_Tenants_ 28), and Lesser wants to get rid of him. Their first conversation puts them both on the defensive. Though Lesser offers friendship, he later regrets it. He considers telling Willie "he had, as a boy, for years lived at the edge of a teeming black neighborhood in South Chicago, had had a friend there. . ." (_Tenants_ 32). Lesser sounds ingratiating and self-conscious like Nat Lime in "Black is My Favorite Color." At first Lesser is kind to Willie out of liberal guilt mixed with sympathy for another writer.

So Willie, gruff and presumptuous, stores his typewriter at Lesser's apartment. Their relationship begins.

Though Lesser and Willie are largely stereotypes of the restrained Jewish intellectual and the radical, inflamed black, the real battle between them is over their differences as writers. Willie does make cracks about the Jewish landlord Levenspiel and about "rat-brained" Jewish publishers (*Tenants* 75); and Lesser is preoccupied with Willie's blackness and his "protrusive" and "tumid" eyes (*Tenants* 34, 75), which are like tics in the book they are mentioned so often. But it is their differences in writing styles and habits that Malamud focuses on.

Ihab Hassan said, "As emblems, the Jew stands for responsible form, the Black for felt experience" ("Fictions Within Our Fictions" 54). However, "responsible form" may be a euphemism, since Lesser is a constipated writer. As he says in the beginning of the book, "Rewriting. That was his forte. . ." (*Tenants* 7). After Willie and his friends destroy all Lesser's manuscripts in revenge for the Irene affair, Lesser struggles to rewrite his novel. In one way this fate is appropriate because Lesser prefers rewriting and revision to completing a work: "A wonderful thing about writing is that you can revise, change images, ideas, write the same book better than before" (*Tenants* 183). Lesser is a fussy writer afraid of completing his work and really in love with the order and discipline of writing, which may explain why he must write about a writer writing. Lesser is not warmed by writing the way Willie is. Lesser's apartment is cold but "His feet froze even with the heater going" (*Tenants* 37).

Willie is at first so warmed by his writing that he declines a spare heater offered by Lesser. He writes passionately, largely from his experience. When he is at work he is totally absorbed and does not seem to see or hear anything around him. He starts out on an eight to twelve schedule and works confidently. But in no time the writers are competing and Lesser is transferring his habits and constraints to Willie. Lesser reads Willie's first manuscript, a seemingly autobiographical section followed by five short stories. Though Lesser is moved by the work, he feels Willie "has not yet mastered his craft" (_Tenants_ 66). Lesser tells Willie to work on form and technique, to revise. Willie naively believes, "I am art. Willie Spearmint, _black man_. My form is myself" (_Tenants_ 75). But soon Lesser creates a more anxious Willie who works endlessly and sports new creases on his brow. Bill, as Willie starts to call himself, works on a second book. Lesser admires the first chapter but pans the second which "although worked and reworked, was an involuntary graveyard" (_Tenants_ 161). When Lesser reads the second chapter he is involved with Irene, Willie's girlfriend, and may have mixed motives in his judgments. Still, it seems likely that Bill has contracted the sterile preoccupation with form from Lesser.

Robert Alter has compared Willie's apprenticeship to Lesser with Frank Alpine's apprenticeship to Morris Bober ("Updike, Malamud and the Fire This Time" 70). There are some similarities. Willie deeply respects Lesser's first novel, "that first one you wrote, man, I got to tell you it's a cool piece of work" (_Tenants_ 80). Willie continues to respect Lesser's judgment until Lesser reveals his love for Irene and the murderous hatred between the two writers begins. However, Willie's respect for Lesser is for his technique, his education in form; Willie does not revere Lesser personally the way Frank reveres Morris. There is less warmth between Willie and Lesser and almost none of the father-son relationship of _The Assistant_. Willie's respect for Lesser is based on craft, not on morality.

Willie and Lesser are bound by their subject matter. Both write about themselves and are especially vulnerable to each other's critical attacks.

Lesser's writer is struggling to put love in his book if he cannot put it in his life, and he is struggling with the conclusion of his book. Lesser's writer shares Lesser's character.

Because Malamud does not get inside Willie's head as he does Lesser's, the reader is left to surmise how much of Willie's writing is autobiographical and what sort of life he has had. But it seems a good deal is autobiographical, despite some of Willie's disclaimers. Bill Spear is Willie's pseudonym, suggesting a spear and William Shakespeare. Willie wants to be identified with what is tribal and primitive as well as with what is literary. The first manuscript he gives Lesser depicts a young boy growing up in redneck Mississippi, who later escapes to Detroit and depression, pimping, dope, thievery and prison. In prison he discovers great books and begins to write. Five short stories with five violent deaths come next. Willie tells Lesser that four stories are true but that the long "autobiographical" section is made up: "Myself, I was born on 129th Street in Harlem and moved to Bedford-Stuyvesant with my mama when I was six years old. . ." (*Tenants* 72-73). Willie's second book opens with a solid chapter in which a young boy Herbert Smith, is forced into a sex act by his alcoholic mother's sleazy white boyfriend. Irene later confirms Lesser's suspicions that some of Willie's work is autobiographical. She says Willie came from Georgia to Harlem with his mother and sister when he was sixteen and later served two years in prison. But Willie changes the name of the southern state each time he mentions it, so it is not certain just when he is telling the truth.

Still the image of Willie as coming from a disadvantaged, unhappy background rings true. He has the respect and passion for books and writing typical of Malamud's self-educated characters who do not take the printed word for granted. And Willie's rough, single-parent childhood, his waywardness as a young man, and his solitariness all mark him as a Malamud hero. Malamud creates some depth within the stereotype of the intensely committed, direct, passionate black militant. While Pearl Bell claims Willie is more "an intransigent force of history" than a realistic portrait, she does find his idiom believable (18). Willie's speech is generally realistic, but at times he is hopelessly jivey. At the party at Mary's, after Lesser has slept with Mary and insulted Sam's manhood, Willie calls Lesser a "bleached out Charlie" among other things (_Tenants_ 133). However, some critics like Sidney Finkelstein view Malamud's portrait of Willie very negatively:

> The portrayal of Willie Spearmint is a racist one. He is uncouth, talented but, in Lesser's words, inartistic; and his politics degenerates into anti-Semitism. He typifies, not the Black writer or intellectual, but Lesser's fears, and through this, Malamud's fears (14).

I see both Willie and Lesser as stereotypes to a large extent, but not racist, or even particularly negative stereotypes. They are stereotypes due to the rather abstract nature of the book and to the artificial and limited involvement of the characters in each other's lives, but not because Malamud is expressing bigotry or exorcising personal fears. On the contrary, Malamud is attempting to deal rather straightforwardly with the issues of Lesser's neuroses and Willie's rage.

Lesser's writing reflects his neuroses. He is contemplative and withdrawn and so creates a character with the same reserve, someone alienated like himself. His failure to complete his book in nine and a half years reflects his perfectionism and also his insistence on the type of life writing a book seems to demand of him. He fears completing the book because it might reveal his own artistic limitations, his life as a shallow waste, and at the same time remove his excuse for being so alone. He has come to define himself by his book.

Many of Lesser's characteristics suggest a parallel to Arthur Fidelman, though Lesser is more substantial, someone the reader tends to take more seriously. Both suffer blocks in their work as artists and both fear they will be revealed in their creations. Lesser experiences "Fear of the ultimate confession" (*Tenants* 184). But the most striking similarity is in the shallowness, the triteness of their own comments about their work. Both of them sound quite egocentric. At the party Willie brings to Lesser's flat, the writers get stoned on Lebanon hash and Lesser compares himself to King David and his fiction to the *Psalms*. He tells Willie, whose thoughts are on making money as a writer, "What of remembrance in a future time, a small immortality? Consider the human condition and how soon gone" (*Tenants* 50). And Lesser's literary pretensions spill over into his relationship with Irene: early on "He feels in himself a flow of language, a surge of words toward an epiphany" (*Tenants* 119).

Lesser's relationship to Willie is in some ways similar to Fidelman's relationship to Beppo. Willie destroys Lesser's book as Beppo destroyed Fidelman's paintings and sculpture. In both books the men compete for dominance in art and in sex. And both relationships have a sexual component though it is somewhat repressed in *The Tenants*. Lesser, like Beppo, gives flowers, here carnations when Willie must move headquarters after Levenspiel discovers him. Willie does not acknowledge the flowers. Willie is Lesser's apprentice as Fidelman was Beppo's. And Willie and Lesser are involved with the same woman as were Fidelman and Beppo. When Lesser begins his affair with Irene he has a nightmare of Willie eating a "Kosher" white leg bone and foot (*Tenants* 144-45). Willie is gnawing on Lesser's slightly displaced sex.

This sexual component in Lesser's relationship to Willie is most close to the surface when Lesser, having just told Willie of the affair with Irene, struggles with a naked Willie bent on throwing Lesser out the window. They are saved by Levenspiel.

At times there is some warmth between Lesser and Willie. One time they shared wine and "talked about being writers and what a good and great thing it was" (_Tenants_ 105). Lesser has just praised the first chapter of Willie's second book. Lesser quotes from a John Keats' letter to John Hamilton Reynolds on the importance of the artist's life: "I am convinced more and more day by day that fine writing is next to fine doing the top thing in the world" (_Tenants_ 105). Willie heartily agrees, and because Lesser has not yet slept with Irene the friendship between Lesser and Willie still has some innocence. But a different Keats' letter might be more suitable for Lesser to be quoting: "That if poetry comes not as naturally as leaves to a tree it had better not come at all" (1215).

In the opening of the book creativity and sex are linked, and later, as the struggle for artistic dominance becomes a sexual vendetta between Lesser and Willie, their relationship deteriorates beyond repair. Early on Lesser is sexually aroused by the act of writing: "He also masted an erection -- creativity going on" (_Tenants_ 15). Later both Willie and Lesser deny themselves sex with Irene in order to reserve their energies for writing.

As always, Malamud uses the heroes' relationships with women as measures of their emotional range. Willie's relationship with Irene is depicted as alternately stormy and cool. She suffers a great deal from him including three black eyes, and he appears to give her little warmth in return. He thinks it is unsuitable for a black militant to be seen with a white woman. But Irene cares for him. As she tells Lesser:

> Willie's struggle to be a writer -- from being in prison to
> actually writing the kinds of things he is, his stories and
> novel, is one of the most affecting things I know about
> anybody's life. It moves me an awful lot. He has to go on
> (*Tenants* 147).

Irene worries about who will support Willie. Her attitude is motherly and liberal. But she comes in such a distant second to Willie's all consuming work that by the time Lesser pursues her she is virtually alone.

First Lesser has a brief sexual adventure with Mary Kettlesmith at her party. Sam Clemence is Mary's boyfriend. When Lesser hears someone crying, Mary says, "Usually it's Sam out in the hall, kneeling by the keyhole and crying. . ." (*Tenants* 129). When Mary and Lesser return to the party Sam's friends, led by Willie, engage Lesser in a contest of threats and name calling. Lesser has been eager for "a lay with a little luck; with more a bit of human love in a mad world" (*Tenants* 16) since the opening of the book and has hoped for a black girl's favor. "He had never slept with a black girl" (*Tenants* 37). But sex with Mary is disappointing even though Lesser says, "This is good, Mary" (*Tenants* 128). Mary is frigid and their sex turns into a logistical discussion of coming and not coming.

The encounter with Mary leads indirectly to Lesser's involvement with Irene. Though Lesser has been attracted to Irene all along, the verbal put downs from Willie like "Let the white spook exit out" (*Tenants* 135) seem to heighten Lesser's hunger for her. Later, on the night of the party, Lesser discovers "from the weight on his heart he knew he was in love" (*Tenants* 136). Syrkin says that "kinship" draws Lesser and Irene together (66). Both Lesser and Irene are white and Jewish. But there are more obvious reasons for the stepping up of Lesser's passion -- revenge on Willie and a working out of his attraction to Willie through Irene. In addition, Lesser's failure to satisfy

Mary is no secret and Lesser may want to prove himself a man again. All this suggests a shaky beginning for Lesser's affair with Irene. But Lesser is uninformed of his own motivations, and his near separation from the human race has blurred his poor perspective. The competition between Willie and Lesser has become the driving force for both men.

Lesser's sudden declaration of love for Irene, when he hardly knows her at all, shows how out of touch he is and contributes to the novel's unreal quality. This love is so abstract and unclear that it is laughable. Even Irene says, "Are you in love with me because I'm Willie's Jewish white girl?" (_Tenants_ 139). Lesser proposes immediately and then they make love. Sexual satisfaction comes easily, but in no time Lesser is worried about how and when to tell Willie. Irene wonders what Lesser wants to tell Willie and suggests, "Couldn't we let it die naturally?" (_Tenants_ 146). This discussion of marriage and telling Willie seems so premature; the affair has barely begun.

But Lesser is obsessed with telling Willie and chooses the worst possible time, after he pans the second chapter of Willie's new novel and goes to find Willie naked and grieving over the manuscript. Willie almost manages to throw Lesser out the window, and the fight is eventually finished in one of the endings of the book when Willie castrates Lesser while Lesser axes Willie in the brain. Earlier the unreal nature of Lesser's affair with Irene, its sudden onset and gradual decline after Willie and his friends vandalize Lesser's apartment and burn his manuscripts in revenge, and Lesser's timing in telling Willie suggest Lesser is getting to Willie through Irene. Like Willie, Lesser becomes a neglectful lover and soon Irene is helping to support him.

Lesser's feelings toward Willie are intense and mixed from the outset of the book. When Lesser first hears Willie's typing, he feels "competitive envy" (_Tenants_ 26) before he lays eyes on the man. After finding fault with Willie's first manuscript, Lesser speaks of "being human," but soon "The black, his eyes tumid, beats his head against Lesser's wall, as the writer, not without pleasure, looks on" (*Tenants* 75). Later when Willie wants Lesser to look at the second book, Lesser "beheld in his dark thoughts Bill Spear, potential executioner, requesting him to midwife his bloody fable" (*Tenants* 83).

However, in spite of Lesser's fears, he treats Willie very well in some ways. He allows Willie to store his typewriter in the apartment. Early in the novel he warns Willie of Levenspiel's presence and hides the typewriter in the bath tub. When on another visit the landlord discovers Willie's makeshift office and calls a cop, Lesser hides Willie. Lesser explains his generosity: "We're both writers, Bill" (*Tenants* 95). Then Lesser offers to let Willie work in the apartment after they see Willie's smashed furniture, broken up by Levenspiel and the cop. Lesser goes so far as to buy Willie a table, chair, cot, and floor lamp.

Lesser's generosity to Willie, seemingly odd in so withdrawn a man, can be explained in several ways. First Lesser is patronizing and generous to Willie because he feels sorry for him as a black, as a poor man, and as a writer struggling in Spartan conditions. Lesser has some advantages including a comfortable apartment and at first some financial security, yet he has had difficulty completing his work. Lesser seems to feel that Willie's claim to a space in the building is legitimate. Generally the novel questions notions of private property and comes down on the side of squatter's rights.

Seeing Willie struggle, Lesser acts out of charity and guilt, guilt for his own prosperity and his white skin. The guilt is especially evident when Lesser puts up with Willie's rudeness. Once the writers are drinking and listening to records when Lesser puts on a Bessie Smith album and Willie gets annoyed: " 'Lesser,' he said in a slow burn, 'why don't you give that record away or break it up or eat it? You don't even know how to listen to it' " (_Tenants_ 86-87). Lesser puts on Lotte Lehmann singing Shubert lieder. He is a model host despite Willie's rudeness. It is hard to believe Lesser would accept this sort of behavior from a white man, though Lesser's condescension does make him more believable if not more likeable.

Lesser also feels that Willie is haunting him and that he is inextricably bound up in Willie's fate and so must deal with him. When Lesser suffers a bout of writer's block, "Lesser felt depression sit on his head like a sick crow" (_Tenants_ 106). Willie is part Poe's raven, harbinger of death, and part a feathery yarmulke reminding Lesser of his obligations to the human race. Later Lesser also wonders, "Who's hiring Willie Spearmint to be my dybbuk?" (_Tenants_ 163). A dybbuk, a demon who takes possession of someone, is an apt description of the psychological burden Willie has become to Lesser. So Willie may also be an evil spirit causing havoc in Lesser's life. In general Willie and Lesser bring out the worst in each other.

One other reason that Lesser puts up with Willie is that he is in awe of him. He is drawn to Willie's passion and drive. Lesser sees Willie as a more vital person than himself. When the two men are stoned on hash they rephrase William Blake's "The Tiger":

> Willie
> Nigger, nigger, never die
> Shinin face and bulgin eye.
> Lesser
> Nigger, nigger shining bright
> In the forest of the night. (_Tenants_ 51)

Willie is absorbed by the fact of his blackness in a racist world, while Lesser is drawn to Willie's blackness. Lesser sees Willie as powerful and mysterious. The passive, bookish Lesser feels pale in comparison. Lesser also has some fear of Willie, another reason he is patient.

Lesser does begin to build up a gradual resentment of Willie and all he feels he has done for him. While Willie withdraws more into his work and becomes obsessed with form, Lesser becomes more angry and active. The affair with Irene is a sign of Lesser's loneliness but also of his growing anger at Willie. Early in the novel he took pleasure in Willie's beating his head against the wall, but at the end of the novel Lesser stalks the tenement, ax in hand, and hacks up Willie's typewriter in revenge for the burned manuscripts. "Though Lesser shivered feverishly, he felt for a while an extraordinary relief. He did not care for what he had done; it sickened him deeply, but for a while he thought the writing might go well thereafter" (*Tenants* 227-28). Though he is justifiably angry for all the years of his work that Willie and company destroyed, by demolishing the ancient, pitiful machine Lesser will not bring back the muse or erase Willie from his life.

The theme of competing writers continues until the last pages of *The Tenants* as both Willie and Lesser rummage in garbage cans reading each other's manuscripts. And the theme of blacks and Jews at war becomes more pronounced toward the end of the novel in Willie and Lesser's last two encounters. When they meet accidentally on the stairs Lesser offers forgiveness. Willie counters, "No Jew can treat me like a man -- male or female" (*Tenants* 224). Lesser urges them to be civilized: "Let's talk to one another like men who write" (*Tenants* 224). Willie accuses Lesser of ruining his style. And in their final murderous encounter their only words are "Bloodsuckin Jew Niggerhater" and "Anti-Semitic Ape" (*Tenants* 229).

The issue of race is handled strangely throughout the novel. Lesser does fit the somewhat negative stereotype of the neurotic Jewish intellectual, but in most ways he does not seem especially Jewish. Someone like Morris Bober, though not conventionally religious, is still markedly Jewish. Even Sy Levin is more conscious of himself as a Jew than is Lesser. Lesser is closer to Fidelman--deracinated, modern and rather removed from the Jewishness of a Shimon Susskind. Lesser is largely Jewish in the eyes of Willie and of Levenspiel, who works on Lesser's Jewishness in order to get him to sympathize and move out of the building.

The distinctions between blacks and whites seem rather bizarre in this novel. Mary will not go to bed with Lesser at the first party because he smells white, as she says, like "No smell at all" (_Tenants_ 47). In an incident reminiscent of Nat Lime's abuse from the blind man in "Black is My Favorite Color," Lesser hands a black woman a broken piece of a mirror she has dropped and she spits on it. Then when Lesser and Irene become involved, "Lesser once asked her whether she missed the mood, the pitch of black life --" (_Tenants_ 153). And she asks Lesser, "Do I smell black to you?" (_Tenants_ 142). Willie stays away from Irene when he is writing about Herbert's mama in the second chapter of his novel, "so I could write it pure" (_Tenants_ 159). He wants a purely black book. In some ways Malamud presents race as a skin disease, an impediment in the eye and nose of the beholder. Malamud is pointing out how ludicrous perceived racial differences are -- but how absolute and ingrained.

In this morass of artistic and racial conflict one man speaks for a more human point of view. Levenspiel the landlord, though not without self interest, speaks constantly of reality, decency, and mercy. Levenspiel visits, calls, and sends notes to Lesser exhorting him to move out. Levenspiel wants to knock down the old building and put up a new one with larger apartments. Because the new building will have fewer units, the District Rent Office forbids Levenspiel to evict Lesser.   Levenspiel's anticipated project will be financed by Metropolitan Life, naturally.

Unlike Lesser, who at the outset of the novel has no personal obligations, Levenspiel has a sick wife, a sixteen-year-old daughter suffering the aftereffects of a botched abortion, and an insane mother eating herself to death. He begs Lesser to sympathize, and at times Lesser feels guilt over the difficulties he has caused the landlord. Levenspiel becomes especially angry when he discovers evidence of Willie's presence. He calls Willie a "gorilla" and Lesser's "nigger friend" (*Tenants* 91-92) though he has not met him. Understandably he does not want to deal with two entrenched writers. Through large portions of the book Levenspiel disappears, but he does show up in time to prevent Willie from heaving Lesser out the window. Levenspiel is shaken by the violence and by Willie's nudity. He says to Levin, "You're your own worst enemy, bringing a naked nigger into this house" (*Tenants* 169). Toward the end of the novel Levenspiel writes Lesser a letter offering him $10,000. Levenspiel explains the offer: "But I am a mensch" (*Tenants* 193). He claims it is the last offer.

Lesser envisions Levenspiel setting fire to the building, but it is Lesser and Willie who bring on the cataclysm. When he sees them hacked up " 'Mercy, the both of you, for Christ's sake,' Levenspiel cries. 'Hab rachmones [have pity or compassion], I beg you. Mercy on me. Mercy mercy mercy. . .' " (*Tenants* 230). One hundred and fifteen mercies in all.

Levenspiel is a type of Malamud *mensch*-teacher. He is the voice of human sympathy. Though he is calling for Lesser and Willie to have mercy on him, he is also begging them to be decent human beings. Levenspiel represents the larger world outside the tenement, in part the world of commerce. But he also is portrayed as caring for a family and having many responsibilities. Both Lesser and Willie see morality as something totally abstract; they are alienated from their families and their communities. Willie has some friends, but neither Willie nor Lesser gives much of himself to anyone else.

That Levenspiel has some selfish motives puts him right in line with other Malamud teachers like Shimon Susskind, who gets money from Fidelman, and Rabbi Lifschitz of "The Silver Crown," who gets money from Albert Gans for healing crowns and then likely uses the money to buy new clothes for himself and his daughter. Malamud presents all these men as justified in their requests and as wiser men than the heroes. Levenspiel's relationship to Lesser and Willie also resembles that of Marcus, the clothing store owner in "The Death of Me," and his two warring assistants. Marcus begs them to treat each other with decency; they keep fighting and he has a heart attack. Syrkin finds Levenspiel "the sole human voice heard" (68).

Throughout the novel Lesser struggles with the ending of his book. Bell has suggested, "Clearly Lesser is not alone in his trouble with endings" (18). She finds Malamud's conclusion disappointing. Actually Malamud offers three or four endings, depending on how one counts. The first ending features Lesser opening his apartment door to find his building engulfed in flames lit by Levenspiel. This nightmare ending occurs early in the novel but is clearly labeled "End of Novel" (*Tenants* 23).

The second dream-like ending is the rather hilarious but incongruous double wedding of Lesser to Mary, conducted by a skinny tribal chieftain, and Willie to Irene, performed by a Litvak rabbi with a fedora and a grizzled beard. The cow dung fragrance in the air means the "The omen is of plenty" (*Tenants* 208). Much of this scene is very funny. Lesser wears "a smoked raffia skirt from waist to knees over his jockey shorts" (*Tenants* 210). Mary is noticeably pregnant. But in the middle of the wedding Lesser misses his book.

The priest speaks of forgiveness and has a few wise sayings like "The mouse which thinks he is an elephant will break his back" and "Eat the fruit where you do find it. The tiger which tears his gut do not digest his food" (*Tenants* 212). These sayings would seem coined for Lesser, but the priest forbids Lesser to put the words in his book. Soon Lesser's father appears and blames the mixed marriage on Lesser's non-Jewish education. Irene's family is sad she is marrying Willie, but the rabbi says, "Someday God will bring together Ishmael and Israel to live as one people. It won't be the first miracle" (*Tenants* 216).

In the third ending Lesser and Willie meet among the spreading trees and bushes in the tenement. The image is gruesome: "Lesser felt his jagged ax sink through bone and brain as the groaning black's razor-sharp saber, in a single boiling stabbing slash, cut the white's balls from the rest of him. Each, thought the writer, feels the anguish of the other" (*Tenants* 229-230). The thinking writer is likely Lesser, but the felt anguish is small compensation for either man. After the murders and "The End," the final ending is Levenspiel begging for mercy.

The endings are no more or less believable than the rest of the book. Violence is inevitable as the relationship between Willie and Lesser steadily deteriorates. It is particularly tragic that two writers cannot communicate. But the novel becomes so grim that I think Malamud balked at a totally despairing ending and threw in the wild, upbeat wedding scene as a slight antidote. Still, as Bell has said, the novel is a "desperately honest and bitter vision of our day" (17). Though the characters are weak at times, Malamud's portrayal of hatred and frustration is honest.

In many ways *The Tenants* stands in opposition to most of Malamud's work. Malamud usually leaves his characters with some uncertainty but with considerable hope. They have changed, grown from their experiences. But while Lesser and Willie have many of the markings of the Malamud hero, they lack the most basic ingredient of compassion. They are self-absorbed at the opening of the novel and even more so at the conclusion. Even Irene sees them as "such self-conscious characters" (_Tenants_ 116). Each is a half-baked _mensch_, a person with potential sacrificed to pride.

It is easy to see why Malamud would be moved by the climate of the late sixties and early seventies to write a book like _The Tenants_ even though it is one of his weakest books. In the novel he does raise many worthwhile questions. Malamud questions the value of a writer's life, largely spent alone, removed from the needs of the world. Malamud suggests the writer is a lesser human being and a lesser writer if he becomes paralyzed by his work. Malamud also asks what can possibly control the violent, primitive side of every man. But when even writers cannot talk things out, the outcome appears hopeless. And once again Malamud raises the issue of one man's obligation to another and again suggests we are all hopelessly indebted and interdependent. Lesser and Willie should have cared more for each other.

The novel falters because Malamud allows his concerns to make the book didactic and abstract. And while most of Malamud's characters are so sympathetic, Lesser and Willie leave the reader with a bitter aftertaste. Lesser as an ordinary writer is a somehow uninteresting figure. Though Lesser has published two novels, he still sounds mediocre when he talks about his work. An ordinary store owner or fixer is one thing; but an ordinary writer who strains and poses gets tiresome.

Malamud does succeed in depicting the endless measuring of guilt and suffering that goes on in the world. Six million exterminated Jews are measured against millions of American blacks suffering hundreds of years of slavery and poverty. Both Lesser and Willie feel they have the bigger pain in their guts. But they see only their personal sufferings and have no real right to speak for mankind. Though they are both tenants of this house, of this decaying civilization, neither has a monopoly on getting the human story, on crying out in grief. In a contest of suffering both Lesser and Willie lose. For Malamud the issue is not simply Jews or blacks but humankind. As always Malamud speaks for the hope of human communion.

But a change is taking place in Malamud's fiction. He is steadily less optimistic about the possibility of people communicating. The dire tone of *The Tenants* is continued subtly in *Rembrandt's Hat*, where the stories deal mostly with failed communications.

A CROWN FOR MALAMUD IN *REMBRANDT'S HAT*

In *Rembrandt's Hat*, published in 1973, Malamud deals with familiar themes in varied settings. The characters are all locked in some sort of prison. Most endure horrible suffering and loneliness. They are eager to communicate, to shove a printed or blank message into someone's hand, to discover a secret in someone else's mail. They are desperate and frantically seek help, often from strangers. Though the collection of stories has some humorous and absurd moments, it is generally an extended lament on the sorrow and separation in the world.

The title is taken from a story in the collection, "Rembrandt's Hat," in which an art history teacher incorrectly identifies his artist colleague's hat as resembling a white hat in a Rembrandt self-portrait. A silent feud ensues as the artist apparently feels insulted, embarrassed and hexed. As a title for the collection *Rembrandt's Hat* suggests the rich variety of art, all that might come out of the master's hat. But the title also invites sad thoughts of how things often fail to measure up to the grand old days of art.

Malamud must have been aware that readers might find these stories pessimistic. The second of two epigraphs for the volume comes from James T. Field's exhortation to Henry James: "What we want is short cheerful stories." But as usual there is a human hum in Malamud's work, a quickening of life in all its pettiness and grandeur, that keeps these stories from being totally despairing. As Malamud emphasizes in the first epigraph in a possibly cheerful quote from T. S. Eliot's otherwise gloomy "The Journey of the Magi," "And an old white horse galloped away in the meadow," the collection ends on an uplifting note as the "Talking Horse" is freed from slavery and gallops away a centaur.

The characters in these stories bear some resemblance to the earlier heroes. They are in unhappy predicaments and they long to escape. They seek to communicate with each other. But most of them will not find a new life, either because their prisons are shut tight or because they lack the strength or courage to break out. John Leonard has said, "These are unfinished or malformed people, tense from trying to make sense of their situations, suspicious of their emotions" (116). In fact, the situations these characters find themselves in are not really unique; and most of the characters are ordinary and typical people, not half-formed. A number of them are guided largely by their emotions.

Generally the collection was well-received when it first came out and has been regarded as closely related to the rest of Malamud's fiction. The critic in *The Times Literary Supplement* had a typical reaction. He felt the book compared favorably with Malamud's earlier collections: "But if the surrounding atmosphere has thinned, the human atmosphere has become sharper and more extraordinary" (1158). The critic said the style "retains lucidity, strength and truthfulness" (1158).

The first story "The Silver Crown" ranks among Malamud's best. Like "The Magic Barrel," "Angel Levine" and "Idiots First," it too mingles old world and new and touches on the supernatural. Again Malamud has a perfect pair of characters in the young skeptic Albert Gans and aging healer-rabbi Jonas Lifschitz. In keeping with the theme of the collection, the story dramatizes big hopes pinned on a small message and the ultimate and inevitable failure to communicate.

Gans is a rather unpleasant person though he does have some of the common markings of the Malamud hero. He is isolated and estranged from his father who is in a hospital dying. Albert appears to be without close friends: he considers approaching a faith healer for his father on the advice of "A female colleague, an English teacher he had slept with once. . ." (*Rembrandt* 4). He feels guilt about his father; "He had done nothing for him all his life" (*Rembrandt* 4). His father suggests he may be dying of cancer of the heart, implying a broken heart. Gans, frustrated by his inability to help his father and by the heavy burden of his guilt, is drawn to any help he can get and so accepts a soiled card thrust at him by a fat girl who appears to be retarded. The message in Hebrew, English, and Yiddish reads, "Heal the Sick. Save the Dying. Make a Silver Crown" (*Rembrandt* 5).

This story is built on many ironies. Gans, a biology teacher who considers himself an empiricist, seeks out a faith healer and then attempts to bargain on rational terms. He decides to buy the mystical crown. He needs the help of a stranger, the rabbi, a religious man, to prove his love for his own father. The old rabbi and his feeble-minded daughter are devoted to each other; they share the love Albert lacks. But Albert feels superior to their shabbiness and eccentricity. The final and most appropriate irony is that Gans does not love his father after all. He has merely been paying off a guilty conscience. Gans decides he has been swindled out of $986 for the crown. He finds the rabbi who suggests Albert think of his father's love. But Albert Gans says, " 'He hates me, the son-of-a-bitch, I hope he croaks'. . . . An hour later the elder Gans shut his eyes and expired" (*Rembrandt* 29).

Jonas Lifschitz and his daughter Rifkele are among Malamud's most memorable characters. The rabbi, complete with his involuntary winks and magical previews of the healing $986 crown, fits squarely into the tradition of the *mensch*-teacher. He appears either suspect or otherworldly. He finally defends his crown by reading hilarious testimonials from lawyers and college teachers who praise the efficacy of the crown and recommend it to all their friends. Even though he and his daughter may be wearing new "glad rags" (*Rembrandt* 26) as Albert calls them when he returns either to see the crown or get a refund, the rabbi and Rifkele are still depicted as genuine, warm, and wise.

Rabbi Lifschitz has "a thickened left eyelid" (*Rembrandt* 6) and is prone to wet eyes, but he sees Albert Gans clearly enough. Several times the rabbi mentions how important it is that Albert love his father for the crown to work, but Albert mostly sidesteps the issue and instead haggles over the prices of the crown. When Albert goes on and on about the "principle, or rationale" of the crown, "The rabbi, with an absent-minded start, seemed to interrupt himself about to pick his nose" (*Rembrandt* 9). He does not think much of Gans' scientific approach. Gans asks how things work while the rabbi speaks of love. Lifschitz reads to Albert from a mystic book, "The crown is the fruit of God's grace. His grace is the love of creation" (*Rembrandt* 12). Lifschitz is a third generation healer-rabbi whom Malamud suggests has at least one foot in an ancient and mystical world.

Throughout the story the rabbi is subtly identified with the elder Gans. Albert notices the smell of old age in the storefront synagogue. When the rabbi's face appears in the mirror during the preview of the crown, Albert sees "his old man's lined and shrunken face, his sad eyes, compelling, inquisitive, weary, perhaps even frightened, as though they had seen more than they had cared to but were still looking" (*Rembrandt* 19). When the crown appears on the rabbi's head Albert should feel the healing power of love, for the rabbi, for anyone. When Albert first saw the mirror he noticed "a single oval mirror, framed in gold-plated groupings of joined metal circles, large and small; but no pictures" (*Rembrandt* 8). Albert and his father are pictured in the wise rabbi's mirror, but Albert will not look into his own heart. The synagogue is a barren room filled with empty chairs. Albert is merely one of many unbelievers.

Rifkele is not so simple as she appears in Gans' eyes either. In her primitive, awkward way she reacts to him most appropriately. She thrusts the card at Albert in the first place; he needs Jonas Lifschitz even if he does not realize it. And most of Rifkele's boohooing and ear slapping comes on cue to Albert's coarse pronouncements. As his father says, "In her way she is also perfect" (*Rembrandt* 7). Her seemingly involuntary movements are linked to her father's expression. Understandably, they both find Gans hard to take. When Albert doubts the crown and insists on a demonstration, the rabbi reminds him that it is not a Chevrolet automobile and asks again if Albert loves his father. Albert says, "Don't be stupid. . ." (*Rembrandt* 16). At that the rabbi's beard quivers and "Rifkele, in a nearby room, moaned" (*Rembrandt* 16). Rifkele does pant after Gans "like a cow for a bull" (*Rembrandt* 22), but she also claps her ears to keep from hearing his crack about their glad rags. She later cries "Booo-ooo" when Gans threatens to call the Bronx County District Attorney and report the rabbi (*Rembrandt* 28). When Gans accuses the rabbi of magic "with an idiot girl for a come on" the rabbi begs, "Be merciful to an old man. Think of my poor child. Think of your father who loves you" (*Rembrandt* 29). Albert curses his father and unwittingly condemns him to death. Lifschitz and his daughter rush into each other's arms, horrified by Albert's hate. Rifkele may not speak but she sees, hears, and understands. She is less an idiot than Albert in some ways.

Albert's grip on reality is actually tenuous. He tries to explain everything in terms of science even though at the outset of the story the reader learns that medical specialists cannot even diagnose Gans senior. Albert Gans is frozen to the world of love and emotions. In spite of seeking out Lifschitz, Gans reverts to a rational approach and tries to get his money back. "He felt he did not, in essence, trust the rabbi; and suspected that Rabbi Lifschitz knew it and did not, in essence, trust him" (*Rembrandt* 22). In his relationship with the old rabbi, Albert reenacts his resentment and mistrust of his own father.

Albert Gans' main failing is pride. He quickly feels superior to the rabbi and his daughter. He appraises them and judges them mercilessly. Though Gans' very presence before a faith healer indicates the rational approach has failed him, he tries to deal with the rabbi on strictly business terms. And the simple, rather sad circumstances of Jonas Lifschitz and Rifkele lead Albert to look down on them.

Albert is an angry man: "He was easily irritated; angered by the war, atom bomb, pollution, death, obviously the strain of worrying about his father's illness" (*Rembrandt* 4). Albert is the Malamud hero unredeemed. The *mensch*-teacher finds him, but Albert does not hear the message of love and compassion. In the rabbi's room, "The shades resembled faded maps of ancient lands" (*Rembrandt* 6). But Albert misses the simple and ancient message.

The story is really an example of Malamud the alchemist at his best, mixing the wild comedy of the ragged rabbi and the ear clapping Rifkele with the straight man approach of the modern Albert Gans. The arbitrarily priced crowns, the testimonial endorsements, the rabbi and his daughter worshipping in a palatial synagogue on Mosholu Parkway, and other beautiful details lend renewed life to Malamud's old theme of the primacy of love and communion. Albert takes the long way around to learn that he has not loved his father after all. He is left with "a massive, spikeladen headache" (*Rembrandt* 29) and little hope of a new life.

The second story is a long one, sixty-two pages, entitled "Man in the Drawer." Its narrator is Howard Harvitz, a recently widowed, forty-seven-year-old free-lance writer from America who is touring the Soviet Union. When he is in Moscow he hails a cab driven by Feliks Levitansky, a half Jewish Russian in his thirties, a translator and a writer of short stories. The story hinges on Levitansky's pleas that Harvitz smuggle out some short stories that the Russian cannot publish in his own country. Harvitz, a nervous man, worries constantly about air crashes, wars, and KGB plots. He admires Levitansky's stories but is afraid of being caught by Soviet authorities and imprisoned. After changing his mind several times, Harvitz finally heads for the airport with Levitansky's stories in his suitcase.

Though the story lacks Malamud's usual economy, much of the dialogue is excellent and Levitansky has a wonderful non-native command of English. As Howard Harvitz says of Levitansky: "His accent was strong, verging on fruity, but redeemed by fluency of tongue" (*Rembrandt* 36). Typical of someone a little uneasy in a language, Levitansky laughs even when he does not understand the joke, as when Harvitz says he is a free-lance writer. Malamud also includes some of his classic elements in this story. First, two strangers are quickly and inextricably bound to each other; their connection seems fated. The claim that the stranger Levitansky makes on Howard Harvitz is seen as a legitimate one; as usual in Malamud's fiction, man is his brother's keeper. Again Malamud deals with a struggling artist, here a writer who, unlike Fidelman, appears to have considerable talent. And once again the chance encounter between two men radically alters both their lives.

Howard shares some of the qualities of the aging Malamud heroes like William Dubin. He is personally fastidious and cautious, but politically liberal. He hopes for yet fears excitement in his love life. He has fantasies of being engaged to a Russian girl; he invites a woman who phones him speaking Russian to "lunch or whatever you like" (*Rembrandt* 44). And later he becomes attracted to a shapely woman of around thirty years who sits next to him at *Tosca* at the Bolshoi, but then he backs off when she suggests that after he leaves the U.S.S.R. he mail a letter to her husband in Paris. In the last case Howard fears a trick and hands back the letter.

Howard is ripe for his encounter with Levitansky. Typical of many Malamud characters, Howard hopes for and expects change. He finds himself suddenly alone, recently widowed, and as he says, "I'm traveling partly to relieve my mind" (Rembrandt 36). Though he has many fears he wants something to happen to him. This sense of expectation is similar to Fidelman's hopes when he first arrives in Rome. As Fidelman is quickly spotted by Susskind who affixes himself to the Jewish American abroad, Howard is soon in the clutches of his *mensch*-teacher Feliks Levitansky, who immediately says "Shalom!" (*Rembrandt* 34).

Though Howard hailed Feliks' cab, he feels that Feliks picked him, "maybe somebody he had mistaken for a friend" (*Rembrandt* 34). In the universal fashion of cabbie and lone rider, Levitansky and Harvitz are quickly engaged in an intimate conversation. As Howard says, "From the moment we met, our eyes were caught in a developing recognition although we were complete strangers" (*Rembrandt* 34). Displaced, in a country of strangers, Howard is eager for a friend. And in Malamud's use of the attraction of opposites, the worrywart Howard is driven around by the reckless and distracted Levitansky.

Levitansky is a lean, hungry looking type who seems to be everywhere at once. Like Susskind in his freezing knickers, Feliks wears sandals and shirt sleeves when the temperature is in the fifties. He seems always to be wearing red, white, and blue socks, either as an affront to the Soviet system or as a reminder to Harvitz of the obligation of the free to the censored. Again Malamud emphasizes how rich even middle class Americans seem compared to many in the world who must struggle for the necessities. Levitansky makes a bit of a living by borrowing his brother-in-law's taxi for a couple of hours every day, but mostly his wife supports him. He has the frail yet somehow hearty quality common to Malamud's teacher figures. Levitansky has a head which "seemed pressed a bit flat by somebody's heavy hand although protected by a mat of healthy hair" (*Rembrandt* 35). The heavy hand of government oppression has flattened his head and pushed him into a drawer. Of the manuscript, " 'The mice should read and criticize,' Levitansky said bitterly. 'This what they don't eat they make their drops -- droppings -- on. It is perfect criticism' " (*Rembrandt* 48-49).

Levitansky suggests the possibilities of communism and Howard admits flaws in the U.S. system but claims it is more free. When Howard insults him by offering him a ruble tip, Levitansky is furious: " 'Hiroshima! Nagasaki!' he taunted as the Volga took off in a burst of smoke. 'Aggressor against the suffering poor people of Vietnam!' " (*Rembrandt* 49). But Levitansky later admits of the Soviet system, "I do not believe in partiinost, which is guided thought, an expression which is to me ridiculous. I do not believe in the bolshevization of literature" (*Rembrandt* 71). And Howard admits he wishes he had spoken up firmly against Vietnam: "In a curious way I am just waking up to the fact that the United States Government has for years been mucking up my soul" (*Rembrandt* 70). So in a smaller way Howard identifies with Levitansky's oppression and moves to free himself as well as Levitansky when he agrees to take the manuscript.

As in many stories in this volume a message, here a manuscript, a suitable symbol for the writer Malamud, is passed back and forth by people attempting to communicate. But this story holds more hope than most in the collection because a friendship develops and the manuscript is en route to freedom and likely an American publisher at the conclusion. However, Malamud emphasizes that the inability to communicate is not always the result of personal failing. Governments conspire to keep many people locked in drawers if they criticize the system, however implicitly.

Levitansky's stories, briefly sketched by Howard, are sharp and compelling. Malamud is able to suggests a story in a nutshell, as he did with the summaries of Willie's fiction in *The Tenants*. Levitansky's stories deal with an old man's unsuccessful attempts to contact his son, a government official; with another old man hoping to have matzos for Passover, though the state laws ban them; with a young man caught by government officials as he seeks to sell a tallith, or prayer shawl; and finally with a writer, half-Jewish, who burns his work in the sink because he is unable to find a publisher. Like "Man in the Drawer," these stories deal with the general difficulties of communicating and with the special terrors of government suppression.

"Man in the Drawer" once again demonstrates Malamud's belief in the possibility of people to change. Howard Harvitz is a rather pinched, rigid man at the outset of the story. He is afraid to remarry his first wife Lillian. When she presses him he reflects, "I warned myself afterwards: Beware of any more contemplated entanglements" (*Rembrandt* 39). Later when Levitansky bursts forth with his troubles Howard thinks, "I have never cared for confessions such as are meant to involve unwilling people in others' personal problems" (*Rembrandt* 62). When Levitansky appeals to Howard as a fellow humanist, Howard says, "What exactly is my responsibility to you, Levitansky?" And Levitansky responds, "We are members of mankind. If I am drowning you must assist to save me" (*Rembrandt* 72). Howard has recently changed his name from Harris back to Harvitz, but Levitansky accuses: "All I wish to say, Gospodin Harvitz, is it requires more to change a man's character than to change his name" (*Rembrandt* 73).

Yet Harvitz does change. Levitansky and his fiction, the discussions of other banned writers such as Boris Pasternak, the pleas of Levitansky's wife Irina, the brother-in-law Dmitri with "sad Jewish eyes" (*Rembrand*t 81), all conspire to convince Howard to take the chance. He feels particularly vulnerable because when he arrived in Kiev officials confiscated five copies of *Visible Secrets*, a high school poetry anthology he edited. But in daring to smuggle out Levitansky's stories, Harvitz becomes a new man. Suddenly he decides to ask Lillian to marry him when he gets home. And though he is still frightened, he wants to be as courageous as Levitansky: "When one thinks of it it's little enough he does for human freedom in the course of his life" (*Rembrandt* 81-82).

This story emphasizes that communication is difficult but not impossible. A person of integrity and feeling like Levitansky can draw out someone rather unwilling like Harvitz. Levitansky becomes Howard's political and artistic conscience. But the prison motif prevails at the conclusion of the story because while his stories may find freedom, Levitansky remains trapped. As Howard tells himself, "I wished for a courage equal to Levitansky's when they discovered he was the author of a book of stories I had managed to sneak out and get published, and his trial and suffering began" (*Rembrandt* 83).

"The Letter," a very short story, deals with the prison of a mental hospital and the difficulties the patients have in communicating with each other and with their visitors. The story has two sets of fathers and sons who are incommunicado. The tone is alternately humorous and grim as once again a rational person attempts to deal with an irrational world.

Newman, the straight man of the piece, visits his father in the hospital every Sunday afternoon for two and a half hours. The father attempted suicide after his wife died. Like Albert Gans in "The Silver Crown," Newman seems bound to his father by a guilty sense of obligation. Newman implies that visiting his father is a chore when he asks his father for a Sunday off: "But if you want a week off sometime let me know. I want a Sunday off myself" (*Rembrandt* 100). Newman brings his father a pineapple tart "but the old man wouldn't eat it" (*Rembrandt* 99). Sadly, they sit on a white bench with little to say to each other. The hospital setting only slightly magnifies the common alienation of father and son.

The father's colorful speech is somehow oddly sensible. He is hurt by his son's request for a day off and says, "Your mother didn't talk to me like that. She didn't leave any dead chickens in the bathtub" (*Rembrandt* 100). Presumably she did not stink up the place with half-camouflaged resentments the way Newman does.

As usual Malamud casts his lot with the irrational folk, the outcasts, the dispossessed. The asylum and its inmates, at first so ridiculous, begin to seem like the true world, the world unmasked. Newman, modern man, cannot cope with the suffering and despair he sees in the patients.

Teddy is a patient in his fifties who, like Lifschitz in "The Silver Crown," has odd eyes; "One of his eyes was a fleshy gray, the other was walleyed" (*Rembrandt* 101). Teddy wants Newman to post an unstamped, unaddressed letter: "Inside were four sheets of cream paper with nothing written on them" (*Rembrandt* 101). A mailbox is hung on the other side of the road, outside the gate. Teddy doesn't want the doctor to "read" his letter so he will not mail it on the ward. Teddy and Newman pass the soiled envelope back and forth each week, the way Levitansky and Harvitz play hot-potato with the manuscript.

Soon Ralph, Teddy's father who looks about eighty, gets involved. Ralph says he fought at the Marne and in the Argonne Forest, and Teddy fought in Iwo Jima and Guadalcanal. They must have seen enough grief for more than two lifetimes. Both men want to know where Newman and his father fought. Newman says, "No war at all" (*Rembrandt* 104). His father fought "The war in his head" (*Rembrandt* 106). When Ralph begs Newman to mail Teddy's letter, Newman says he will write out a message if Ralph will say who he wishes to communicate with. " 'He wants to communicate with me,' says Ralph" (*Rembrandt* 105). But Teddy does not want anything written: "There's a whole letter in there. Plenty of news" (*Rembrandt* 106).

"The Letter" suggests several things. First, a blank letter in an unaddressed envelope is the ultimate in existentially absurd communications. Nothing is left to say; the emptiness itself is the horror. But the letter is no less empty than Newman's obligatory attempts to communicate with his father. And that Teddy would want a blank letter sent out of the hospital in order to communicate with his father who is a patient in the same hospital is no more strange than that Albert Gans in "The Silver Crown" would attempt to reach his own father through Jonas Lifshitz, the supernatural faith healer.

Though the mental patients are somewhat ridiculous Malamud still imbues them with a certain charm. Death, wars, and illness are too horrible to face. There is some comfort in the elder Newman's refusal to accept his wife's death. The younger Newman accepts all with the calm dispassion of those dead to feeling.

The story fits squarely into the theme of this collection. The characters struggle to communicate, to leap out of their individual prisons of emotional despair. They send messages, blank pages and pineapple tarts. But in the end even those confined together suffer separately.

"In Retirement" also emphasizes the lack of communication, the deep sense of sorrow and separation in the world. A sensitive retired man, Dr. Morris holds out for the dream of a new life and is left, instead, lonely, humiliated, drifting into old age. At 66, Dr. Morris is a widower who retired after a heart attack. His only daughter lives in Scotland and his life in an apartment near Gramercy Park is lonely and endlessly the same. He uses routine to give himself a sense of purpose but even his morning walks sadden him: "What was difficult was that it made no difference where he went" (*Rembrandt* 110). Dr. Morris is like an older Howard Harvitz, a reserved, meticulous man secretly drawn to danger and intrigue. Dr. Morris wants to reread the *Odyssey* in Greek, likely to find the adventure his life lacks.

His adventure begins when he sees an attractive young woman leaving the apartment building, "In fact he held the door open for her and got a breath of her bold perfume" (*Rembrandt* 111). Later he finds a letter she had dropped. He slips it into his pocket and reads in his apartment. It is to a girl named Evelyn from her father with a P.S. from her mother reading, "Your sex life fills me full of fear" (*Rembrandt* 113). The father begs his daughter to stop sleeping around and to marry someone decent: "I don't want to think of you any more as a drifting semi-prostitute" (*Rembrandt* 113). The letter excites Dr. Morris' imagination. At first he sympathizes with the girl and with her parents.

But soon Dr. Morris is obsessed by erotic thoughts of Evelyn and his fantasies quickly cure his depression. "The hunger he felt, a hunger for pleasure, disruption of habit, renewal of feeling, yet a fear of it, continued to grow in him like a dead tree come to life and spreading its branches" (*Rembrandt* 115). "He woke with desire mixed with repulsion and lay quietly mourning himself" (*Rembrandt* 116). Like other characters in these stories, Dr. Morris is excited by the thinnest of messages, not even addressed to him, and he hopes for a new life. But he is also frightened by his reawakening: "The doctor felt he was caught in an overwhelming emotion, a fearful dark wind" (*Rembrandt* 115).

The next day Dr. Morris steals a letter for Evelyn Gordon from a pile of alphabetized mail in the lobby. In his room he steams the letter open. It is an account of business dealings with a quite personal closing: "Be in your bed when I get there tonight. Be wearing only your white panties. I don't like to waste time once we are together" (*Rembrandt* 118). The lover is a Lee Bradley. Dr. Morris finds the letter coarse and disgusting. He reseals it and puts it in Evelyn's mail box. Suddenly Dr. Morris is "more than half in love with her" (*Rembrandt* 119).

Dr. Morris observes Evelyn for months and imagines that he could give her the steadiness, respect, and love she needs. When spring arrives he writes her a letter of introduction, explaining his honorable intentions, all the while fearful he will mention the white panties. He waits in the lobby for her to receive her letter. Dr. Morris is a vision of spring: "He had on a new green suit, blue striped shirt and a pink tie. He was wearing a new hat. He waited in anticipation and love" (*Rembrandt* 122). But ah, Evelyn comes down with a man, perhaps Bradley. She reads the letter, shows it to her companion and rips it to bits, flinging the pieces at the doctor. "He thought he would sit forever on his wooden throne in the swirling snow" (*Rembrandt* 123).

Dr. Morris comes sharply to life in this brief story. Like Leo Finkle, Morris is drawn to a woman who has lived fully. His nosiness and spying as well as his compassion and erotic dreams all serve to make him sympathetic. But like several other characters in this volume, Dr. Morris is so isolated that he pins all his hopes on a stranger and is inevitably rebuffed. Because he so wants to live, it is especially sad to see him pushed back into more sorrow and isolation. Malamud suggests that often when people try to climb out of their living graves, the graves simply deepen.

There is some warmth in the story between Dr. Morris and Flaherty, the kindly, aging doorman who is dying of cancer of the jaw. The doctor would like to console Flaherty in some way. As the story closes they do speak to each other of death and old age; but "The doctor tried to say something kind to him but could not" (*Rembrandt* 124). Although Morris and Flaherty seem to care a bit for each other, they still suffer separately. And Morris is a particularly pathetic Malamud hero. Although he has the capacity for love, the capability to be a *mensch*, he is locked out of life and has no avenue by which to express his sensitivity.

"Rembrandt's Hat," the title story, also emphasizes the difficulty of people communicating and the special difficulties of the artist's life. A more subtle point is that art historians, like Arkin in this story, should have little to say about art: they have no idea how hard the life of the artist is. And once again Malamud shows his sympathy for an artist of minimal talent. Like Fidelman, Rubin the sculptor in "Rembrandt's Hat" produces little that is worthwhile and gains negligible satisfaction from his work.

Both Arkin and Rubin teach at an art school in Manhattan. Arkin is thirty-four; Rubin around a dozen years older. Arkin is "a hypertensive impulsive bachelor" (*Rembrandt* 127). He is talkative, aggressive and outgoing. He wants always to be liked and cannot believe he has offended Rubin by comparing the sculptor's hat to Rembrandt's. Arkin is quite unaware that he can be obnoxious. Early in the story he offends Rubin by asking if he is working and what he is doing. Rubin responds with "Of course I'm working" and "I have a thing going" (*Rembrandt* 128). Years before, Arkin attended Rubin's one gallery opening but disliked the pieces of altered driftwood Rubin displayed and never commented on the show to Rubin. So Rubin must suspect that Arkin dislikes his work, making the Rembrandt remark more galling. Once when Arkin discourses on Jackson Pollock in the faculty cafeteria, Rubin angrily replies, "The world of art ain't necessarily in your eyes" (*Rembrandt* 128). And he asks Arkin, "Have you ever painted?" (*Rembrandt* 128). Arkin thinks he has strong feelings, but he cannot begin to imagine the torture Rubin is going through.

Rubin is a more typical Malamud sufferer, though older and more worn. He is a private person who looks away as he talks to Arkin, perhaps offended by Arkin's judgments of art. Rubin's wife has recently abandoned him and he has taken to wearing hats. He is trying to start up a new life in new hats. But Arkin's comment about the white hat must suggest to Rubin that he looks silly and pretentious, as though he were trying to jump under Rembrandt's hat. Arkin says:

> I'll tell you why I like it so much. It looks like Rembrandt's hat that he wears in one of the middle-aged self-portraits, the really profound ones, I think the one in the Rijksmuseum in Amsterdam. May it bring you the best of luck (*Rembrandt* 129).

As Renee Winegarten said of Arkin, "Thus he stands in for the critic who not only fails to hit the nail on the head but strikes the practitioner's thumb . . ." (99). After Arkin's remark, Rubin for a time wears no hat at all and then the feud begins. Arkin is at first bewildered but then becomes increasingly angry. The bulk of the story is taken up with the hat and with Arkin's attempts to discover its meaning. Malamud picks up on some humorous and typical details of academic feuds: Rubin takes a new route to his studio to avoid passing Arkin's open door, they refuse to serve on committees together, and they avoid each other in the men's room. When a student gives Arkin a Stetson hat, Rubin glowers at it and it is soon stolen from Arkin's office. They meet in a mock-western stand off, Arkin in a black wool hat and Rubin in an engineer's cap. They see by their headgear that they have artistic pretensions. Later Arkin calls Rubin "murderer" and the sculptor responds with "thief" (*Rembrandt* 136).

Finally, after more than half a year of the feud, Arkin sneaks into Rubin's studio, discovers the sad and mostly disappointing flower sculptures, and then looks at his own slides of Rembrandt's self-portraits and realizes he was mistaken about the hat. "Rubin's white thing, on the other hand, looked more like an assistant cook's cap in Sam's Diner than it did like either of Rembrandt's hats. . ." (*Rembrandt* 138). Arkin finally has insight into Rubin and imagines how he has irritated the sculptor, who might well think:

> The mention of Rembrandt, considering the quality of my work and what I am feeling generally about life, is a fat burden on my soul because it makes me ask myself once more -- but once too often -- why am I going on this way if this is the kind of sculptor I am going to be for the rest of my life (*Rembrandt* 139).

This story offers some hope of communication and reconciliation. Arkin goes to Rubin's studio and apologizes for mixing up the hats and "Also for letting things get out of hand for a while" (*Rembrandt* 140). Rubin, so much more tied up in knots than Arkin imagines, first says "Damn right" and then cries: "He wept silently, his shoulders shaking, tears seeping through his coarse fingers on his face" (*Rembrandt* 140). A pleasant, though distant relationship ensues and they meet one day in the men's room, the conference room of academe in this story. Rubin is looking in the mirror, in his white hat: "He wore it like a crown of failure and hope" (*Rembrandt* 141). That hat neatly sums up the failure and hope expressed in many of the stories in this collection, a humble dream that life can be better than it is.

In some ways both Arkin and Rubin are humanized by their feud, unlike Willie and Lesser of *The Tenants*. Though Rubin turns out to be the real injured party, both men are more sympathetic by the end of the story. Again, so much hinges on a brief message, here verbal; and people who are practically strangers are deeply changed by their encounter. Arkin, whose profession it is to rank and categorize art, learns how to be the friend of someone who has tried but mostly failed to be an artist. Malamud emphasizes how hard the life of an artist is and how few will become Rembrandts. But for Malamud art remains a noble calling, one most human and filled with hope.

In "Notes from a Lady at a Dinner Party" Malamud again deals with isolation, frustration, mistaken paths, traps. The title seems to echo Dostoyevsky's *Notes from Underground*. In Malamud's story lives are depicted as often more miserable than anyone might expect, if not quite as sordid and evil as Dostoyevsky's narrator suggests. An unhappy young wife thrusts notes into the pocket of a man she hardly knows. Again these characters are desperate to communicate, even with strangers; in this story, as in "Man in the Drawer," the stranger responds.

This story is really more titillating than humorous. The story hinges on two improbabilities: that a man and woman could pass notes at a dinner table and be undetected by the guests and, more unlikely, that a woman six months' pregnant would not show. Karla Harris, the pregnant young wife, spends the evening seducing Max Adler, her husband's former pupil, and then bows out of a rendezvous by revealing that she is pregnant. Her messages turn out to be a game, false promises for herself and Adler.

Max Adler is a chunky, thirty-two-year-old architect. His work is admired both by Clem Harris, his former teacher, and by Karla Harris, wife and former student of Clem. Adler is divorced and seems ready for new connections. He is fond of Harris and feels guilty to be carrying out a flirtation with Harris' wife but "She wants someone young for a change, he thought. It will be good for her" (*Rembrandt* 160). He already feels "as though he were in love with her" (*Rembrandt* 159). Love at first sight is fairly common in Malamud's fiction.

Karla Harris is a woman in a trap. Now twenty-five or six, she has been married to Clem for several years and seems to adore their two little children. She hints to Adler that she admired Clem but that their marriage was a mistake; "Clem married me when I was very young. . ." (*Rembrandt* 155). She has given up her dreams for work and burnt her diary: "I had to. It beat me up badly" (*Rembrandt* 158). But her attraction to Adler is based on his accomplishments as well. She admires his work and seeks vicariously to assume his talents as she earlier tried to do with her husband's. She has not found the courage to be herself.

From the very beginning of the story Karla makes her interest in Adler obvious. When she asks him his age and he says it is thirty-two, "Karla remarked it was a fine age for a man" (*Rembrandt* 146). She implicitly expresses dissatisfaction with her husband's sixty-four years. Her first note to Adler makes her unhappiness clear: "Why do we all think we *should* be happy, that it's one of the necessary conditions of life?" (*Rembrandt* 147). Later after several notes and after Karla shows Adler her babies, they go to her study. She praises Adler's work and soon "They embraced forcefully. She dug her body into his. They kissed wet-mouthed, then she broke with an embarrassed laugh" (*Rembrandt* 155). If she had not appeared pregnant to Adler, she ought to have felt six months' pregnant in such close proximity. Her secret pregnancy strains credulity. Still, the flirtation seems quite realistic, fueled by the complications of the dinner party and everyone's respect for the fatherly Clem Harris, who is drinking himself into a flushed and watery-eyed state. When Karla says she is experiencing anxiety, Harris advises, "Take a pill" (*Rembrandt* 159). He seems to believe their marital estrangement has a chemical cure. Karla appears ready to jump through the roof or hop on any passing stranger.

Adler realizes he has been arbitrarily singled out and decides not to read the last note, which falls on the floor. "She'll write forever, he thought; that's her nature. If not to me, then to the next one who comes into the house who's done something she wishes she had" (*Rembrandt* 160). Shirley Fisher, Harris' secretary with a son on LSD, picks up the note and asks Harris if he dropped it. He hands it to Adler. The note reads, "Darling, I can't meet you, I am six months' pregnant" (*Rembrandt* 161). Shirley suspects Adler and Karla, and Adler suspects Shirley of being involved with Harris. It would seem that Adler has jumped in to a hot pot of frustration and intrigue. Harris does not open the note, perhaps suspecting its contents and preferring to remain half-deluded. As the guests leave Karla sings, "Love, marriage, happiness" (*Rembrandt* 161), from the stairs.

The surprise ending of a pregnancy is ineffective. It does neatly keep Karla in her trap, but it also suggests she is even more neurotic than she has appeared. The pregnancy is no surprise to her and if she prefers not to have an affair because of her condition, she has simply been pretending to break out. She may be using Adler to make Clem jealous. She says of her husband, "It might do him good" (*Rembrandt* 157). Karla is much less sympathetic than someone like Pauline Gilley in *A New Life*, who is also escaping her unhappy marriage. Pauline is sensitive and warm; Karla is flighty and immature. And though Max Adler is sweet, he is also somehow innocuous and does little thinking for himself.

The story is perfectly true in some ways, yet it is not as rich and suggestive as the others in the volume. While Karla's predicament could be made compelling, it is not. Generally it is hard to care about the characters in this story and the tone is rather distant and cold, unusual for Malamud. But "Notes from a Lady at a Dinner Party" is still connected to the other stories in the volume. A person who feels imprisoned believes notes sent to a stranger will serve as a magical S.O.S. Again the Malamud characters become quickly and deeply entangled in each other's lives. Max Adler is chosen by fate and by Karla to be the agent of her escape, if only for one night; but he is let off the hook as the needs of a baby-to-be take precedence.

The next story is the excellent "My Son the Murderer," a most explicit handling of two themes that thread throughout the volume: the alienation of father and son and the terror of war, here the Vietnam War. Albert Gans and his father, Newman and his father as well as Teddy and Ralph, and Harry and Leo in this story all face a wall of silence that has grown up between them. And as these stories were written during the Vietnam War years it is not so surprising that war contributes heavily to the gloom of this collection. Albert

Gans and Howard Harvitz worry about Vietnam. Teddy and his father, psychiatric patients in "The Letter," seem to have been mentally unhinged by World Wars I and II. And in "My Son the Murderer" Harry, recent college graduate, is expecting his draft notice any day. He watches the television news from Vietnam and thinks: "It's a big burning war on a small screen. It rains bombs and the flames go higher" (*Rembrandt* 167). The war is a monumental grief weighing down a young man; it renders him speechless, without feeling for his family or friends.

Since Harry graduated from college he has remained at home, mostly in his room -- his trap. He corresponds with the draft board, perhaps hoping to get conscientious objector status. He won't work because he says, "It's not that I don't want to work. It's that I feel bad" (*Rembrandt* 167). When his mother suggests temporary work Harry yells, "Everything's temporary. Why should I add more to what's temporary. On top of that I don't want temporary work. I want the opposite of temporary, but where is it? Where do you find it?" (*Rembrandt* 167). Depressed, deeply moved and frightened by the war, Harry angrily withdraws from everything.

Malamud uses no quotation marks in this story and the point of view shifts from father to son to narrator. So their anxieties become closely identified, but the father and son remain estranged. The father Leo actively seeks to help his son and to show him love, but he is constantly rebuffed by Harry. Leo says, "Harry, we live like strangers. All I'm saying is I remember better days. I remember when we weren't afraid to show we loved each other" (*Rembrandt* 169-170). Even the older sister says of Harry, "I used to like him when he was a little boy but now it's hard to deal with a person who won't reciprocate to you" (*Rembrandt* 168).

Because Leo cannot reach his son his methods have become rather bizarre. He listens in the hallway and by his son's door, he tails Harry to Coney Island twice, and he resorts to steaming open a letter marked "personal" from a girl Harry once knew named Edith. She simply requests that Harry return two books he borrowed over six months ago. Leo's snooping is similar to Dr. Morris' snooping in "In Retirement"; in both cases older men hope to establish connections by reading someone else's mail. In Malamud's world spying is the sort of thing an alienated person does. And as with the other messages and manuscripts in *Rembrandt's Hat*, the mail and the printed word in general seem to excite the characters' highest hopes. Though Harry's letter turns out not to be very personal at all, Leo probably hoped it would hold a key to Harry's depression. The other letter Harry receives is from the draft board, presumably his draft notice.

Harry discovers his father reading the girl's letter and says, "I ought to murder you the way you spy on me" (*Rembrandt* 172). After Harry tears up the letter and leaves the house, Leo, apparently unrepentant, snoops around in Harry's room and finds a note: "Dear Edith, why don't you go fuck yourself? If you write me another letter I'll murder you" (*Rembrandt* 172). Even the reader is shocked by the tone of the response to Edith. Harry is more deeply disturbed than anyone has suspected. Everything is judged by the magnitude of the war; the two books seem insignificant to him.

Sadly, when Leo had opened the mailbox he was hoping for a letter from his son Harry, explaining why he acts the way he does. Earlier in the story Leo hoped for such a letter beginning "My dear father" (*Rembrandt* 166). Of course such a letter never arrives. In one way Harry is murdering his father Leo by cutting off the father's love.

The conclusion is the most touching one in the whole collection. Leo follows Harry to Coney Island amid snow flurries on a cold winter day. The amusement park is closed up and "The gunmetal ocean, moving like melted lead, looked freezing . . . The wind white-capped the leaden waves and the slow surf broke on the empty beaches with a quiet roar" (*Rembrandt* 173). The "leaden" and "gunmetal" ocean is a reminder of the war. Appropriately enough, when Leo finds his son, Harry is "standing in the water to the tops of his shoes" (*Rembrandt* 173). Harry is testing the currents, likely with thoughts of suicide.

> Harry, I'm frightened. Tell me what's the matter. My son, have mercy on me.
> I'm frightened of the world, Harry thought. It fills me with fright.
> He said nothing (*Rembrandt* 173).

Malamud beautifully suggests the degree of the father's grief with a simple prop, a hat. In the middle of this tragic scene Leo's hat is blown off his head and carried along the wet sand. "He chased it one way, then another, then toward the water. The wind blew the hat against his legs and he caught it. By now he was crying" (*Rembrandt* 174). He cries that his son is so lonely and unhappy. At the height of Leo's despair the lost hat makes him look ridiculous; it accentuates his absurd isolation, his hopelessness. Frustrated, Leo resorts to the age old and mostly useless parental exhortation: "All I can say to you is who says life is so easy? Since when? It wasn't for me and it isn't for you" (*Rembrandt* 174). Harry does not respond and the father leaves. Once again Leo's hat is plucked from his head.

Malamud presents these characters as isolated, even from those who could be close. Communication seems impossible. Leo, the father, sells stamps at the post office, but he opens his son's mail and hopes Harry will write to him, though they live under the same roof. And as in "Man in the Drawer," politics and wars tear up people. Here Harry is presented quite sympathetically. Who can blame him for not wanting to fight in Vietnam? Like Malamud, Harry is frightened by the horror and violence in the world. In this story the mail brings only bad news from the draft board. Harry and Leo end up at the Atlantic, on the edge of an endless ocean of grief. Yet they cannot share the grief and, like most characters in this volume of stories, must suffer alone.

In the final story, entitled "Talking Horse," Malamud again features someone in a special type of prison, but this time the character has the ability to communicate and is finally freed. Abramowitz, the talking horse, is in bondage to Goldberg, "a deaf mute from way back" (*Rembrandt* 178), who uses the horse in a sideshow act. The story seems a mixture of Dostoyevsky's "The Crocodile," television's "Mr. Ed," and Kafka's *Metamorphosis*, and old vaudeville acts where two men made up a horse. Malamud's horse is uncertain whether he is simply a horse "with a complicated voice box" (*Rembrandt* 177) or a man in a horse. Abramowitz thinks that if it is a man in a horse "Jonah had it better in the whale -- more room all around; also he knew who he was and how he got there" (*Rembrandt* 177). But though he has a Biblical sounding name and may be in a predicament like Jonah, Abramowitz says "he's no prophet" (*Rembrandt* 178). The story has the mixed comic and serious tone that characterizes Malamud's last novel *God's Grace*, which also features talking animals.

In this story the horse has all the humanity and Goldberg, the trainer, is the true beast, though speech and thought ordinarily define what it means to be human. Goldberg is a violent man of limited insight pounding Morse code messages onto a horse of greater sense. Goldberg can only "geee, gooo, gaaw"

(*Rembrandt* 181) and Abramowitz says, "When he laughs he sounds like a horse, or maybe it's the way I hear him with these ears" (*Rembrandt* 183).

Malamud suggests that Goldberg is a perverse God. When Abramowitz insists on knowing where he came from, Goldberg taps on the horse's skull: "In the beginning was the word" and "NO MORE QUESTIONS" (*Rembrandt* 185). In fact, their circus act is a mock liturgy of staid and stale jokes like "Why does a fireman wear red suspenders?" (*Rembrandt* 188). Goldberg beats Abramowitz if he mixes up the riddles or makes up new ones. Goldberg counsels the horse, "Don't try to know everything, you might go mad. . . . Follow the rules of the game. . . . The law is the law, you can't change the order" (Rembrandt 193). He mocks Abramowitz' dream of becoming a race horse or a poet.

Abramowitz, the man trapped in the horse, comes to represent human aspiration, imagination. "Sometimes I think of myself as an idea, yet here I stand in this filthy stall, my hoofs sunk in my yellow balls of dreck" (*Rembrandt* 190). The talking horse is weighed down in the small, vindictive world of his simple-minded keeper, who wears yellow gloves like Lodovico the procurer in "A Pimp's Revenge" from *Pictures of Fidelman*. Abramowitz aspires to a better life; he dreams of freedom. He imagines how he came to be a talking horse after a battle on horseback or after seeing a goddess bathing naked. Beaten with Goldberg's bamboo cane, Abramowitz says, "But the true pain, at least to me, is when you don't know what you have to know" (*Rembrandt* 179). This talking horse suffers from existential *angst*. Goldberg tells Abramowitz, "you think too much, why do you bother?" (*Rembrandt* 194). And in the true spirit of a god Goldberg warns, "Watch out for hubris, Abramowitz" (*Rembrandt* 198).

The talking horse makes one escape but is recaptured. Finally when Goldberg is watching an astronomy program on educational television, Abramowitz brings his hoofs down on Goldberg's head; Goldberg grabs the horse's ears and in the struggle Abramowitz emerges to the waist. "He was in his early forties, with fogged pince-nez, intense dark eyes, and a black mustache" (*Rembrandt* 204). "Departing the circus grounds he cantered across a grassy soft field into a dark wood, a free centaur" (*Rembrandt* 204).

The image of Abramowitz throughout the story is really a positive one, especially compared to the brutish and ignorant Goldberg. Abramowitz' metamorphosis to centaur is a step up for him: he is more human with his intense eyes and pince-nez. He has not become more brutal. If the new world he enters is "a dark wood," it represents the constant danger of further oppression and slavery, Abramowitz' unknown future, not a darkness in the centaur's nature.

Much of this story is humorous: the deaf-mute reads the *Daily News* and keeps an eye out for astronomy programs, but the horse has the horse sense. The story also has its serious elements and is closely connected to others in the collection. Two very different types of characters are locked into a struggle. It is a story about communication: a deaf-mute communicates through Morse code and instructs a talking horse on what to say. Though the horse wants to speak for himself, he seldom gets to. He is a slave to Goldberg who derives his total existence from Abramowitz; the oppressor simply vanishes without a trace when Abramowitz becomes a centaur. Malamud suggests that man, part animal, part poet, is often imprisoned in a rigid life governed by the mindless. Though sometimes the audience weeps as the horse says he wants to be free and once the band plays "The Star-Spangled Banner," no one comes to aid Abramowitz. He must struggle violently to free himself.

Rembrandt's Hat depicts a Malamud hero whose roots go back to the earliest works but who is steadily evolving. Consistent with heroes like Alpine and Hobbs, these people are mostly loners, alienated outsiders seeking connections. They have the makings of decent caring people; but unlike Sy Levin or even Arthur Fidelman, most seem unable to change their circumstances. Here, more than in any other of his short story collections, Malamud presents the heroes as trapped, sometimes by circumstances beyond their control such as repressive regimes, wars, mental illness. Others are in emotional prisons. Albert Gans, without emotions, has killed his own humanity as he has precipitated his father's death from a broken heart. Dr. Morris is unable to break out of his frozen life as a widower. Rubin, the failed artist, is in emotional isolation, fearful of revealing his failures. Karla Harris is afraid to disrupt a marriage which is bringing her little fulfillment, afraid of trying her own work rather than envying the work of others.

The image of the hero in this collection is of a stifled, trapped *mensch*, with some emotional sensitivity, who finds difficulty in expressing himself. He cannot break out due to feelings of insecurity, fear of failure, or self-consciousness about age. Or he is under pressures which he cannot control, like Levitansky in "Man in the Drawer" or Harry in "My Son the Murderer," both men of feeling tortured by wrongminded regimes.

Still Malamud emphasizes the possibility of the human. It takes courage for a person to become a real *mensch*, to radically alter his life, even with misgivings the way Levin did in *A New Life* when he drove off with Pauline and the children. Harvitz finds that courage in "Man in the Drawer" when he smuggles out the manuscripts; he is transformed by his commitment to Levitansky and by Levitansky's humanity and courage. Abramowitz attacks his oppressor Goldberg and becomes a new man, a centaur. And in "Rembrandt's

Hat," in a smaller way, Rubin and Arkin gain some understanding and humanity.

Again, as in *Pictures of Fidelman* and *The Tenants*, Malamud deals with the life of the artist, here a writer, a sculptor, and a talking horse who would like to be a poet. Malamud emphasizes the isolation and struggle of the artist. In *Dubin's Lives*, the next book, Malamud pursues much that is brought up in this volume. The hero is another writer, this time a biographer, who yearns to have a fuller life of his own. And as in *Rembrandt's Hat*, Malamud holds onto his hopes for the *mensch*-hero but emphasizes that most people are locked in and isolated and that change in life is rare and difficult.

DUBIN'S LIVES: THE MALAMUD HERO COME OF MIDDLE AGE

In William Dubin, of *Dubin's Lives* published in 1979, Bernard Malamud created his most complex and fully drawn hero. Dubin is an introspective yet passionate man, something of an older Sy Levin. Malamud generally fit the fate of his heroes into a moral scheme, demanding discipline and devotion from men who seem poorly suited for altruism. He has shown the greatness of the little man, the simple, earnest Morris Bober. However, in Dubin, a man with a talent for biography, with a devoted wife, and with fairly secure finances, Malamud presents a person who is happiest and most fulfilled when he appears least moral and most selfish. Though Dubin never sinks to thievery or rape as does Frank Alpine in *The Assistant*, neither is he capable of the self-sacrifice of a mature Alpine or a Yakov Bok of *The Fixer*. The biographer Dubin is a natural outgrowth of the steady movement of the Malamud hero toward a more flawed and complicated person. Dubin is a direct descendent of Arthur Fidelman, Harry Lesser, and many of the characters in *Rembrandt's Hat*. Though Dubin appears more gifted in art, here the art of biography, than either Lesser or Fidelman were, he shares with them the lonely, often blocked life of the artist, or in Fidelman's case, the would-be artist. Dubin also shares the private, mental prison typical of the characters in all Malamud's work since *The Fixer*.

Just before *Dubin's Lives* was published Malamud said: "The texture of it, the depth of it, the quality of human experience in it is greater than in my previous books" (Tyler 32). Certainly Malamud never focused in such detail and so convincingly on one person. Dubin quickens the pages as his consciousness pervades them.

Many critics praised *Dubin's Lives*. Saul Maloff called it "Malamud's most ambitious and richest novel" (246). The critic in *The Atlantic* claimed: "It is Malamud's simplest novel since *A New Life*, and maybe his most affecting" (132).

Those who found fault with the novel tended to dislike most the characterization of William Dubin and to be unsure how seriously to take him. As Robert Towers asked: "How ironically are we meant to perceive him? How sympathetically?" (31). Towers raised another interesting point: "Malamud, I believe, has positioned himself too close to Dubin to get him in perspective -- either for himself or the reader" (31). Joseph Epstein complained, "Worst of all, William Dubin is a selfish charmless man, and it is far from clear that Malamud is aware of this" (52). Richard Locke saw *Dubin's Lives* as a symptom of Malamud's decline: "Over the years he has lost his sense of humor and become self-important, sententious, morally vain" (67).

I admire *Dubin's Lives*, with a few qualifications. The book does have its slow, sticky parts, with Dubin whining, in decline, near creative paralysis. Yet Dubin emerges fully drawn and mostly likeable. Perhaps critics who saw a diminished Dubin were searching for someone more heroic. In fairness, it might be said that Malamud himself set up these expectations. Frank Alpine approaches sainthood; Yakov Bok, revolutionary martyrdom. But Dubin moves in small steps to his desk and at a quicker pace to his lover. Dubin is ordinary, flawed, of two minds, deceitful, kindly, warm, and worn. His thoughts are sharp, if literary. He is, in short, the Malamud hero come of middle age.

Though it seems clear that Dubin is of the same family as the other Malamud heroes, can he be considered a *mensch*-hero? Robert Towers claimed, "Though given to psychological and moral self-scrutiny, Dubin is the bearer of no superior moral insight; he is, in short, a man, not a *mensch*" (1). For Towers a *mensch* may not be simply a man. But it is clear that Malamud's morality is evolving. Dubin, by his very age, is more tested, more vulnerable than many of the younger early heroes. But he is no less a *mensch*; he has moral thoughts even if he does not act on them. For Malamud, some of Dubin's weaknesses attest to his humanity, to the amount of life he has left in him. Malamud appears more broad-minded but not necessarily any less moral in this novel. He has eased away from the grin and bear it morality of *A New Life*, where Levin leaps into an uncertain future with Pauline. Malamud has moved to a morality acknowledging the common compromises of life. Generally his view of life has become more complex and realistic. The *mensch*-hero is aging and maturing.

Before *Dubin's Lives* Malamud held up a standard for his heroes: he moved them toward love and commitment. Even *The Tenants* is a negative lesson in the importance of fulfillment in love and work. But in William Dubin, Malamud shifted his emphasis to the primacy of sexual fulfillment rather than love. D. H. Lawrence, the subject of the biography Dubin is writing, is something of a volcano in this book. Dubin likely chooses Lawrence because of an unconscious desire for a model when breaking out of his own dull regime of marriage and work. Near sixty, Dubin finds sexual passion in his on and off affair with Fanny Bick, his young lover. The affair leaves Dubin alternately exhilarated and devastated. He sinks into depression, is impotent and aloof with his wife Kitty, and is for long, cold, wintry periods often unable to write. Dubin needs Fanny desperately, yet it is as unlikely he will live with her or marry her, as it is unlikely his mostly sad marriage will improve or dissolve. Malamud presents this impossible situation with conviction and sympathy. He appears less optimistic about the possibility of people to radically alter the circumstances of their lives. Though Malamud still holds to the importance of human communion, the novel is riddled with broken promises and lost connections.

Dubin is a departure from most of the earlier heroes in a few significant ways. He is in his late fifties, considerably older than the heroes of the other novels. Some Malamud characters like Morris Bober, Rabbi Salzman of "The Magic Barrel," and Rabbi Lifschitz of "The Silver Crown" all are close in years to Dubin, but Malamud depicts these as old men. Dubin is livelier, really middleaged. And though the Malamud hero has typically been a late bloomer, Dubin blooms later than most. Dubin's age provides Malamud the opportunity to test some of his earlier assumptions. For example, the Dubin and Kitty marriage seems like the Sy Levin and Pauline Gilley marriage-to-be, twenty-five years later. Both marriages are almost acts of will, the couples seeking love through commitment. The Dubins' marriage is failing badly, its slow, deadly decomposition the subject of much of the novel.

Dubin is also more established, more secure financially than the earlier heroes. Though money begins to run short toward the end of the novel as Dubin slowly endeavors to complete his life of Lawrence, the Dubins appear to live comfortably in the middle class. Perhaps because Dubin is established in his profession, his thoughts turn more easily to sexual diversion. Most of the earlier heroes are struggling to begin a worthwhile work, to establish a life. Though Roy Hobbs devotes much of his time pursuing Memo Paris, he is mostly frustrated. Dubin, however, wants to escape the life he has established.

And most importantly, Dubin is the only hero in a Malamud novel who is married throughout the book. The earlier heroes were marked by their isolation; they were outsiders. Dubin is isolated in his marriage, an altogether more gloomy situation. Because William and Kitty Dubin are both sensitive, intelligent people hoping for love, their failures are more sad.

In spite of his several differences from most of the Malamud heroes, Dubin still bears many of the heroes' significant markings. He had a troubled childhood and youth, he has surrogate father figures, he is geographically displaced, and he seeks fulfillment in his work and in love.

First, Dubin's youth was typically tragic and fractured. Thoughts of his parents thread throughout the novel. Dubin was ashamed of them. His father Charlie Dubin was a waiter in Jewish dairy restaurants, and his mother Hannah became insane after the drowning of her nine-year-old son Leo. William Dubin looks back on them with guilt, warmth, and sympathy.

From his father, Dubin inherited the waiter's disposition, "an overly patient nature" (_Dubin_ 67). Charlie Dubin got fired from jobs because he refused to joke with the customers. William thinks, "His life has made me a deadly serious man" with "an inclination to a confined lonely life" (_Dubin_ 68). Charlie had disapproved of William marrying Kitty, a goyish woman with a young son. But William Dubin countered: "Dear Papa, How can a man be a Jew if he isn't a man? How can he be a man if he gives up the woman he wants to marry?" (_Dubin_ 69).

William Dubin's thoughts about his mother Hannah are more complex. He was understandably embarrassed by her when he was a young man. In her insanity she would shout at strangers and make odd pronouncements: "The steak is in the bathtub, she whispered in the dark" (_Dubin_ 69). Mostly she feared that she would lose him, too, to pneumonia for example. Once young

William saved her life by inducing vomiting with citrate of magnesia after she had swallowed half a bottle of disinfectant. As a teenager he avoided her on the street. But an older Dubin, caught up in his own despair, seems to look back with sympathy and fear. Dubin recognizes the seeds of his mother's illness in his own depression and hysteria. Though she died when Dubin was fourteen, she is still close to him: "He loved and feared her. He forgot words, to forget her; but she, with her fears, lived in his flesh" (*Dubin* 312). And a mature Dubin has come to respect his parents and their struggle. His father kept his mother home in an attempt to protect her. Finally Dubin forgives Hannah "her insane life." "It was the only life she had to live" (*Dubin* 312).

With both Charlie and Hannah long dead, an adult Dubin turns to surrogate fathers, the subjects of his biographies. He is most influenced by Thoreau on nature and D. H. Lawrence on sexuality, but he also quotes constantly from the letters and writings of other famous men and relates incidents in their lives. Whether he seeks to counsel or impress someone, Dubin refers to the subjects of his biographies. Dubin's writers influence him the way the lives of St. Francis and Morris Bober influenced Frank Alpine and the lives of Spinoza and Shmuel influenced Yakov Bok. But Dubin has also lived in his biographies at times, rather than in his own life. As Dubin tells himself: "Language is not life. I've given up life to write lives" (*Dubin* 316).

Though Dubin must learn that work is not a substitute for a personal life, he, like Malamud, still values work highly. All of the heroes of the novels are hard workers. They tend to be serious and dedicated, though often frustrated. The ones who have the greatest work struggles are the later heroes who attempt artistic work. Typically they suffer blocks and must discover the interrelationship of life and art. Malamud suggests that Dubin must learn from Thoreau, Lawrence, and others just how to be truly Dubin. The last page of the novel indicates that Dubin has found some balance and fulfillment. He has completed *The Passion of D. H. Lawrence: A Life, The Art of Biography*, and *Anna Freud* (with his daughter Maud D. Perrera). So Dubin prevails as a biographer, an achievement that Malamud respects.

Like most of Malamud's heroes in the novels, Dubin is geographically displaced. He is a Jewish city boy from Newark and Bronx tenements who has lived for fifteen years in Center Campobello, a small town in New York State near the Vermont border. Like Sy Levin venturing to the Northwest, Dubin often sees the natural world with fresh and appreciative eyes. But the country life is not completely idyllic. Though Dubin and his wife Kitty have some friends who share their intellectual and artistic interests, many of the neighboring farmers are primitive folk who sic dogs on trespassers and fear Jewish conspiracies. One "overalled horseman" points out to Dubin that bulldozers are leveling the earth: "Look there! Them Jews are crucifyin' the earth" (*Dubin* 307).

Dubin has many personal traits common to the Malamud hero. He is introspective and fastidious, yet volatile and passionate. His compulsiveness about his work seems, in part, a way of keeping his desires in check. He wants to break free of his confined life, yet is fearful and self-conscious. Oddly, he changes underwear frequently and likes both his underwear and socks ironed. He sees himself as overweight and aging and frequently starts on austere regimes. He wants a new life; but unlike the earlier heroes he is tied by marital vows and children to his past life. Yet like all the Malamud heroes, Dubin is searching for a reason to live, for something or someone to make his life significant. But for most of the book, Dubin sits on a thin limb, perched between Kitty and Fanny.

His love life and marriage also link him to other Malamud heroes in several ways. First, Dubin had the typical bad luck in love when he was young: "Dubin said it wasn't a happy time of his life" (*Dubin* 228). In the early part of the book, when Fanny works as a housekeeper for the Dubins, he tells her about his past, confessing he often fell in love and seldom had sex: "It was a different world in those days, Fanny, though perhaps I was not as daring as I might have been. There was much I missed" (*Dubin* 37).

And as Pauline Gilley had picked out Levin's picture from a stack of job applications for Cascadia College, William Dubin picked out Kitty's personal note to *The Nation*, where he was an assistant editor. Her second note, requesting that her first be destroyed, landed on Dubin's desk and he answered both notes. He wrote to her without laying eyes on her: "You seem to be capable of a serious act of imagination: To be willing to love someone willing to love you. Plato in the *Republic* says that marriages between good people might reasonably be made by lot" (*Dubin* 47). They arrange to meet and soon marry. For Dubin, "All it takes is character" (*Dubin* 48). But a wiser Kitty says, "That's not all it takes" (*Dubin* 48). Dubin is thirty-one when he first writes to Kitty. Like all the heroes of the novels, Dubin is a late bloomer. He blooms late in love with Kitty, later in sex with Fanny. He sets out on daring and risky courses. And Fanny is impulsive and daring like Dubin and Kitty. She becomes interested in Dubin after reading his *Mark Twain* and sets off for Center Campobello in hopes of meeting the author.

Dubin's Lives contains some of Malamud's fullest and most detailed writing on the subject of sex, but the treatment is similar to the treatment in the earlier works. Sex does not come easily to the Malamud hero. As Sy Levin's sexual escapades are often interrupted and Fidelman is prematurely spent with Annamaria, Dubin is cuckolded by Fanny in Venice and suffers impotence with his wife at home. Though Dubin has had a number of affairs in the last twelve years of his twenty-five year marriage, he first rejects Fanny when she offers herself nude in his study. Later Dubin takes Fanny to Venice where she, perhaps sensing he is using her, outwits him; she avoids sex with Dubin though he soon discovers her on the floor of their room making love with the gondolier. And like Harry Lesser of *The Tenants*, Dubin is accused of caring more about his work than about women and sex: Kitty says, "That's your grand passion -- if you could fuck your books you'd have it made" (*Dubin* 337). However, Dubin does find a great deal of sexual fulfillment in his relationship with Fanny, more than any other Malamud hero finds.

As usual, Malamud presents women as crucial to the development of the hero. Iris Lemon offered a better life for Roy Hobbs, as did Helen Bober for Frank Alpine, and Pauline Gilley for Levin. Yakov Bok's forgiving his wife Raisl and his acceptance of her illegitimate child as his own were presented as measures of Bok's new maturity. Esmeralda tried to teach Fidelman about life, as Irene cautioned Harry Lesser. However, Kitty, Maud Dubin, and Fanny Bick are Malamud's most fully drawn women. Their influence pervades Dubin's consciousness and the book itself. Kitty is sensitive, over-refined, full of character. Maud, their daughter, is sharp like her father, yet delicate like Kitty. Fanny, something of the new woman of the book, is at first all sensuality and cunning; but toward the end of the book she is depicted as practical and intellectual as well. Dubin measures himself in the eyes of these women. And for the first time Malamud gives the women characters a significant portion of the book; they are almost as palpable as Dubin himself.

The particular nature of William Dubin which pervades the novel is revealed in his roles as biographer, husband, father, and lover. First, Dubin sees himself as a professional biographer, and his thoughts on the subjects of his books permeate nearly every page of the novel. He identifies closely with his subjects. Early in the novel Dubin has a minor traffic accident on the icy highway. When a young woman stops to help him he introduces himself, "I'm a biographer" (*Dubin* 7). He is a craftsman who has proudly accumulated endless information about the lives of famous men. And whether he is arguing with his wife, advising his children, or courting his lover he quotes freely from the lives and writings of others and readily falls back on the role of lecturer. Because Dubin is tied so closely to his work, Malamud avoids his earlier troubles in depicting writers or artists convincingly, especially when they suffered from artists' block. Dubin and Dubin's work validate each other.

Dubin as biographer is especially convincing because he is the most educated, the most intellectual of the Malamud heroes. Dubin's thoughtful, refined sensibility is the stuff of the novel. The reader also senses a kinship between Malamud the novelist and Dubin the biographer, making Dubin all the more believable. And as Robert Towers said, "Throughout, Dubin's relationship to his work is a major concern" (29). Towers approves of Thoreau as an influence on Dubin but has reservations about D. H. Lawrence: "Of all the risks that Malamud takes in this book, the constant evocation of an angry genius like Lawrence is the most audacious -- and possibly the most damaging" (31). Even Ondyk, Kitty's psychotherapist and lover, cautions a depressed Dubin, "you and he are two radically different types, and living every day with the anger and spleen, and hostility of this enraged man is bound to exacerbate your other day-to-day problems" (*Dubin* 304).

In fact, the subject of Lawrence for Dubin's biography is a wise choice on Malamud's part. Lawrence lights a fire under Dubin while providing Malamud a reason to deal more fully with the sexuality of the hero. In the earlier novels Malamud emphasized the importance of the hero finding commitment and love; but sex was under-emphasized, except perhaps with Fidelman. Only Levin and Pauline found a degree of sustained sexual fulfillment, but it was interrupted for a time by the tension-induced fiery pain in Levin's rear. Dubin says of Lawrence, "At his best he wants man to risk himself for a plentitude of life through love" (*Dubin* 303). Dubin takes some risks with Fanny but at the conclusion races back, half-erection in hand, toward his wife. The novel is a merging of Malamud and Lawrence, with no simple answers. Because Kitty Dubin is not a one-dimensional and unsympathetic character like Clifford Chatterley was in *Lady Chatterley's Lover*, Malamud seems reluctant to have William Dubin leave her easily as Connie left Clifford.

While Malamud got bogged down on the subject of writers at work in *The Tenants*, by placing Dubin in a home with a wife, a lover, a visiting daughter, and a distressed son in Sweden and later in the U.S.S.R. Malamud complicates and enlivens Dubin's days. Harry Lesser and Willie Spearmint were largely in a grim vacuum. Dubin also makes trips to Venice, Sweden, and New York City, all providing variety for the reader. In addition, the rural New York setting and Dubin's Thoreau enhanced sensibilities attune Dubin's work and mood to the rhythms of the seasons.

Dubin's role as biographer also underlines the major preoccupation of the Malamud *mensch*-hero: How is man to live his life? Dubin searches among past lives for clues of how to live his own life: "He felt that the pieces of his own poor life could be annealed into a unity. He would understand better, be forewarned. He felt he had deepened, extended his life; had become Dubin the biographer" (*Dubin* 98). He is deeply and understandably touched by the lives of people like Thoreau and Lawrence, both passionate, solitary men wary of civilization. The mention of Lyndon Johnson, Richard Nixon, and Vietnam suggest that Dubin feels greatly at odds with his government. And Lawrence's belief in the primacy of the love of woman and man is close to a view seen throughout Malamud's fiction, though the love is somewhat romanticized and idealized prior to *Dubin's Lives*.

Generally, Dubin the biographer is revealed as a serious, hardworking man. He tries to anchor himself in his work but ironically chooses Lawrence as a subject and soon is looking for a new life of his own. His marriage fails as he struggles to become a new man, in part in Lawrence's image. Dubin, typical of the Malamud hero, seeks a *mensch*-teacher who will provide a model for a new life. Dubin's teacher is Lawrence with a dash of Thoreau. Never before has Malamud so thoroughly combined the hero's life work with his ethical and spiritual quest. Dubin the biographer is a professional student of life. And as Barbara Koenig Quart said, "Finally, the love of work is again the most enduring and believable love in the book, the love of words, of beautiful thoughts, of the lives of writers" (148).

Dubin's second most important role is as husband. His wife Kitty is both a secondary hero and a measure of the hero Dubin. The marriage of William and Kitty, in painful disrepair, takes up much of the book. It is amusing that many critics found Malamud's depiction of marital unhappiness very convincing -- attesting, perhaps, to the pervasiveness of marital woe. In fact, Mark Shechner claimed *Dubin's Lives* is Malamud's best novel precisely because of its picture of a marriage in decline ("The Return of the Repressed" 279).

When Kitty and Dubin first married they were both lonely people with a history of sadness. Dubin had his unhappy family and his few disappointing early affairs. Kitty's father committed suicide when she was four and her mother went abroad with a lover when Kitty was nine, leaving her to be raised by a loving grandmother. Kitty's first husband Nathanael died of leukemia at forty. She was twenty-six and left alone to raise her three-and-a-half-year-old son Gerald.

Kitty and William began their marriage on unreal footing, not knowing each other well. However, one senses that they were basically good for each other at first, despite their bitter accusations twenty-five years later. Early in the novel, before he becomes involved with Fanny, Dubin thinks about how good Kitty has been for him and about how he may have failed her. He finds her "kind," "generous," "empathetic":

> When Dubin was thinking of gains over losses in marriage, he felt he had honed his character on hers. In all she helped to stabilize and enlarge his life; but he was not sure, after a generation of marriage, that he had done the same for her or why wasn't she at peace with herself? (*Dubin* 17).

At their wedding Kitty wept, Dubin felt "inspired" (*Dubin* 90).

Kitty is in some ways a better person than Dubin. She is more sensitive; she tries to mend. When things between Kitty and Dubin have gotten rather hostile she says: "William, let's be kind. Let's not be nasty. . . . Let's be considerate and kind" (*Dubin* 298).

However, Kitty's dissatisfaction is intense, measured in sleepless nights, dreams of her idolized first husband Nathanael the doctor, and her sniffing the gas burners and stove, fearing, yet almost hoping for asphyxiation. She is neurotic and compulsive, fearing death by cancer. And Dubin feels Kitty is attractive but limited sexually, especially as he becomes more experienced. He thinks, "The more experienced he became, the less she seemed to be. Though Kitty called herself passionate there were areas of sensual experience she made no attempt to know" (*Dubin* 348). Kitty has a birthmark on her left thigh and buttock. She says, "It inhibited me sexually when I was young" (*Dubin* 90). Barbara Koenig Quart claims the blemish and Kitty's signs of age are "the

physical flaws of Malamud's defective women" (147). This is further evidence
for Quart of Malamud's negative view of women. Like Pauline Gilley, Kitty
does have long, narrow feet and small breasts. But, generally, these flaws
humanize the women. Malamud's men are not without physical flaws,
including the balding, spreading Dubin; they are simply seen in a less physical
light because the novels are almost told from their points of view.

In addition to her alleged sexual inhibitions and her fears of death, Kitty's
neurotic attachment to the memory of her late husband Nathanael is extreme:

> In bed one night Kitty said, "You mean a lot to me,
> William."
> "How much?"
> Because I haven't put Nathanael out of my mind doesn't
> diminish my feeling for you.
> "Is it love?"
> That was the wrong question: She said, "I'm not sure
> what or how much of something is something,
> philosophically speaking."
> "Speaking simply, like now in bed?"
> She admitted she couldn't say she loved anybody without
> qualification. One had to be honest.
> When she asked him, Dubin said he loved her (*Dubin* 93).

Later she tells Dubin of Nathanael: "We would have been gayer,
certainly less tense. I was gayer with Nathanael. And more carefree in sex"
(*Dubin* 102). But Dubin doubted it: "He said he hadn't much use for the kind
of honesty that crapped on experience because it had occurred one way and
not another" (*Dubin* 102). Near the end of the book, with accusations of
marital failings flying loose and free, Dubin asks Kitty,

> "Who would you have done better with?"
> Her eyes were moist. "If Nathanael hadn't died."
> "I wish to God he hadn't" (*Dubin* 336).

After twenty-five years of marriage they both deserve more than the ghost of this long dead man. Because Kitty in part keeps Dubin at a distance, measured by her first husband, Dubin's distance from her and his infidelities are made more understandable and are somewhat justified.

Though Kitty remains largely sympathetic, in her delicate, refined way she can be brutal and abstract. When Dubin suffers impotence with her, Kitty reads compulsively on the subject in Nathanael's old medical texts, in plain view of Dubin. Once she tells him, "If I'm the cause of your discontent, and/or sexual problem, I'm willing to let you go. Some men are impotent only with their wives" (*Dubin* 315). Though she is understandably hurt, she speaks to him coldly and clinically.

However, Dubin can be equally abstract, especially toward the end of the novel. When Kitty and Dubin discuss whether or not they ever loved one another, Dubin says, "Maybe at most I was thinking I was giving love, a rationale or self-deception suiting your needs to my ethic or aesthetics, or both" (*Dubin* 337). They distance each other with words.

As with other Malamud women, Kitty is used to define and sharpen the hero. She is a mirror to Dubin: "One of his problems, Dubin thought, was that he too often saw himself with her eyes" (*Dubin* 315). And Kitty is a parallel hero to Dubin. They share many qualities. Both are sensitive, intelligent people who have spent years trying to will a good marriage. In middle age both look for affection and sex outside of their marriage. They are mostly polite and considerate of each other, yet often lonely under the same roof.

While Dubin is preoccupied with Fanny, Kitty falls for Roger Foster, the librarian she works with; and later she has an affair with her psychotherapist Evan Ondyk. When Kitty confesses to Dubin her feelings for Roger, which were unacknowledged and came to nothing, she explains that she feels guilty and fears Dubin has sensed something. Dubin, preoccupied with his own disappointments with Fanny, of course has noticed nothing. Kitty's confession of a wished for affair elicits a confession from Dubin that he had a girl with him in Venice. But Dubin manages to imply sex when there was none. Though Kitty and Dubin had parallel difficulties, each yearning for a younger love, unattained, Dubin preserves his ego and dignity by concealing his frustrations. The next day when Dubin tells Kitty he once slept with Flora Greenfield, his best friend's wife, Kitty faints.

Much later in the book Kitty confronts Dubin about his affair with Fanny. Belatedly she has realized that Fanny was the girl in Venice and later in New York. Dubin admits all, a simple task since Fanny's whereabouts are then unknown. But when Fanny is back in town, involved with Dubin again, Dubin overhears Kitty on the phone arranging a rendezvous with Ondyk. Dubin considers their affair fuel for divorce and has some nasty and petty thoughts about Kitty, especially considering his own marital record: "You wanted to go on respecting her whether she was still your wife or not. He hoped she would not spoil that for him" (*Dubin* 350).

Malamud excels in this depiction of Dubin and his wife in their rocky marriage. Dubin sighs and talks to himself in the bathroom mirror. Kitty says, "We used to talk about everything in the world. We talk about nothing now" (*Dubin* 142). She shows her dissatisfaction in very believable ways: "She no longer set up his breakfast dishes for the morning. She no longer paired his washed socks; she dropped them in a heap on his dresser" (*Dubin* 359). The growing silence, the awkwardness between Dubin and Kitty is felt on every page of the book. Malamud creates the climate of marital disappointment with all the attention to human detail that brought to life Morris Bober's grocery store. Yet in *Dubin's Lives* the characters are more complex and the answers to their pleas, less certain.

Malamud also focuses on Dubin as a father. In the earlier novels only Morris Bober was a father throughout. Hobbs and Levin were fathers-to-be and Cohn is something of a surrogate father to some of the primates in *God's Grace*. Dubin is a father throughout the novel, though his daughter and step-son no longer live at home.

Just as Malamud illustrates the difficulties of marriage in *Dubin's Lives*, he illustrates the difficulties of parenthood. Both Kitty and Dubin love their children, yet whether they stand next to them or are separated by the Atlantic Ocean, the parents and offspring are truly in different universes. And Dubin, particularly, is tested in his love of the children: Can he love them when he disapproves of them? Does he have a right to disapprove of them at all? Curiously, Malamud stacks the deck against Dubin as his children's lives take increasingly melodramatic turns.

Gerald is Dubin's adopted stepson. Kitty, in her warped preoccupation with the deceased Nathanael, has taught Gerald to love a father he barely knew. Yet Gerald must have felt warmth for Dubin, apparently more than Dubin remembers. Once Dubin looks for an old valentine from his daughter but finds it was really from Gerald: "Willyam, Be My Valentine" (*Dubin* 120).

Though a young Gerald asked Dubin to adopt him, an adolescent Gerald became distant and silent. Dubin offered his own experience and advice but was rejected. Early on Gerald became fearful of the Vietnam War, but Kitty encouraged him to enjoy his youth. But "Dubin, peacemaker, rattled on about the miserable youth of Edgar Allen Poe; his mother had died young. Kitty asked him to change the subject" (*Dubin* 107). The young Gerald is reminiscent of the son in "My Son, the Murderer," who was also angry about the war and alienated from his parents. When Gerald is drafted he is stationed in Germany until three months before his term of enlistment is due to end; then he has orders for Southeast Asia. He goes AWOL to Sweden. Kitty and Dubin feel Gerald should have endured the three months; but as Gerald later tells Dubin, "If I had stayed in another month I'd have killed somebody, not necessarily a Viet Cong" (*Dubin* 110-11).

After Dubin's Italian fiasco with Fanny he stops in Sweden to see Gerald; "He wanted her [Kitty] to be grateful to him before he lied to her about Venice" (*Dubin* 95). On his first night, in search of a restaurant, Dubin misses a double step and has a mean fall. When Dubin does find Gerald Willis, as he calls himself now, their conversation is strained, with Dubin limping along as the son walks away. This walk in Stockholm, in the rain, down to a bridge echoes the father chasing the son to Coney Island at the end of "My Son, the Murderer." Gerald disapproves of his parent's disapproval. He is a bitter, lonely young man who does not want his situation pointed out to him. Dubin implies that Gerald is in prison. But Gerald counters, "I am where I choose to be" (*Dubin* 111). This failed communion between two people who have reason to care for each other, to comfort each other, is the stuff of later Malamud, as the characters' prisons become more personal and mental.

Toward the end of the novel, in a plot twist that Saul Maloff understandably found "sheer melodrama" (245), Gerald writes to his parents, revealing that he was recruited by the KGB and flown to the Soviet Union. He became disenchanted, quit, and is now a non-person, living in parks. Though Gerald's lot is hopeless, he now thinks warmly of his family: "My mother is my mother, and you are my father, William. Some simple things take a long time to get thought out" (*Dubin* 354). Though these circumstances are rather exotic, the movement through suffering to love is a common theme in Malamud's fiction.

Dubin's relationship to his daughter appears strained by the very intensity of their love for each other. Quart calls Dubin's feelings for Maud "vaguely incestuous" (146). Dubin remembers Maud as a child, warm and laughing. He tells a mature Maud: " 'I loved you more than anyone.' 'Papa,' Maud said, 'I'm not your wife' " (*Dubin* 172). Later Maud cautions Dubin, "You neglect Mother. She's lonely" (*Dubin* 172). She tells Dubin: "I'm trying to live my life without you" and "Pay attention to your wife . . . She's not a happy woman" (*Dubin* 341). Like Gerald, Maud grew distant from Dubin when she was in her teens. Dubin accepts some blame for her troubles: "He sometimes thought his life had pressed hers too strongly. He was too intensely aware of Maud, had made her self-conscious" (*Dubin* 167). When Dubin lectures Maud about the importance of work, how Twain and Fitzgerald had wasted much of their talent, Maud says, "Why didn't you learn about some of the fun they had, especially Fitzgerald?" (*Dubin* 166). Ironically, Maud is more serious than even Dubin. She approaches her life with grim determination. Maud later explains why she plans to enter a Zen commune: "I want discipline" (*Dubin* 280). Dubin is touched: "He felt a sorrow of sorts for what she had of him in her" (*Dubin* 280).

The intensity of Dubin's feelings for Maud is underlined by the parallels between Dubin's affair with Fanny and Maud's on and off affair with her sixty-year-old, married, black Spanish teacher from Berkeley. Both Fanny and Maud try Zen communes. Perhaps Malamud emphasizes the intensity of the father and daughter relationship to suggest that the gradual, semi-secret breakdown of affection and sex between Kitty and Dubin started years ago.

Late in the novel when Maud visits her parents in New York she is pregnant by her married lover and determined to keep the child. Her parents disapprove; she feels uncomfortable and leaves. Like Gerald, Maud leads an unpredictable, even melodramatic life.

Generally, the Malamud hero as father fares poorly. Dubin genuinely loves his children, but unfortunately he has imparted to them his own propensity for being tied up in knots. Like him, Gerald and Maud are highly serious, often noble, and tense. Their relationships with Dubin emphasize a basic Malamud premise: true communication is rare. And naturally, Dubin, ever the student of life, tries to teach his children from his own experience. Like many parents, he is spurned.

Dubin experiences more closeness, joy, and fulfillment in his relationship with Fanny than with anyone else. She is looking for a lover, father, and teacher; and Dubin seems eager to serve in all these roles. Her seeking him out because of the Mark Twain biography suggests that she wants guidance. And in their relationship Malamud emphasizes that it is often easier to be close to a stranger. As Dubin tells himself after Fanny asks him if he has enjoyed sex: "How intimate strangers can be" (*Dubin* 218).

Critical reaction to Fanny was mixed. Maloff claimed, "she's a woman in her own right, an entirely believable if sometimes nutty one" (245). Others had serious reservations. For Richard Locke, "Fanny is much too promiscuous to inspire our affection or respect, and this of course, diminishes Dubin in our eyes" (69). Locke also regrets "Fanny's unfortunate slang" (68). For Robert Towers,

> Fanny is never endowed with as much substance as Kitty
> . . . We are told that she sees Dubin as lover, friend, father,
> but the dynamics of her personality are insufficiently
> dramatized for us to understand fully her need for a lover
> thirty years her senior (30).

I find some truth in the criticism of the character Fanny. Malamud tried to capture a type, a free floating latter day hippie. Fanny uses all the expressions of her time "flaky," "dig that," and "It's cool" (*Dubin* 194, 195, 232); "Her orgasm, she swore, spaced her" (*Dubin* 219). She tells Dubin, "And we get along swell in bed --" (*Dubin* 265). This sort of language becomes distracting, annoying; it does diminish Fanny. And Fanny is promiscuous with a vengeance in the first part of the novel. Especially in Venice, she seems to be evening a score her new relationship with Dubin cannot altogether account for. However, she does present herself as someone at loose ends, looking for guidance. Dubin, for his part, also thinks of sex as revenge. When Fanny does draw down her underpants for Dubin, half a year after Venice, "This evens it, Dubin thought, for the cruel winter" (*Dubin* 208).

Yet Fanny does serve a useful and credible role in the novel. It takes someone rather wild to enliven a repressed, orderly Dubin. He is attracted to a vitality he lacks. Fanny is his teacher in sex and more importantly, in a greedy zest for life. And Fanny herself has several characteristics of the *mensch*-hero. She has had a sad past, parent problems; she is something of a drifter; she is talented but lacks direction; and she is seeking someone to model her life after. In the course of the novel, Fanny, more than any other character, changes and matures. By the end of the book she has worked hard on the Wilson farm she has bought, and she will likely begin legal training, eyeing public service.

Dubin's affair with Fanny has several stages. They meet at the novel's start, when she stops to ask Dubin directions to town. Later Kitty hires Fanny as a cleaning woman and soon an awkward courtship begins, Dubin quoting the words of famous men while taking careful note of Fanny's charms: "it annoyed him a bit that he had felt her sexuality so keenly" (*Dubin* 23). Once, he is embarrassed to discover Fanny in the kitchen ironing his underpants. Later when Fanny asks what Thoreau did for sex, Dubin defends Thoreau's literary accomplishments. But Fanny answers: "I don't care what he accomplished in his books, when you get right down to it he missed the most satisfying pleasure of life. I mean we're human, aren't we?" (*Dubin* 30). Fanny emphasizes what Malamud emphasizes in the novel: to be a human being is to be a sexual being. The hero can no longer live on mere ideals and the hope of love, as did Frank Alpine. And for the first time Malamud's hero thinks of sex more than of love. Even Fidelman's encounter with Beppo was immediately elevated to the plane of love.

But the course of Dubin's affair with Fanny is so rocky that it strains credulity at times. When Fanny offers herself in his study, throwing her underpants at him, Dubin solemnly declines. She leaves, quits housekeeping. But when he spots her in Center Campobello one evening, he asks her to meet him for a drink at the Gansevoort bar in New York, where he first arranged to meet Kitty. Fanny stands him up, claiming later that she lost the name of the hotel. Though being stood up leaves Dubin feeling grim, he next asks Fanny to go to Venice. He tells himself that he is "Enjoying myself. I have it coming to me" (*Dubin* 55). He imagines saying, "-- Kitty, I'm going off with a chick for a week. A night out in life. I want an experience before I'm too old to have it. Don't fret, I'll be back soon as good as new and as loyal as ever" (*Dubin* 56). But Dubin has more coming to him than he realizes.

The Venice episode, one of the liveliest chapters in the novel, is a series of frustrations for Dubin. Fanny dresses provocatively when they go out, apparently to provoke interest from waiters, bell hops, and gondoliers rather than from Dubin. She eats and drinks too much, makes herself ill; and Dubin serves as a nurse. She quizzes Dubin about Kitty. She tells him she doesn't want to be a "diversion" or "a hooker" (_Dubin_ 59). After Fanny is ill the first time she says, "I also feel I am tripping. 'Seize the day,' hump your lay" (_Dubin_ 64). Yet Dubin persists in attempting to buy rights to Fanny, not only in taking her to Italy but in buying her "a twenty-two carat gold band overlaid with a spiraling coil, which surprised and delighted her" (_Dubin_ 79). It is the only thing that Fanny is wearing when Dubin returns late to the room to find her on the floor with the strong-backed gondolier: "The biographer felt as though he had wasted every cent of a large investment and stood on the verge of desolation" (_Dubin_ 82). When Dubin next returns to the room, Fanny claims he does not own her and she accuses him of loving his wife.

Though it seems odd that Dubin would risk taking to Europe someone who does not manage to meet him for a drink, the events in Venice are still credible. As usual, Malamud brings a fresh touch to what could be a trite situation. Dubin wants leverage, prestige to assure him a place in Fanny's bed. At first Fanny is not primarily looking for sex. She wants respect, companionship and friendship. She correctly senses that Dubin initially has a limited use for her. She tells him, "All you wanted was cunt" (_Dubin_ 83). And by foiling him, she increases his need for her: "He sensed a more intense commitment to the girl than he had guessed, or perhaps permitted, and wondered if he had been almost in love with her -- sad pattern of long past" (_Dubin_ 82).

Oddly, Fanny writes many letters to Dubin when she stays on in Murano and then Rome. After the first letter detailing her life with Arnaldo, the capitano of the motorboat, Dubin responds with a curt note, including: "You've cheapened and shamed me. Please don't bother writing again" (_Dubin_ 115). But throughout Dubin's desolate winter of diet and exercise, the letters continue to arrive. During this winter Dubin nearly freezes to death, lost in a blizzard; but Kitty arrives miraculously to save him.

Fanny writes asking for advice: "Could you specifically say what I ought to be thinking about in the way of a job or a career, or recommend books that might be helpful? Or give me names of courses that I could take when I get back to New York City?" (*Dubin* 135). She claims in her final letter to be writing to him because she respects him, even if he does not respect her. All this seems weirdly out of touch, considering their past relations. She may want to improve the quality of their relationship by making it more formal, by denying their past. She writes to him as though he were simply her guidance counselor. Yet her letters manage to keep Fanny on Dubin's mind.

Then one April morning Dubin spots Fanny in town with Roger, and Dubin's preoccupation with Fanny begins anew. He decides to act his age but promptly drives onto the highway in the wrong direction. In May, Dubin on his long walk is spotted by Fanny. She joins him on the walk and they discuss Italy. Fanny asks, "Who was protecting me?" (*Dubin* 197). As they walk, Dubin names the wild flowers. Fanny details her early sexual exploitation by Mitchell, the Jersey City orthodontist. Soon she touches Dubin, he touches her, they make love. The affair continues on Dubin's visits to Fanny in Manhattan. He discovers "the fountain of youth is the presence of youth" (*Dubin* 209). He again has confidence, feels himself "an excellent biographer" (*Dubin* 211). Magically, sex soothes over their earlier differences. When Dubin stays in Fanny's apartment he straightens up, does dishes, writes, while she works as a secretary in a law office. He buys her window shades, always conscious of the davening Jews in the synagogue across the street.

Fanny's sexuality helps Dubin -- "He understood Lawrence more fully, his religion of sexuality: a belief in the blood, the flesh, as wiser than the intellect" (_Dubin_ 219). Malamud, too, would seem to smile on Dubin's sexual fulfillment. Still, Dubin claims to be in love with Kitty as well. And Dubin is wary of Fanny's sexual expertise: "But when he asked whether she was teaching him the orthodontist's repertory, Fanny denied it" (_Dubin_ 218).

In the winter Fanny visits Dubin in his barn study. They are interrupted by Kitty, Fanny hides, and Kitty says, "The room smells sexy" (_Dubin_ 250). The gas sniffer has quite a nose, though Dubin claims the smell is his erotic thoughts. Dubin becomes impotent with Kitty; and Roger Foster confronts Dubin, declaring love for Fanny. Roger functions in the novel as something of a ubiquitous clock, warning Dubin that age will out.

When Kitty goes to Stockholm to visit Gerald, Fanny visits Dubin at home. The weekend brings out the extent of Dubin's guilt. Understandably, he does not want Fanny in Kitty's bed, in Kitty's robe -- where Kitty wants to be. More than ever, Fanny resents the fact that Dubin is married. She says, "I am entitled to an open ordinary and satisfying life of my own" (_Dubin_ 268). And she leaves Dubin; she cleans out of her New York apartment and leaves no forwarding address. Dubin suffers his worst depression.

Dubin becomes acutely conscious of his age, his two years to sixty. He groans over hairs on his comb, his wrinkles, his belly: "He was less vital than a year ago" (_Dubin_ 285). He backs the car out over Lorenzo, the stray cat Kitty is so fond of. Years before he ran over Maud's cat. He has a predilection to crush something in the women he loves. His impotence becomes chronic. He puts the blame on Kitty for thinking of him as "spinach" (_Dubin_ 291). But he fears his lies have wilted his organ. He feels wounded, crippled, and suggests separation.

Then Dubin decides that "When he felt better he would ask her to divorce him" (_Dubin_ 309). Several times in the novel Dubin is nasty and self-serving in this way. But he is deeply disabled: he sobs at his desk, unable to work. His memory fails him. This depression is his most severe: "As the days went by, the depression he had held off with upraised hands, as though it was a poisonous cloud, slipped through his fingers and smote him with suffocating force" (_Dubin_ 317). Malamud spares the reader none of the lurid details of Dubin's decline: "He pissed in a limp stream dribbling in his underpants. Dubin had discovered his prostate" (_Dubin_ 318). At one point Malamud's description is excessive. The specter of D. H. Lawrence appears to Dubin spouting anti-Semitic garble, including:

> You rat-faced Jew. . . . Your Jew mind is antagonistic to the active Male Principle . . . Sex, to you, is functional, equivalent to passing excrement . . . You write muckspout lives because you fear you have no life to live. Your impotence is Jewish self-hatred (_Dubin_ 318-319).

This nightmare sends Dubin flying out into the night for fear of destroying himself or his book. As Dubin breaks down, so does his car -- out of gas. He wanders, runs near mad from an open grave, and is soon treed by a dog. A farmer appears and shoots into the woods but ends up hitting his dog rather than Dubin. The farmer chases Dubin yelling, "I'll git you, you-Jew-son-of-a-bitch, one way or t'other" (_Dubin_ 322). Malamud's rural setting is crawling with anti-Semites, real and imagined. When Dubin escapes the farmer he is rescued by Fanny who is returning to live on the Myra Wilson farm she has just purchased with money her mother left to her. Fanny's happening along in the pre-dawn hours is the single most improbable event in the novel.

Dubin recuperates from bacterial pneumonia in the hospital, and one of the warmest scenes in the book occurs when Oscar Greenfield, his friend and neighbor, visits. He suffered a heart attack and is now sympathetic to Dubin.

Greenfield plays a Schubert song on his flute and treats Dubin warmly, apparently forgiving the encounter between Dubin and Flora. Dubin confesses: "I'm an odd inward man held together by an ordered life" (*Dubin* 326). Dubin cries and he and Oscar kiss. In the renewal of this friendship the novel comes full circle from the comradeship of two men, bundled against the New England winter on the opening page when Dubin said, "This has to be the center of the universe, my friend . . . This road as we meet" (*Dubin* 3). In this lasting friendship Malamud strikes one optimistic chord.

But in the final renewal of the Fanny and Dubin affair Malamud sends mixed messages. The epigraphs for the novel suggest the conflict: "What demon possessed me that I behaved so well?" -- Thoreau, and "Give me continence and chastity, but not yet" -- Augustine. Though Fanny quickly puts an end to Dubin's depression, Malamud seems unwilling to accept her as a permanent solution to Dubin's problems and especially unwilling to allow Dubin to leave Kitty.

When Dubin first visits Fanny at the farm she claims that she is starting a new life which does not include resuming her affair with Dubin. However, as usual, Fanny is determining the course and nature of her relation with Dubin. She hardly would have become Dubin's neighbor unless he still interested her.

Fanny's return sets Dubin to peeping again. Earlier in the novel he looked for Fanny at Roger's. Now every night he waits for Roger's truck to appear at Fanny's farm. He even peers in the windows and is recognized by Fanny. The hero as the Peeping Tom was featured prominently in *The Assistant*, where Frank Alpine repeatedly spied on Helen Bober in the shower. These images suggest the hero as a pathetic outsider, lonely and alienated.

Fanny is unwilling to continue the affair, until Dubin arrives with a $450 gold band with six rubies. He also brings a gardenia. As always, he is buying her affections. But she takes the gifts, thinking of marriage: "It looks like a wedding ring. I feel like a bride" (*Dubin* 332). They make love, oddly enough, to "A Mighty Fortress is Our God" in German, blaring forth from the stereo.

Dubin's impotence with Kitty continues; and she, probably accurately, accuses him, "You're doing this to punish me" (*Dubin* 333). Kitty claims their marriage was always disappointing: "We pretended a better relationship than we had" (*Dubin* 335). Dubin counters, "Doesn't everyone?" (*Dubin* 335). Both stand bickering about the long marriage as though it were an icy cadaver.

After Dubin realizes Kitty is having an affair with Ondyk, he outlines the steps for a divorce, relying on his own training as a lawyer. But before Dubin can confront Kitty she confesses the affair and says it is over.

Dubin does chores at Fanny's and offers her money, but she rejects it: "I'm not your goddamned wife -- I don't want your money" (*Dubin* 357). Soon Dubin sets off to visit attorneys in Vermont, to arrange not a divorce, but a legal career for Fanny. She will be an apprentice to a lawyer, a friend of Kitty's no less; in four years Fanny will be able to take the bar exam. In apparent celebration, when Dubin returns Fanny puts on a Mozart flute concerto and she and Dubin get in bed. As soon as Dubin is aroused he dresses and departs: "Roger Foster waited in the shadow of a long-boughed two-trunked silver maple as Dubin ran up the moonlit road, holding his half-stiffened phallus in his hand, for his wife with love" (*Dubin* 362).

It is a comical and somewhat ambiguous ending for the book. Conveniently enough, Dubin feels benevolently toward Kitty when he has just arranged for Fanny to embark on legal training within commuting distance, thus assuring her continued presence in Center Campobello, N.Y. Fanny appears to believe that Dubin is truly returning to Kitty, for more than just one night, because she calls to him from the window, "Don't kid yourself" (*Dubin*

362). All in all, this system hardly seems a practical method of foreplay or a method likely to insure marital fulfillment. And given Dubin's tendency to deceive himself as to the degree of his need for Fanny, it does not seem likely he could so easily walk away from her.

The conclusion is strong testimony to Malamud's mixed feelings on the subjects of marriage and sexual fulfillment. While the novel testifies to the importance of sex and Dubin degenerates without sexual fulfillment, the sex also brings great guilt and many complications. Malamud still believes in the importance of promises and commitments. He cannot easily allow Dubin to walk away from Kitty after twenty-five years of marriage. Yet whatever promise of fulfillment Dubin's final half-erection brings, it hardly seems enough to mend a marriage in serious decline. In general, *Dubin's Lives* suggests marriage and sexual fulfillment are strange bedfellows: Dubin and Kitty, Ondyk and Marisa, Oscar and Flora are all dissatisfied. Dubin and Fanny find sexual satisfaction but would likely find marriage to each other disappointing.

However, *Dubin's Lives* does contribute to Malamud's portrait of his hero and to his image of men and women in general. Throughout the novel the characters cry out for love, for communion, for sex. But most people want more from love than they are likely to get. And often one person's fulfillment is someone else's betrayal: both Oscar and Kitty are betrayed by those they trust. Though Malamud celebrates sexuality in this novel, he also seems to fear it. And Dubin feels more guilty about his affair with Fanny than he admits, as evidenced by his preoccupation with the praying Jews in the synagogue across from her Manhattan apartment. Malamud insists on sex and then qualifies his insistence. The Malamud hero cannot live by sex alone, and there are no easy answers for the Fanny-Dubin-Kitty triangle. As Fanny matures, becomes more

substantial toward the end of the book, Dubin's decision to stay with Kitty
simply seems less solid, less likely to prevail.

Several themes do emerge which are consistent with all of Malamud's
fiction. Malamud emphasizes the importance of friendship and communion:
"William, Oscar cried, let's not forget our friendship. William, it's a lonely
world!" (*Dubin* 133). And the few moments of true communication between
Dubin and his children hold out a poignant hope. However, as always, the
Malamud hero remains a loner in many ways. Even when Dubin's affair is
going well he thinks: "Although he missed Fanny he sometimes thought that
so long as they cared for each other, admitted the reality and importance of
their relationship, he did not always have to be with her" (*Dubin* 234). After
Fanny breaks it off with Dubin, at his house, "He had liked that day alone:
the company of Wm. Dubin, who'd been with him all his life -- nobody's father,
husband, or lover" (*Dubin* 271). At times Dubin seems to enjoy the thought
of the affair rather than the affair itself. There is a core of aloneness and
isolation in Dubin that no one seems to reach.

And finally Malamud emphasizes the importance of the hero's work, a
marked theme in the later books. By closing *Dubin's Lives* with a list of
Dubin's books, Malamud sends a pointed message. Dubin's success in work
is crucial and lasting. At the conclusion of the book both Kitty and Fanny are
looking for productive work.

Dubin is the most complex and fully drawn hero in the later works. He
suffers mostly from his neuroses rather than from deprivation or persecution.
Like Fidelman and Lesser, Dubin sets high standards for himself in his creative
work and is in despair when his work does not flow smoothly. The prison he
suffers from is largely mental. While he is not as displaced as many of the
other heroes, Dubin, intellectual in the natural world of rural New York State,

is never altogether at home. At times he makes a chore of nature, listing flowers, stomping through long walks as part of his regimes. He seems uncomfortable with himself, with his own body; so his affair with Fanny, with all its sexual openness, brings him a kind of new life. Malamud also adds his usual comic touches to his portrait of the hero; here these touches keep Dubin from appearing hopelessly stuffy and withdrawn. Dubin himself is deeply rocked by the absurdity of his near affair with Fanny in Venice. And when Malamud has Dubin up a tree, chased by a farmer and his dog, Dubin is humanized.

The movement of the Malamud hero toward commitment in human relationships is handled differently in _Dubin's Lives_ than in Malamud's other work. Dubin's long-standing commitment to Kitty appears shaky; his love for Fanny, more tenuous. Dubin is a dedicated, if somewhat distant father. But the strongest long term commitment of the book is really Dubin's commitment to his work.

However, Dubin is a Malamud hero in terms of his humaneness, his general decency. He does want to behave well; he is concerned with moral issues -- personal and political. But in keeping with the general trend of Malamud's later work, Dubin is a _mensch_-hero primarily because he is a rather ordinary person who desires a full life, who despite his age and disappointments hopes to give and receive more in love and life than he has in the past. Dubin is sensitive and alive to the possibilities of human life.

In Calvin Cohn of _God's Grace_, Malamud continues the theme of a rather ordinary, even inept hero who hopes to lead a full life. Cohn is under forty when the book opens, much younger than Dubin, but he is both more serious and more ridiculous than Dubin. Cohn's task is doomed: he attempts to build a more humane society as the sole human survivor of the nuclear Holocaust.

His community is composed of chimps and a gorilla. Sexual fulfillment figures prominently in *God's Grace* as it did in *Dubin's Lives*. But in terms of its serious preoccupations, *God's Grace* is a more didactic and a less satisfying book than *Dubin's Lives*.

COHN'S FALL FROM *GOD'S GRACE*

In 1982 Malamud published his last novel, *God's Grace*. The human hero of the piece is Calvin Cohn, sole *Homo Sapiens* survivor of the nuclear havoc brought on by the Djanks and the Druzhkies. Cohn attempts to build a new life for himself and his primate cousins on a jungle island. Again Malamud raises the question of what it means to be human, of what man is capable of for good or ill. The novel is distilled, quintessential Malamud. And Cohn is a *mensch*-hero in the Malamud mold. Cohn also represents the somewhat unhappy culmination of a view of human nature that Malamud moves toward in his later work.

When *God's Grace* was first published it received a rather mixed reception. Alan Lelchuk claimed:

> *God's Grace* seeks to be a cry in the moral wilderness, a cry on the part of God's beasts as well as man, and this ambition may be outside the realm of literature. . . . If religious and prophetic urges sometimes conflict with literary purpose, that may be the price paid in the endeavor. Rewriting the Bible is no easy matter (15).

Lelchuk also questioned Malamud's decision to have the chimpanzees talk. Still he had much praise for the novel, especially Malamud as "an epicure of the ordinary" in his depiction of daily life on the island (14). John Updike admired the chances that Malamud took in *God's Grace*, yet he had contradictory feelings about the book: "As a cosmic fable, *God's Grace* -- a tender retelling of Noah's shame and a comic sketch of final horror -- is a muddle, but therein lies its mercy" (170). Joseph Epstein greatly disliked the novel: "Once the chimpanzees are allowed to speak, *God's Grace* takes on something of the quality of a situation comedy, with symbolism added" (53).

Though most critics noted similarities in *God's Grace* to other Malamud novels and heroes, they seemed generally troubled by its heavily allegorical and didactic quality. Malamud does draw extensively from Old and New Testament mythology while dabbling with one hand in *Robinson Crusoe*, whose hero is quoted in one epigraph -- "I came upon the horrible remains of a cannibal feast," and another hand in Torah and Midrash scholarship of the Abraham and Isaac story. Malamud noted *The Last Trial*, by Shalom Spiegel, as an influence, a book which raises the issue of where Isaac ends up after Abraham returns from the mountain. Another influence on *God's Grace* which Malamud credited was Jane Goodall's *In the Shadow of Man*. Several incidents in *God's Grace* are lifted directly from Goodall, especially the chimps hunting of and feasting on the young baboons, relishing the brains (Goodall 197-213). Finally, a more silent influence would seem to be Jonathan Swift, whose *Gulliver's Travels* made use of exaggerated human and non-human creatures in order to more closely define humankind. Like Swift, Malamud seems to be moving with increasing pessimism to an cataclysmic view of man's future. And as a reader would not deny Swift the right to have talking horses, for example, a contemporary reader must allow Malamud his primate license. But Malamud's Cohn is more sympathetic and complex and less innocent than Swift's Gulliver.

Curiously, two novels by James Fenimore Cooper bear some similarities to *God's Grace*. *The Monikins*, published in 1835, featured talking monkey-mannikins from the lands of Leaphigh and Leaplow, near the South Pole. In Leaphigh, a satirical Britain, tail length determines a citizen's rank.

In Leaplow, a satirical America, all citizens are docked of their tails and positions are determined by lottery. In *The Crater*, published in 1847, a Pacific island Utopia is disrupted by the arrival of several clergymen, a lawyer, and an editor. The founder of the Utopia, a shipwrecked man from Philadelphia, leaves as the society is destroyed. When he returns he finds the place literally devastated by a volcanic blast. If one combines the satire of *The Monikins* with the mordant conclusion of *The Crater*, Cooper and Malamud seem to have much in common.

In Voltaire's *Candide* two young girls sob over the bodies of their monkey lovers who have been shot by Candide on what he considered a rescue mission. And in the entire world of the fairy tale, talking animals are the norm. So the animal and human relations depicted by Malamud have many literary precedents.

In an interview with Helen Benedict, Malamud spoke directly as to his intents in *God's Grace*. He was greatly moved and frightened by the first atomic bomb dropped on Japan: "I have a sense now, as many people have, of peril -- it's terribly frightening. I feel it is the writer's business to cry havoc, because silence can't increase understanding or evoke mercy" (Benedict 28). Malamud wanted to deal with what man does with freedom: "I'm not going to gainsay man's accomplishments, but I still feel that there's a vast sense of failure that has clouded his best efforts to produce a greater freedom than he was born with" (Benedict 29). Malamud said he made the book humorous as well as serious: "Not all of us are eager to be reminded how close man has come, through his own madness, to the end of time. So I wanted a little laughter in this serious book" (Benedict 30). Malamud claimed he was influenced by his own short stories about animals, "and I wanted to see how far I could go with that in a novel" (Benedict 32). "The Jewbird" and "The Talking Horse" also mixed the serious and the comic.

The novel does have some flaws. At times the chimps sound "Walt Disneyish," as Benedict noted (31). Mary Madelyn, the lone female chimp, has a lallation which Lelchuk found grating and ridiculous (15). For instance, she says, "I would wike to be Juwiet in wov with Romeo" (*God's* 147). Yet, in general, Malamud is once again entertaining and thought provoking. Malamud said he was asking simple questions in *God's Grace*: "Why does man treat himself so badly? What is the key to a sane existence?" (Benedict 30).

By having Calvin Cohn be the lone human in the universe, Malamud dramatizes modern man's precarious fate much as he used Yakov Bok to suggest the six million victims of the Holocaust. This novel focusing on Cohn as the last human specimen is somehow much more poignant, sad, and hopeful than any novel depicting the global nuclear destruction of millions could have been. Cohn is the last breathing specimen of a species which has endangered itself. And because the nuclear annihilation hovers over the novel, creating a portentous smog, much of the violence among the chimps and baboons is seen in a more human light; the chimps eat baboons but the humans press buttons to send missiles across continents. The violence, chimp and human, which clings to almost every page of the novel sends out a cautionary message much like the message of *The Tenants*: Love and cooperation are essential, or else!

Calvin Cohn survived the nuclear war because he was in a submersible, studying fossils on the ocean floor. God tells Cohn on the first page of the novel: "I regret to say it was through a minuscule error that you escaped destruction" (*God's* 3). This vaudevillian banter between God and Cohn, God rationalizing His behavior and blaming man for succumbing to evil and Cohn quizzing God in Job-like fashion while secretly blaming God for man's fate, makes for some of the sharpest writing of the novel. Malamud claims he would talk back to God, too: "Of course I would! There's a whole tradition of back-talk from Adam to Job. God may not enjoy man as much as we would like Him to, but He seems to enjoy the human voice" (Benedict 31). However, it is uncertain whether Malamud truly believes in God. When asked, Malamud was cryptic: "I think it was Carlyle who said whether he believed in God was his business and God's" (Benedict 31). Generally, God is a character in *God's Grace* and a prop, an ashen canopy providing little protection and fewer answers. His major contribution to life on Cohn's Island is to keep up pollination and decay, without visible evidence of insects, and to cure plant radiation.

Mr. Cohn's plight places him firmly on the genealogical chart of the Malamud hero. He is a loner, he is geographically displaced, he is a sufferer, he is orderly and methodical, and he seeks a new and better life.

Of all Malamud's lonely heroes, Cohn is the ultimate loner, alone on the planet, keeping company with chimps, a gorilla and some baboons. But even his pre-war life was lonely. His wife died in an auto accident: "She had been driving, not Cohn. He mourned her among those he mourned" (*God's* 13). She was pregnant when she died. Cohn takes her ashes ashore and later buries them after he has made love to the chimp Mary Madelyn, but the chimp Buz digs them up and flings them out to sea. Cohn's tragedy goes back even before his birth, to the death of his grandfather the rabbi in a pogrom. Cohn's observances of religious rituals such as the Passover seder in part serve as homage to his grandfather and to Cohn's own dead father, a cantor turned rabbi whose records, prayers of lamentation rescued from the ship, deeply move Cohn and George the gorilla. George shows his appreciation by gobbling up one record and then spitting it out. Cohn is thankful that his religious father died before the nuclear annihilation: "They had serious trouble after the Holocaust" (*God's* 57).

Cohn's aloneness is extreme, more extreme even than that of Job or Robinson Crusoe. Both the *Book of Job* and *Robinson Crusoe* are hymns to man alone. But Job was still a part of the human community and Crusoe had Friday, whom he treated as more or less human. A most poignant example of the degree of Cohn's isolation comes when he says Kaddish for "one hundred souls whose names he had picked at random in a heavily thumbed copy of a Manhattan telephone directory he had snatched from the sea battered Rebekah Q" (*God's* 38). This absurd yet tragic detail is in perfect Malamud tempo.

Cohn's total isolation leads him to believe that chimps and gorillas will behave humanely, even in the face of evidence that humans themselves have betrayed human hope. He rationalizes that he will promote anthropological and moral evolution by fathering a child with Mary Madelyn the chimp.

Typically, Cohn is geographically displaced. Here even the geography may be displaced. Of the island, "Cohn guessed from the vegetation that it lay somewhere in what had once been the Indian Ocean, perhaps off the southeast coast of old Africa. . ." (*God's* 44). While many Malamud heroes move consciously to a new locale to seek a new life, the at first passive Cohn is shipwrecked and as a result must try to build a new world where he is.

Only Yakov Bok suffers in as physical and palpable a way as Cohn. A week or two after Cohn and Buz start to set up camp on the island, they are both laid low by radiation sickness. Cohn asks, "Is it the Swiss cheese ozone or the will of God that makes me ill?" (*God's* 34). He sweats, vomits, stinks, fouls himself, loses his hair. One night when Cohn is delirious, someone enters the cave, feeds him coconut milk and later returns with fruit. After Cohn falls into a coma his protector drags him out into the sun. Cohn recovers. Later, when Cohn meets George the gorilla, he believes George was the rescuer. The mystery is how George stayed well enough to be a nurse. Buz, thin and slightly bald, suffered himself.

Aside from his physical suffering, Cohn suffers perpetual grief, first at the loss of the world as he has known it for thirty odd years, then at the destruction of the new world he tries to create. Whenever possible Cohn rails at God: God responds with pillars of fire, rains of lemons, and obfuscating hokum. Though God generally throws up his hands at man's fate in the novel, "Cohn shook his enraged fist. 'You have destroyed mankind. Our children are all dead. Where is justice and mercy?' " (*God's* 137). God responds that He was using man "to perfect Himself" (*God's* 137). Cohn suffers because of what he hopes for and expects from God but does not get. As always, Malamud's emphasis is really on man, not God. In talking of *God's Grace* Malamud said: "In a sense, blaming man gets you nowhere. But, on the other hand, whom else can you seriously blame?" (Benedict 36). But even if man is responsible for man, Cohn's grief is undiminished.

Unlike many Malamud heroes who look for moral guidance to surrogate fathers or are pursued by teacher figures, like Susskind or Salzman, Cohn's teacher is his own father, the cantor and rabbi. Cohn relates tales of his father to Buz and George. George, in particular, loves these stories. The father sounds like a Morris Bober figure: "he had labored up the stairs of a cold tenement to deliver a pail of coal to an old woman in a freezing flat" (*God's* 79). Cohn is not especially religious himself, though he studied for the rabbinate for a time; but he has a great respect for the lives of the men in his own family and for his people the Jews.

Cohn also shares a number of personal traits common to the Malamud hero. He is orderly, meticulous, a collector -- like William Dubin for example. Cohn collects bones and fossils, maps the island, noting the locations of the fruit trees. As Bober and Alpine created an order in the small yet symbolic world of the grocery store, Cohn organizes the island. Cohn builds bookcases, brings a cot and even a dust mop to his island cave home. In his hut "he had strung up a canvas hammock he had made from a sail, where he often lay, reflecting on his lonely fate" (*God's* 53).

Cohn's role as collector, scientist, organizer of nature, cultivator of rice recalls Robinson Crusoe in some rather unpleasant ways. Cohn considers the island "his domain" and makes a sign "Cohn's Island" (*God's* 32, 45). He seeks to catalog and ration the fruits of the trees and Mary Madelyn's sexual favors. He hopes the chimps and George will conserve fruit and thereby survive, but the chimps are understandably resentful. When Cohn decides to accept Mary Madelyn's romantic advances, he suggests sublimation for a jealous and sexually frustrated Buz. While Cohn is affectionate and even fatherly to Buz, their relationship is more unequal than the Crusoe-Friday relationship was. Even though Buz speaks, he is forever a chimpanzee. Cohn hopes to run the island and bring about a higher and more human level of life in chimpland. The absurdities of thinking of human life as higher than animal life in light of the nuclear Holocaust is underscored when Cohn says:

> "We behaved toward each other like animals, and therefore
> the Second Flood followed hard on the Day of Devastation."
>   Buz hooted, "I'm on onimol and hov always been a
> vegetorion" (*God's* 75).

Cohn shares another personal trait with many Malamud heroes: he is not very worldly. Like Bok, Levin, and many characters in the short stories such as Leo Finkle in "The Magic Barrel," Cohn is a little naive, innocent, even green. The few times Cohn speaks of his days before the nuclear war, he generally mentions his father and grandfather. Aside from his dead wife no other woman is mentioned. And Cohn quite quickly gets caught up in rather absurd schemes, such as his education of the chimpanzees. He has missionary zeal. This innocence often suits Malamud's purposes: it leads to comedy as well as high hopes. Cohn embarks on his primate improvement crusade precisely because he is somewhat innocent as well as desperate. An innocent person may be more ripe for change, for experience.

In *God's Grace* Malamud once again uses the role of *mensch*-teacher. While Cohn is flawed and somewhat egotistical his purposes are serious, even noble. Like many of Malamud's characters from Alpine to Bok, including even Dubin, Cohn tends to be high-minded, concerned with how life should be lived. He sets up a school for chimps in the eucalyptus tree; George is in the cedar. At first Cohn sticks to didactic parables about sharing food and conserving. Eventually he teaches the *Bible* and Shakespeare: "He was no Martin Buber and the apes no Hasidim, though they might someday be, Cohn permitted himself to think" (*God's* 129-30). When Buz asked Cohn what "humon" means, "Cohn said he thought to be human was to be responsive to and protective of life and civilization" (*God's* 70). Cohn shows his preoccupations to be close to Malamud's own.

In spite of Cohn's shortcomings and occasional shopkeeper mentality, he is for a time successful in his role as repository of a valuable tradition. Early in the course of civilizing and sanctifying the chimps and George, Cohn plans an intricate Passover seder, complete with banana wine, matzos, a fossil bone, wooden tumblers he carved himself, and a seat ready for the prophet Elijah. The feast goes smoothly except for Esau, the aggressive Alpha Ape: "My purpose in life right at this particular time is to slip it to Mary Madelyn as soon as she learns the facts of life" (*God's* 116). When George the gorilla arrives, the shrieking chimps scatter and overturn the seder table. But soon George sits in Elijah's spot, munching matzo, teary-eyed over the story of the Prodigal Son and the song of the passionate cantor. The gorilla is deeply moved by Cohn's Passover: "George bonged his chest in joy" (*God's* 124). Cohn is a *mensch*-teacher himself, flawed as are others like Susskind and Angel Levine.

As the Malamud hero in search of a new life, Cohn is unsurpassed. Once again the drive for a new life is partly a result of all Cohn has suffered. None of the other heroes has a more dramatic task. Cohn has a few bare artifacts of the civilization he knew; and after the broken *Rebekah Q* drifts away when Cohn and Buz first settle on the island, the past life is truly gone. Cohn feels sympathy for Buz, who dragged off the ship his old cage that Dr. Bunder, the scientist, had kept him in. Cohn longs for security, too. Though Cohn is slightly more abstract and less appealing than either Sy Levin or Yakov Bok, his task of bringing a moral order to his island places him squarely in the new life tradition. And like other Malamud heroes who seek love for a female as part of the road to the new life, Cohn, after an unsuccessful search for a human female, falls for a chimp, Mary Madelyn, proving that love is often nine-tenths availability and proximity.

The course of events in the novel raises several questions, important to understanding Malamud's view of his hero at this stage of his career. What part do animal nature, human nature, God, and sexuality play in the undoing of Cohn's fairly peaceable kingdom? Are the Judaic and Christian views of man and God, as seen in this book, contradictory or complementary? How is the reader to view the violent conclusion? And finally, how does the novel contribute to Malamud's view of what it means to be human, the major preoccupation of the Malamud hero?

First, Malamud presents an unusual view of animal nature. At the opening of the novel Cohn is alone on the _Rebekah Q_; all the other scientists have deserted the boat before Cohn re-emerges from the sea, an almost protean man, to face a post-nuclear world. After a few days he hears whimpering and soon discovers Dr. Walter Bunder's chimp Gottlob. To Cohn, "He gave the impression that he was not above serious reflection, a quite intelligent animal" (_God's_ 16). The chimp knows sign language. The name Gottlob suggests "God's bumpkin," perhaps one reason Cohn changed the name to Buz, a name from the Torah that Buz objects to.

Dr. Bunder had been a student of Konrad Lorenz and was a great ape scholar himself before switching to prehistoric fish. He had begun an experiment to give his chimp speech. Cohn notices two copper neck wires after he snips off Buz' beloved, decaying neck cloth. When Cohn twists together the wires Buz speaks: "Fontostisch///I con hear myzelv speag///pong-pong" (_God's_ 64). Cohn had already taken to the chimp: "A genius chimp . . . They'd be like brothers, if not father and son" (_God's_ 26). Cohn uses a pair of pliers to tighten the wires and the pong-pong disappears. Buz' speech improves and he and Cohn are even closer: "They laid arms around each other and affectionately kissed" (_God's_ 67).

In addition to speech, Buz has other qualities usually associated only with humans. He uses a hammer as a tool, as Goodall's chimps used grass stems to fish for termites in their mounds. He plays games with Cohn like "tag, hide-and-seek, nut-in-the-hole, an aggie game. . . " (_God's_ 49). He becomes "depressed" by the wet weather (_God's_ 46). And he espouses the Christianity taught him by Dr. Bunder.

The third character to appear still alive on earth is also an ape with some human characteristics. George, a depressive, gassy gorilla, is drawn to the recorded music of Cohn's father, the cantor. The greatest ape is described: "He was a burly beast, almost ugly, with a shaggy blue black head and heavy brow ridges" (*God's* 62). Still " -- there was something gentle about him" (*God's* 63). Cohn picks the name: "I'd like to call you George, after my late wife's father, who was an accomplished dentist, a wonderful man. He often fixed people's teeth for nothing" (*God's* 63). Later Cohn tells Buz that George is also named for George Washington; "he told Buz the story of the cherry tree" (*God's* 81).

Malamud would seem to be suggesting a third source for the gorilla's name. One cryptic epigraph for the novel reads: "Nobody seemed to know where George's name came from" -- Johanson, Edey. Because George is associated throughout the novel with tremendous power and also deep sentiment, with a religious bent, Malamud may be presenting George as a God figure. "By George" is a common substitute for "By God." In any case, George is certainly identified with religion. He attempts to sing along with the cantor record: "It came out a throaty basso aiming an aria to the night sky, possibly pledging his heart and soul to the song of the impassioned cantor" (*God's* 60). At one point Cohn describes George as looking like Mars, "his head helmeted with cockleburs . . . if not a militant Moses of Joshua" (*God's* 97-98). Joshua, Moses' successor, led the Israelites to the Promised Land. When George sits in Elijah's seat during the seder, he would appear to be heralding the messiah. In addition to perhaps saving Cohn's life by feeding him during his radiation sickness, George, with Buz' help, rescues Cohn from the albino ape by beaning the ape with a large coconut or rock. While most of the chimps favor walking erect, George favors his old knuckle-walk; yet "He kept dignity" (*God's* 172). When warfare erupts among the chimps and the less advanced baboons, George remains withdrawn. And when Cohn is sacrificed

on the mountain; George speaks for the first time. He is humanized by Cohn's
suffering:

> In a tall tree in the valley below, George the gorilla, wearing
> a mud-stained white yarmulke he had one day found in the
> woods, chanted, "Sh'ma, Yisrael, the Lord our God is one"
> (*God's* 223).

When Sara, the baby baboon, is killed and eaten by the chimps, George
attends the funeral: "He seemed to have a natural appreciation of funerals"
(*God's* 192). And in his final Kaddish as Cohn is sacrificed, George represents
one optimistic note. In his gentleness despite his strength, George stands for
mercy and for a prehistoric wail against the tragic conditions of life.

Malamud's view of animal nature grows more complex; midway through the
novel five more chimpanzees appear "who looked as if they had recently been
released from a prison pit" (*God's* 94). Buz teaches them English somehow,
and soon Cohn is teaching them in the school tree. Slightly frightened by the
new chimps and the more primitive element they seem to introduce to the
island, Cohn builds a rolling device to move across the door of his cave, "in
case of peril" (*God's* 102). Buz takes the liberty of naming all five: Mary
Madelyn, Esau, Melchior, Luke and Saul of Tarsus -- the twins. Esau sees
himself as the Alpha Ape, and his aggression is a major cause of the undoing
of Cohn's man and chimp society. Malamud's Esau sells his birthright, a right
to a higher, more noble life. Mary Madelyn soon falls in love with Cohn,
suggesting parallels between Cohn and Christ, especially in light of Cohn's
eventual sacrifice. Like Christ's Mary Magdalene, the female chimp offers
pure love -- absolute devotion.

Later three new chimps arrive. Cohn names the grandmotherly one Hattie
and "the males he named Bromberg -- the monkish tall one -- and Esterhazy,
the short other -- after two college friends whose names he liked to be able to

say once more" (*God's* 143). They too soon speak "a human tongue" (*God's* 144). Malamud describes all these primates in wonderful, comical detail. He gives himself wholly over to his far out world. As John Updike said: "Malamud's curious sensual searchingness bestows upon the apes such individuality that the reader can almost tell them apart by smell" (167).

Finally with the addition of the baboons the recipe for catastrophe is complete. They bring a truly primitive, uneducable element into the view of animal nature in the novel. They are not so much evil; they merely elicit the worst in the chimps. The baboons fear the dark and even the falling leaves, their children are undernourished, and their mouths are full of long pointed teeth. Their appearance at the opening of the chapter entitled "The Voice of the Prophet" suggests that they herald some prophesied doom. When the chimps hunt, murder, and eat the baboons, Esau offers his justification: chimps have always hunted small baboons:

> And besides that, those baboons are dirty, stinking, thieving monkeys, interfering into everybody's business. They breed like rats and foul up all over the clean bush. If we don't control their population they will squat all over this island and we will have to get off.
> And further to that, all of us are mighty sick and tired of eating so much goddamed fruit, plus moldy matzos for dessert (*God's* 194).

Esau's other rationale is sexual frustration: "if there was a piece of sex around instead of that horseass sublimation you [Cohn] are trying to trick on us, we would have something to keep our thoughts going. . . " (*God's* 194). Cohn has cornered and been cornered by the sole available female, Mary Madelyn.

Esau's prejudiced view of baboons taken together with Buz' hatred for that "stupid" and "fot" gorilla George who "stinks" (*God's* 81) present a view of primate relations mirroring the human relations of Djanks and Drushkies, whose tribal hatreds were no less primitive. And Esau correctly identifies sexual frustration as a cause of the violence against the baboons. Curiously, sex and lack of sex, play a bigger part in everyone's undoing in _God's Grace_ than the religious and moral ideas and ideals so prominently featured.

While the chimps and George are shown to have many human qualities for good and ill, Cohn is the sole living example of human nature. Other evidence of humankind is the aftermath of the nuclear war as well as the religious and cultural heritage Cohn tries to perpetuate. Generally, Cohn's dedicated, highly social nature is presented positively. He tries to live decently among his primate relations. He wants community and harmony, if on his terms. He cares for Buz, Mary Madelyn and their chimpchild Rebekah. But he will not realistically accept the limitations of nature. He is destined to fail if he seeks equality for chimps and gorillas -- and their eventual humanization.

While Malamud does not seem to believe animals will become human, he does suggest there is more humanity in animals, and animal in mankind than most people realize. Yet when the violence erupts in the chimp community, beginning with the slaughter of baby baboons and ending with the death of baby Rebekah, the chimps revert to chimp-like ways. They lose the power of speech and Mary Madelyn allows Esau and Gottlob to mount her freely. She does not respond to the grieving Cohn when he calls, "Love, Wov, Lwov!" (_God's_ 217). The chimps take Cohn prisoner and he is eventually sacrificed. Still, compared to the human nuclear havoc, the chimp explosion seems a lesser evil.

Malamud's emphasis on sexual frustration and territoriality is a continuation of a theme developed in _Dubin's Lives_. In _God's Grace_ the bestial nature of the relations lends a wilder and funnier tone to the subject of sex.

Initially Cohn is so sexually frustrated that he even considers Buz as a mate: "If you had suckled the lad, could you marry him?" (*God's* 87). Later Cohn's horniness leads him to accept Mary Madelyn's advances and to rationalize the potential evolutionary benefits such a union might bring. He even identifies himself with Lot, whose daughters "lay down with their wine-drunk father after Sodom had been smoked off the map, to preserve the future of mankind and its successors, not excluding the Messiah?" (*God's* 166). Mary Madelyn and Cohn do treat each other with love and respect; he even makes her a dress out of a portion of sail salvaged from the *Rebekah Q*. But it is their union that precipitates the undoing of the community. Esau tells Cohn of the lady chimp, "Your stupid schooltree has made her too proud to dip her butt for friends" (*God's* 153). But Malamud presents Mary Madelyn's constancy as admirable, noble. She understands her selectivity to be a result of her use of language: "If I hadn't wearned to speak and understand human speech, I would have awready presented mysewf to every mawe on the iwand" (*God's* 152). This association of language with what is most noble in the world is seen throughout *God's Grace*. At one point, "Cohn remembered: God was Torah. He was made of words" (*God's* 92). But sexuality, primitive in man and animal alike, is presented in *God's Grace* as volcanic, chaotic, and potentially destructive. Here Malamud closely associates sexuality with violence, as he did much earlier in *The Assistant* when Frank Alpine raped Helen, a woman he loved.

God as presented in this novel does not appear responsible for the global nuclear destruction or the death and destruction on Cohn's Island. He stands mostly in the distance, dismayed that things have gone awry. He allows the natural bounty of the island to continue, but he accepts no responsibility for the Djanks and the Druzhkies. Of man, God says: "I made man to be free, but his freedom, badly used, destroyed him". . . (*God's* 5). Though God frightens and occasionally bombards Cohn, he is seen mostly in a benign light.

One exception to this view of God as a neutral force is the recurring image of human sacrifice which runs throughout the novel. Buz is fascinated with the tale of Abraham and Isaac and demands that Cohn relate in great detail many versions of the story, including Midrash accounts, collections of scholarly rabbinical commentary on Torah stories. Cohn views the original Biblical story as "a protest against the pagan sacrifice of human beings. That's what I meant by man humanizing himself -- if you follow me" (*God's* 73). Naturally, Buz objects to the animal sacrifice. Cohn brings up the old question of what happens to Isaac after Abraham returns from the mountain alone: "Cohn said some Talmudic sages had interpreted it that Isaac had been carried off by the angel to the Garden of Eden, and that he had rested there, convalescing from the bloody wound his father had inflicted on him" (*God's* 74). Cohn mentions the commentary stating Isaac was resurrected: "Given the nature of death -- how long it lasts once it sets in -- who can blame us for inventing resurrection?" (*God's* 75). This controversy over Isaac's fate is discussed in detail in *The Last Trial*. Given the emphasis on Abraham and Isaac and Cohn's sacrifice by Buz in the final chapter of the novel, where Cohn's "Blood, to their astonishment, spurted forth an instant before the knife touched Cohn's flesh" (*God's* 223), Malamud emphasizes that sacrifice is in the nature of life. God and man may insist on it. And given the sacrifice of life on Earth before the novel opens, Malamud suggests the inevitability and uselessness of sacrifice.

God's Grace can be seen, in part, as a discussion of Judaic emphasis on law and Christian emphasis on love. Cohn espouses law writ large in Cohn's Admonitions. Most of his laws emphasize community life, sharing, not killing. But the second admonition reads: "Note: God is not love, God is God.

Remember Him" (*God's* 171). God has not appeared to Cohn as loving or merciful. Cohn baked each letter of his admonitions into clay and assembled them on sentences which he attached to the escarpment with aid of "Twine, pegs, nails, and Elmer's glue" (*God's* 170). It is significant that Cohn comes up with these admonitions soon after he is involved with Mary Madelyn, perhaps sensing jealousy will soon erupt.

Buz, often speaking for Christianity, advises Cohn after the little baboon boy Aloysius has been killed and half eaten: "Buz said it was Cohn's fault for not teaching love. Cohn said he had tried to teach the good life, but it hadn't come to much" (*God's* 203). Buz insists that God is love. Yet along with the other chimps he betrays Cohn. He watches Cohn when Esau attacks him and later he allows Esau and his gang to enter Cohn's cave, where they grab Rebekah and then throw her around until she dies. Mostly Buz talks love, an easy game, but does not live it.

As Buz is associated with Christianity, George the gorilla is associated with Judaism, the law, the music of the cantor, and the final Kaddish for Cohn. When the chimps, led by Esau, ransack Cohn's cave and tie him up, the law still speaks: "But in the place where the wrecked phonograph stood, a rabbinic voice recited the law" (*God's* 218). It is that rabbinic voice, often associated with George and with Cohn's father the cantor, which seems to have moral validity throughout the book.

Yet it is an oversimplification to suggest as Benedict does that the symbolism of the novel is " --- Christians as savages, the Jew as a lonely, kind-hearted outcast --" (31). In fact, Mary Madelyn embodies some positive Christian virtues until she is undone by the murder of her child Rebekah. And there is something rather unloving and pinched about the Jewish Cohn at times, especially in his rage to order and classify all life on his island, though these qualities may be the result of the often abstract and didactic nature of the novel. It seems unlikely, especially considering other works by Malamud such as *The Assistant*, where Franciscan premises are suggested, that Malamud would deny the importance of love. Yet the novel is weighted slightly more heavily in the direction of law, as every page attests to the natural disorder of human and animal life. Malamud, perhaps grown more cynical, no longer places all his hopes on man's ability to find and give love.

As is often the case in Malamud's novels, the conclusion of *God's Grace*, although somewhat enigmatic, helps to define the novel. In this novel Malamud poses a possible future: What if history came down to Cohn's lot -- if his few artifacts and memories were all that were left of humankind? Malamud emphasizes that humans have a penchant for stacking the deck, or the missiles, against themselves. Our annihilation is practically predestined, as Cohn's first name Calvin, as in John Calvin, suggests.

Cohn tries hard to resurrect civilization, though his task is impossible. But he also contributes to his own undoing. Even as he is up the mountain where he will be sacrificed, Cohn refuses to give a blessing to a beggar whom he realizes later might have been "a naysaying angel" (*God's* 223).

The blood spurts forth from Cohn's neck before Buz places the knife to the skin; God must be sacrificing Cohn before Buz gets the chance. God may be anxious to see the last of man unkind. However, Buz, who once again calls himself Gottlob, seems a strange agent for the sacrifice; he has betrayed the love Cohn showed him. On the mountain Cohn says to Buz, "I wouldn't do this if you weren't my beloved son" (*God's* 223). As the blood spots his white beard Cohn feels grateful:

> "Merciful God," he said, "I am an old man. The Lord has
> let me live my life out."

He wept at the thought. Maybe tomorrow the world to
come? (*God's* 223).

As Cohn is sacrificed he still hopes for a new life, a new world. This hope
against hope is Malamud's own, steady from first book to last in spite of his
increasing pessimism. As Cohn hopes for a world to come, George the gorilla
says Kaddish for a world lost with the last human on earth. The conclusion of
God's Grace is not a simple triumph of atavism; it is a warning of how the
human world we know could be so easily lost. Malamud was questioned about
this bleak conclusion:

> "Yes, I am more pessimistic than I used to be," Malamud
> said a little sadly. "I feel that the more the world stays the
> same, the worse it seems to become. Man seems to be a
> constant disappointment to himself" (Benedict 36).

In *God's Grace*, Cohn carries on the tradition of the Malamud hero with
a new urgency. With Calvin Cohn, Malamud contributes to his portrait of the
hero, to his definition of what it means to be human. As always, Malamud
emphasizes love and communion, the importance of being a better and more
decent person, of rising above the circumstances. Yet while Frank Alpine
could build a new life out of so little, Cohn is given less. In his solitariness, in
the absurdity of his task, Cohn is the most doomed of Malamud's heroes.
Even Yakov Bok was enriched by his fate; Cohn is broken by his. In *God's
Grace* Malamud shows a world where the worst in humankind has triumphed
-- a nuclear war has undone the history of human civilization. In this novel
Malamud presents a life of value, the *mensch*-hero tradition, as essential if
mankind is to undo his present course. Cohn tries to be a *mensch*, to carry on
the tradition, but he cannot do so alone.

God's Grace is a violent, cautionary tale, most like *The Tenants*. They are both idea books, even more so than *The Fixer*. Both are topical: *The Tenants* came out just after the racial turmoil of the 60's and early 70's; *God's Grace* appeared amid heightened interest in nuclear proliferation and disarmament. In both cases Malamud was inspired by important ideas which did not, of themselves, diminish the novels. But the didactic tone and the isolation of both Harry Lesser and Calvin Cohn go against Malamud's own talents. Malamud's heroes are most lively when they are in love or in a struggle with one or two other people. Fidelman is most alive when Susskind is on his trail. Sy Levin is best remembered in Pauline Gilley's arms. Because Cohn, like Lesser, is so isolated, he is also less substantial, less warm. Cohn talks of *mensch* values, sharing, communal life; but without a human companion he ends up emphasizing the law, fearing the primitive elements in his primate companions. Cohn's only triumph would appear to be his influence on the gorilla George, who at the novel's conclusion carries on a humane and Judaic tradition.

Malamud's treatment of his themes and his hero in *God's Grace* also suffers because the comedy and tragedy are awkwardly mixed at times. It is often hard to know when Malamud is serious in this book. But evidently he is highly serious: he starts with nuclear war and ends with the bloody sacrifice of his hero. Yet in between, the sexual relations between Cohn and the lady chimp, the monkey seder, the Elmer's glued up Admonitions, all rock the serious foundations of the book. In *God's Grace*, Malamud is mostly very serious but sometimes very silly.

Still, Malamud's work was always worthwhile. And in *God's Grace* he emphasized that the life of value he spoke for over many years is a life and death matter. The question in Malamud's last completed novel is not only how the hero will live his life, but if he will get a chance to live it at all.

CONCLUSION

In more than forty years as a fiction writer, Bernard Malamud produced a sizable body of work. His achievement is rich in the variety of experiences he dealt with. When his subject is somber, heavy, as in *The Fixer*, he never becomes morose; when he deals in comedy, as in "Still Life," he is neither superficial nor facile, and he is never superior to his characters. In his sustained focus on rather ordinary people, in his lack of concern for intellectual answers to life's problems, in his near disdain for the subjects of material success or fame, as reflected in Dubin's guilt over accepting the Medal of Freedom from President Johnson, Malamud was a unique contemporary American writer. He brought Old World values, a preoccupation with morality in daily life, for him tied closely to the history of the Jewish people, and occasionally Old World characters, like Salzman and Susskind who speak with a Yiddish accent and lead others to a greater appreciation of all lives, to settings which were usually New World. He was distinct from most contemporary American writers in that he was seldom satirical; he did not harangue his readers or baffle them with intellectual puzzles. Without being overly sentimental or emotional, Malamud wrote sincerely, directly, straight to the heart.

In his introduction to the 1983 publication of *The Stories of Bernard Malamud*, Malamud wrote of his own struggle to become a writer:

> Some are born whole; others must seek this blessed state in
> a struggle to achieve order. That is no loss to speak of;

ultimately such seeking becomes the subject matter of fiction (*Stories* vii).

That struggle to become a whole person has certainly been the main struggle of Malamud's heroes. The pattern of the struggle remained quite consistent over the years, especially in the novels where there is more time for character development. All these heroes are in the same family, possessed of much the same genetic assets and liabilities.

To a striking degree the particular markings of the hero remain consistent throughout the years. They are sufferers. In part they suffer from past mistakes, but much of their suffering is born of illness, death of family members, grinding poverty. Yet Malamud was not perverse; he did not take pleasure in his characters' misfortunes. It seems to me Malamud took a rather direct look at the degree of sorrow and suffering there is in the world. He did not overstate the case. While the earlier heroes often suffer physically like Bok, or because they make bad choices like Roy Hobbs, the later heroes suffer in very believable mental prisons. While Dubin has more money and prestige than the earlier heroes, he suffers from depression and is once close to suicide. Cohn, the hero of the last completed novel, suffers from impossible circumstances as the sole human left on an earth where mankind has destroyed nearly all human possibilities. All the heroes suffer from traps or prisons they must learn to overcome. But Malamud shows that the trap often leads to a new life.

The heroes are displaced and their discomfort in their new locales contributes to their anxieties and high expectations, their hopes for change. Comically enough, in the late story "A Lost Grave," a man searches for the grave of his deceased wife only to be told by the cemetery director, "Lost is

premature . . . _Displaced_ might be better" (_People_ 249). So Malamud's
characters become displaced even after death.

The general movement of all Malamud's heroes is toward love,
commitment, and communion. Often the hero finds this love in a woman, as
does Sy Levin in _A New Life_. Even Bok, who is isolated in prison throughout
most of _The Fixer_, finds that his forgiveness of his wife and his affection for his
father-in-law give him new peace and strength. When stories end with
isolation, aloneness, and destruction, as in _The Tenants_ and _God's Grace_, they
become even more of a testament to the necessity of love. Some of the short
stories in _Idiots First_ and _Rembrandt's Hat_ depict lonely heroes: Malamud
emphasizes that true communion is rare. The tragedy of much of the later
work is caused by the breakdown of communication between children and
parents, husbands and wives, both featured prominently in _Dubin's Lives_.

Generally the later heroes are more ordinary, their tasks less heroic.
They do not suffer for others like Frank Alpine or Yakov Bok did. With the
notable exceptions of Cohn of _God's Grace_, and Yosip of _The People_, whose
dire situations are extreme, the later heroes are faced with common, ordinary
problems. They have family problems; they have affairs. They long to tear
down the walls which separate them from those they would love. They are
sensitive people who hope to break out of the habit of solitude.

In _The Stories of Bernard Malamud (1983)_, Malamud chose to include two
previously uncollected stories, "God's Wrath" and "The Model." "God's
Wrath" was first published in _The Atlantic_ in 1972 yet is curiously tied to the
later stories he wrote. The protagonist Glasser, "a retired sexton," measures
out a lonely, desperate old age trailing his "heavy-breasted" daughter Lucille,
a prostitute, around her 8th Avenue haunts. Lucille is Glasser's daughter by
his second wife, "a dissatisfied woman" who "bewailed her fate" (_Stories_ 258).

The story is lonely, pathetic, yet angry. As in *Dubin's Lives*, parents have little control over adult children: " 'You're not God,' Luci cried in sudden rage" (*Stories* 264). Still, as Glasser hobbles around after Lucille, he first offers forgiveness of a sort: "come home with your father, we won't tell anybody. Your room is waiting" (*Stories* 264). Again Malamud imagines desperate yet ordinary people. Prostitutes have fathers who once hoped for different lives for their daughters. But this story ends on a note of grief and wrath, not communion or reconciliation: "He [Glasser] punishes by his presence. He calls down God's wrath on the prostitute and her blind father" (*Stories* 265).

"The Model," first published in *The Atlantic* in 1983, features a seventy-year-old protagonist Ephraim Elihu who has much in common with Dr. Morris of "In Retirement." Isolated, lonely, feeling his age, Elihu, once an amateur painter, requests a model he can paint nude. But the model turns out to be a painter herself and she recognizes that he is really watching her, not painting. He becomes embarrassed when she insists that he disrobe; she paints a picture of him and then squeezes black paint all over the canvas. When she leaves he asks himself, "Is there nothing more to my life than it is now? Is this all that is left in me? The answer seemed yes and he wept at how old he had so quickly become" (*Stories* 306). Like Dr. Morris, Mr.Elihu is thrown back into old age, more miserable than ever.

In 1989 Robert Giroux and Malamud's other two literary executors Timothy Seldes and Daniel Stein authorized the publication of *The People and Uncollected Stories*. *The People*, which is a partial draft of a novel, and the stories, including six previously unpublished, contribute to any understanding of Malamud's long and varied career, even if the volume does not represent Malamud at his best. Taken together the draft and all the stories are a skeleton or anatomy for Malamud's work and suggest how he changed over the years.

The earliest stories illustrate that Malamud had found his subject but had not yet found a way to make his heroes' suffering and struggle meaningful and sympathetic. The first two stories in the volume are "Armistice" (1940) and "Spring Rain" (1942), published here for the first time.

In "Armistice" Morris Lieberman, an owner of a small grocery, is deeply disturbed by the surrender of the French to Hitler. As a young boy Morris saw a Jew murdered by a Russian peasant. Now he feels the horror of the Nazis as he listens to midnight news on the radio. His loving son tries to protect him, to make him sleep in peace. The story contains seeds of the Morris Bober and Frank Alpine relationship in _The Assistant_, but in this story the emphasis is on grief and pain, not redemption. The final focus of the story is on Gus Wagner, the meats and provisions deliverer, who is pleased by the German victories. He drives his truck down the street imagining it is a massive German tank on French boulevards. He is contemptuous of the grocer and his loving son who cries for his father. Gus thinks, "It was always like that with the Jews. Tears and people holding each other. Why feel sorry for them?" (_People_ 109).

"Spring Rain" is a poignant story suggesting a degree of communication between a father and a surrogate son. The story opens as the older man George Fisher watches a young man die as a result of an automobile accident. He is moved and shaken into intense thoughts. The war news is again a backdrop as George realizes his isolation from his wife and his daughter who does not want a college education. Paul, a boy who attends Columbia, is dating the daughter Florence but does not love her. When Paul asks George to go for a walk on a rainy spring evening, George is excited and moved.

Malamud beautifully depicts the older man's hunger for a change of routine, for communication. The candid conversation between George and Paul sets an early pattern for the father and surrogate-son communication so common in Malamud's fiction. The men stop for beer and Paul confesses that he does not love Florence, he can't "reach her" (*People* 114). George is moved and quickly identifies with the younger man: "He wanted to tell him how lonely he had been all his life and how he lay awake at night, dreaming and thinking, until the gray morning drifted into the room" (*People* 114).

When George returns to his apartment he is in tears, "Once more he possessed the world and loved it" (*People* 115). The warm and honest conversation with the younger man has brought him to life. But when he tries to speak to Florence he simply stammers and tells her they went for a walk.

"The Literary Life of Laban Goldman," first published in *Assembly* in 1943, is a vivid and comical tale about a dissatisfied man who seeks a new life in night school and in friendship with a younger fellow student Miss Moscowitz. Like "Spring Rain," the story sets an early pattern for the hero wanting a new life, wanting to at least find someone to talk to. But this story is basically ridiculous as the married Laban Goldman tries to impress Miss Moscowitz with a letter to *The Brooklyn Eagle* on incompatibility as grounds for divorce. Laban's wife and daughter bump into him and Miss Moscowitz having coffee in a cafeteria after class. A wild scene follows as Miss Moscowitz flees.

The reverence for learning and the formality of the night school class are charming, even touching. But Laban is limited, even cruel to his wife and daughter. He is self-serving and wants to pretend to be learned in order to impress a woman twenty years younger. In the cafeteria he yells out, "Let them see what a man of sensitivity and understanding has to suffer because of incompatible ignorance" (_People_ 125). Still, as in "Spring Rain," beautiful small touches bring these people to life.

Another early story, "The Grocery Story" (1943) is published here for the first time. The subject matter suggests _The Assistant_ but the tone is more grim and realistic. The suffering in the story seems pointless and the grocer Sam lacks warmth. Ida Kaplan, unlike Ida Bober, looks "at her husband with loathing" (_People_ 128). Sam Kaplan calls the grocery salesman "common" (_People_ 128). And Sam thinks of his impoverished business of nineteen years as pointless--"For what? For what, dear God? The feeling of misery crept into his stomach. Sam shivered. He felt sick" (_People_ 127).

Many details in this story appear in _The Assistant_, altered and enriched. Here Ida forces Sam to sweep snow from the sidewalk and then she begs him not to lie down and rest. When Sam Kaplan nearly gases himself by accident, just as Morris Bober nearly did, Ida Kaplan is frightened and moved to some degree of sympathy. She decides to let Sam sleep in the morning.

The long hours with no customers suggest the despair of _The Assistant_. But when Malamud added a daughter and an apprentice grocer to the equation he opened up a world of possibilities.

In "Benefit Performance," published first in _Threshold_ in 1943, an angry Jewish actor named Maurice Rosenfeld disapproves of his daughter's boyfriend Ephraim "the plum-ber" who is not learned and converses in "yes and no" (_People_ 139). The story suggests the later scene from a play, "Suppose a Wedding," where a father attempts to influence the daughter to marry the struggling writer.

In this story the daughter makes her bedroom in the living room of their tiny apartment by putting up screens. When the actor performs his grief, compares himself to Job, the plumber justly cries, "You cheap actor" (_People_

142). At the conclusion the plumber leaves and the daughter hides from her father behind the scenes.

"The Place is Different Now" was first published in 1943. The relationship between Wally Mullane and Mr. Davido was another early model for Morris Bober and Frank Alpine, though Wally is also close to Ward Minogue, more of a bum than Frank. But the generosity of the barber, his willingness to treat Wally with respect, illustrates how Malamud was finding his theme of meaning through shared suffering. The barber regrets that he chased away his own son Vincent by slapping him and yelling, "You bum, why don't you go look for a job?" (_People_ 152).

After Wally's brother beats him up Mr. Davido takes him in for a shave. Both men think back on a better past as "The barber slowly raised the lather until it mixed with tears" (_People_ 153).

"An Apology," first published in _Commentary_ in 1957, is a very suggestive and symbolic story tied to Malamud's best work. An itinerant peddler of light bulbs is hassled by the police who realize he has no license to peddle. Light bulbs always fascinated Malamud, from Brietbart the bulb peddler of _The Assistant_ to the talking Yiddish light bulb of _Pictures of Fidelman_. Here the peddler brings the light of conscience; he is the ubiquitous reminder of human debt and responsibility.

When the police take the peddler to the station they leave one of his two boxes of bulbs on the curb. Walter, the older policeman, tries to find the bulbs and even offers to pay for them but the peddler Bloostein refuses the offer and haunts Walter's front door. Bloostein is a jewbird, "a skinny owl" (_People_ 160). Finally Walter buys bulbs for Bloostein but Bloostein still stands in the rain outside the policeman's house. Eventually Walter realizes he owes an apology: "Bloostein, I owe you an apology. I'm really sorry the whole thing happened.

I haven't been able to sleep. From my heart I'm truly sorry" (_People_ 162). Bloostein vanishes. Walter "looked again, but the long, moon-whitened street had never been so empty" (_People_ 163). The story is pure Malamud. A person is pursued, haunted, and taught a moral lesson by a threadbare character who would appear to be more needy.

"Riding Pants" was written in 1953 but now appears for the first time. The story touches on a young man's longing for a new life but focuses on the trap of the father's butcher shop. Like Tommy Castelli of "The Prison," Herm of "Riding Pants" has limited dreams. Herm likes to go horseback riding; he would like to ride out of his future as a butcher. Instead, his father chops up his riding pants. He decides to chop up his father's cat in revenge but ends up briefly locked in the meat freezer.

When the butcher father loosely wraps up some liver and the blood stains a woman's mink coat, the son Heim accepts his service in his father's butcher shop: "he got up and reached for the blood-stained apron hanging on a hook. He looped the loop over his head and tied the string around him" (_People_ 170). But unlike Frank's holy apprenticeship in Morris Bober's grocery, this assistance is filled with resentment and resignation.

"A Confession of Murder" is a section of an unpublished novella _The Man Nobody Could Lift_, written in 1952-53. The excerpt focuses on the estrangement between father and son, like Albert Gans and his father in "The Silver Crown," and Gerald and William Dubin in _Dubin's Lives_, among others. But here the father has been an abusive brute and the son imagines he has killed him. The reader learns that the crime is a delusion near the end of the piece.

The section has the feel of a Dostoyevsky work, with its vivid portrayal of the young Edward Farr's guilt and obsession. He hides the window sash he believes he used as a weapon. He visits Gus's tavern and is reminded of his past, his great punch-ball life, his singing and mandolin playing, as well as his failure to consummate sex with a girl who offered herself nude on a tar-papered roof. Gus sentimentally recalls the old days; he chased his own son away much like Mr. Davido in "The Place is Different Now." Gus's son Marty was later killed in the war.

The richness of this selection is in the depiction of the younger Farr's guilt and the older Farr's terrible remorse. Herman Farr beat his son and his wife. In a drunken fit he swung the same window sash at her and later she tried to kill him with it. Though she has been dead sixteen years, both father and son are haunted by her memory. The father has nightmares, including that the son has murdered him.

The disturbed son Edward Farr, who reads books, who wanders the streets, unemployed and obsessive, is insane according to Detective Wolff. When Wolff says he'll call an ambulance, Edward Farr knocks him over and runs out into the streets: "In the street he flung his coins into the sky" (*People* 190). The father shouts that he is the real guilty one, the one who deserves hanging.

The selection is grim and hinges on the surprise finding that the older Farr is alive, the son insane. As with much of Malamud's earliest work, this piece is without hope. The suffering is endless and inevitable.

"The Elevator" was first written in Italy in 1957 and was published in *The Paris Review*, fall 1989. It is closely tied to two other Italian stories, "The Maid's Shoes" and "Behold the Key," where Americans struggle with Italian mores. Once again the Italians seem to have hard lives. Here the maid Eleonora wants to use the elevator to bring the wash up five flights. The signora who owns the building wants all maids to use the stairs.

George, the American who has employed the maid, is more sympathetic than Orlando Krantz of "The Maid's Shoes," and feels uncomfortable having a maid at all. But like Krantz, he does consider becoming caretaker of his maid's morals, though his wife advises against it.

Eleonora has "lost" one husband and had a baby by another fellow who deserted her. She keeps the child in a convent school. When she becomes involved with a plumber's helper who worked on the washtub, he takes off on his Vespa with a girl from Perugia.

The signora calls her a "whore" and advises, "don't steal the privileges of your letters. Use the stairs" (*People* 197). George fights for the girl's rights, and after threatening to break the lease has victory over the signora. But the owner is furious--" 'Your money is your dirty foot with which you kick the world. Who wants you here,' she cried, 'with your soaps and toothpastes and your dirty gangster movies' " (*People* 199).

In this story, Malamud once again depicts Americans abroad as more sheltered, cushioned from life's hardships, than Italians who live in a stratified world, most of them scraping by as best they can. The Italians shake up the Americans. As this story ends, a beggar plays a flute and George is depressed by his victory.

"An Exorcism," first published in *Harper's* in 1968, is closely tied to Malamud's other work about writers including *The Tenants* and *Dubin's Lives*. Like *The Tenants*, this story centers around two writers, one more experienced, who are friends and competitors. Here Eli Fogel, the older man, is a fine though not so "successful" fiction writer. Like William Dubin, he emphasizes discipline and invention. He wants a fuller life, including sexual fulfillment. But he is single, has a noticeable limp, and encounters difficulties with women. Gary Simson is a young would-be writer who first ingratiates himself to Fogel, gets letters of recommendation from him and then betrays the older, kinder man by detailing in a "story" Fogel's unhappy sexual adventure. A young college girl working as a chambermaid, who once slept with Fogel, had her boyfriend call "fire" to get Fogel locked out of his room, naked. This is a misadventure Dubin might have.

Gary Simson is always with a new sexy girl and Fogel is angered and envious. At the conclusion of the story Gary Simson once again seeks out Fogel for a recommendation and reads a draft of a story about a young man who has sex with three roommates in one night--the final consummation in a van. Disgusted by Simson's exploitation of people, Fogel sets his van ablaze with a fifth of bourbon.

In Fogel's preoccupation with his age and his physical shortcomings, this story is tied to Malamud's later work. Like Dubin, Fogel gets offers from women because of his status as a writer. One student from a writing conference offers herself for "art and truth" (*People* 206). But Fogel declines, realizing she is not "aroused" by him.

Like Malamud himself, Fogel emphasizes that the work, not the writer is most important: "Memory is an ingredient, Gary, not the whole stew; and don't make the error some do of living life as though it were a future fiction. Invent, my boy" (*People* 204).

Though "An Exorcism" is a good story with many fine details, it is not one of Malamud's best. It is a little stiff, a little long and suggests to me that Malamud may have been searching for material for a longer work. Both William Dubin and Harry Lesser many contain a bit of Fogel.

In "A Wig," first published in *The Atlantic* in 1980, the protagonist is a fifty-year-old woman named Ida with thinning hair. Like many other Malamud parents, she is alienated from her child, here a twenty-eight-year-old daughter.

After Ida's husband dies she tries to express her worries to her daughter but notices the girl's hair is also thinning, a circle of scalp becoming visible. Ida rushes out to buy herself a wig. Again Malamud focuses on the physical effects of aging and the general loneliness of older people.

The last four short stories of this collection suggest Malamud was still concerned with the same themes in his treatment of the hero. "Zora's Noise" was first published in *Gentleman's Quarterly* in 1985. Dwoskin, a cellist, and his wife Zora live in a country house. She is kept awake at night by a noise of "utter misery" (*People* 245). At first they believe it emanates from the paint factory, but when that noise ceases she still hears her noise.

Finally Dwoskin is awakened by "a burst of cello music in the sky" and observes his personal constellation "the Cellist" (*People* 243). He goes down to the music room to play Schubert's B-flat major trio. The music summons Zora from bed and later "a fleeting figure" of Ella, his departed first wife, who previously lived in the house (*People* 245).

It is a thin story but it focuses on two of Malamud's common themes, the strength of the past and the physical manifestation of grief and despair. Zora hears the first wife's cry; Kitty Dubin, unsettled and unhappily married, constantly smells gas. For Malamud the past is palpable and dangerous. His characters must learn to live and love in the present. Dwoskin and his wife Zora put their house up for sale.

"A Lost Grave," first published in *Esquire* in 1985, is a brief but sharp story depicting a man's attempt to dignify and define his past. Hecht, the hero, long ago buried his wife from whom he had been separated for several years. Now Hecht, "a born late bloomer" (*People* 247), has the desire to visit her grave but cannot locate it. This sort of intense feeling for a long dead spouse comes up a couple of times in Malamud's fiction: in "Life is Better than

Death" and in Kitty Dubin's love for the long dead Nathanael. Here Hecht's grief is mixed with anger: "she had spoiled his life" (*People* 250). She had left him twice in her life and now after death she has hopped into a grave with another man. Her lover before her death requested that she be buried with him. Now they lie together, adulterers in death. But the story emphasizes how life sometimes softens people: "Hecht had lately been remembering his life more vividly, for whatever reason. After you hit sixty-five some things that have two distinguishable sides seem to pick up another that complicates the pictures as you look or count" (*People* 250).

Suddenly, late in life, Hecht may feel more compassion for his wife. Still, the events disconcert him. "he felt he had lost a wife but was no longer a widower" (*People* 251). The story is comic and ironic: even in death one cannot control a loved one. But in terms of the hero reevaluating his life and having warm, if frustrated, feelings late in life, the story continues Malamud's tradition.

The last two selections are biographical stories: "Kew Gardens" is about Virginia Woolf and "Alma Redeemed" is about Alma Mahler, Gustav's wife, and her various other husbands and lovers. Malamud became interested in mixing biography and fiction when he worked on *Dubin's Lives*. "Kew Gardens" mentions pieces of Virginia Woolf's life, from her early closeness to Vanessa to her life with Leonard and his love and care for her. Though Malamud briefly depicts Woolf's depression and suicide, complete with the large rock she put in her pocket before she drowned herself in the river, he ends on a rather odd note, one supposes in Virginia's words: "I don't think two people could have been happier than we have been" (*People* 257). In this brief sketch Malamud outlines a despair which knows no cause, something akin to Dubin's depression. "Alma Redeemed" is far lighter: Alma survives

Mahler and his ghost, plus Walter Gropius, Franz Werfel, and Oskar Kokoschka, and lives to be eighty-five. Alma has mostly lived fully, but she has suffered guilts and losses. Two of her children die and when her husband Werfel dies Malamud says: "there is no beating out illness and bad health" (*People* 268). While the story is mostly humorous, including a walk with Freud and Mahler who discuss the psyche, Alma does look back on her life wondering who she really was: "Where is *my* truth?" (*People* 268). In her search for herself she ended up dominated by the famous men she loved.

Malamud was working on a draft for a novel entitled *The People* when he died. It is difficult to know what the work would finally have become if he had been granted the health, the energy, and the time to complete it. It is based on an idea Malamud had after hearing a joke about a "Jewish Indian" in the 1940s (Introduction, *The People* xii). Later while teaching in the Northwest he did research on the Nez Percé tribe. Then in 1983-84 Malamud decided:

> I may have done as much as I can with the sort of short story I have been writing so long--the somewhat mythological, biblically oriented tales I have been writing. These become more and more difficult to do and I feel I must make a change. What I see as possible is another variation of the comic-mythological--possibly working out the Chief Joseph of the Nez Percé idea--in other words, the Jewish Indian; or the igloo piece of the race to the North Pole. Possibly both, but I must recover the voice I need. I have reached a dangerous place for a writer to be, that means I should search for a new material (Introduction, *The People* xiii).

So while *The People* represents an old idea it also represents Malamud the experimenter, author of wild fables like *God's Grace*. The hero of *The People* is Yozip Bloom, a refugee from Russia, an itinerant peddler, a socialist, and a Jewish Indian, striking out for a new life. As a Jew in the West he is at first self-conscious, believing people regard him uncomfortably: "He did not like saying his name in public" (*People* 7).

Like most Malamud heroes, Yozip does find a new life, though not in the terms he envisioned. After five years in the U.S., he is hoping for American citizenship. Instead, he is mistaken for a marshall, accosted by two gun-slingers whom he miraculously punches out, and finally kidnapped and drafted into an Indian nation after an older Indian sees his performance against the gun-slingers. The Great Spirit has spoken and Yozip will be an Indian after surviving ritual competitions and initiation.

Unfortunately Yozip speaks with a thick, supposedly Yiddish accent. Through he quickly picks up the Indian language, she still says "denks" for "thanks," "tulk" for "talk," and "of cuss" for "of course." Usually Malamud handled the Yiddish accent with great subtlety and ease. Here Yozip speaks as stiffly as Gottlob the chimp in *God's Grace*. Of course Yozip's "tulk" may have changed in subsequent drafts.

But the heart of the draft is pure Malamud and tied quite closely to *The Fixer*. The old chief is like old Shmuel, a wise teacher. His daughter One Blossom is drawn to Yozip as was Raisl. In Yozip's desire for a new life and a decent living he is caught up in the Indian cause and takes on the U.S. Government, as the fixer Bok became a symbolic Jew and defied all of Russia.

Malamud also manages to suggest the horror of the 19th century west --passengers on trains are passed rifles to slaughter buffalo, the army is just as brutal to the Indians. When old Chief Yoseph dies, Yozip becomes Chief Jozip. He tries to negotiate peace and later tries, unsuccessfully, to lead the tribe to safe haven in Canada. In the author's notes for the conclusion of the novel, Yozip wants to become a lawyer and mourns the murder of One Blossom.

The draft suggests the creativity and daring that Malamud still possessed, but it cannot be compared to his finished work. It is more of a sketch and at times reads like a synopsis or like stage directions. From the first line--"Here's Yozip rattling around in his rusty wagon" (_People_ 3) to the conclusion, little of the work is fleshed out, full Malamud. As Philip Roth told a weak and ailing Malamud when he read Roth the opening pages, "it seemed to me a beginning like all beginnings" ("Pictures of Malamud" 41).

Malamud died at his desk while completing a draft of _The People_. He curiously foretold his death in the story "An Exorcism." The writer Fogel had visions of himself dying before the work was complete:

> It was a terrible thought: Fogel seated at the table, staring at his manuscript, pen in hand, the page ending in a blot (_People_ 213).

On March 18, 1986, Bernard Malamud died, after several years of struggle with a stroke, bypass surgery, and the side effects of heart medication. The vision of Malamud dying at his desk is not a terrible one. It is testimony to his character and his courage. Like his heroes who struggled against hardship and infirmity, Malamud fought to complete his book despite his failing health. His passing left an emptiness in the scene of American writing not likely to be filled. One feels the loss of the man as well as the world he represented. Who will speak up as clearly, as magically for second chances, for ordinary people, for love and redemption? Two other American writers were grieved by Malamud's death and saluted him in print.

Philip Roth struggled over the years with Malamud and his work. Roth resented the many unfortunate comparisons between himself and Malamud, the moralist, the more serious writer. Roth claimed that Malamud sometimes praised suffering and heaped too much sorrow on his lowly heroes. Yet Roth greatly respected Malamud the man and the writer and over the years Roth and Malamud managed to sustain friendship and respect. In his memoir of Malamud, Roth recalls the impact Malamud had on him from the start, his love of the "masterpiece" *The Assistant*, of the early stories, "four of the best American short stories I'd ever read or ever will" ("Pictures of Malamud" 1). As Roth recounts Malamud's failing health, he speculates:

> It couldn't help but appear as though the pursuit of that unremitting aspiration that he shared with so many of his characters--to break down the iron limits of circumstance and self in order to live a better life--had finally taken its toll (41).

Cynthia Ozick recounts her long enchantment with Bernard Malamud and his work. She called him "Maestro":

> This after all, was the very writer who had brought into being a new American idiom of his own idiosyncratic vision; this was the writer who had introduced the idea of blessing--virtue as insight, virtue as crucible--into the literature of a generation mainly sunk in aestheticism or nihilism or solipsism (464).

Ozick notes that Malamud was a unique American master as well as a Jewish writer: "He not only wrote in the American language, he augmented it with fresh plasticity, he shaped our English into startling new configurations" (465).

Malamud reflected on his own life in "Long Work, Short Life," an address at Bennington College, published posthumously. In this brief memoir he celebrates his vocation as a writer and describes what a large part of his life writing always was. He recollects the early days, in his twenties:

> One night, after laboring in vain for hours attempting to bring a short story to life, I sat up in bed at an open window looking at the stars after a rainfall. Then I experienced a wave of feeling, of heartfelt emotion bespeaking commitment to life and art, so deeply it brought tears to my eyes. For the hundredth time I promised myself that I would be a very good writer ("Long Life" 604).

Over the years Malamud made good on his promise. His own career reflects the discipline, courage, and imagination he demanded of his heroes. As Saul Bellow wrote: "The accent of a hand-won and individual emotional truth is always heard in Malamud's words. He is a rich original of the first rank" (Introduction, *People* xv).

Malamud was an American master, a Romantic, a humanist in the tradition of others like Walt Whitman. Malamud dealt with basic, almost conventional, themes, making him something of an anomaly among contemporary fiction writers; yet he was always fresh, inventive, full of the dance of the imagination. In his search for a better, fuller life for himself and his heroes, he has enriched us all. And in his hero, Malamud brightened the American landscape with new vigor and old values. He has given American fiction a new type of hero, a flawed and fully human person, still capable of fashioning a new coat for himself out of old disappointment and fresh longing.

LITERATURE CITED

Alter, Iska. *The Good Man's Dilemma: Social Criticism in the Fiction of Bernard Malamud*. New York: AMS., 1981.

Alter, Robert. "Malamud as a Jewish Writer." *Commentary* 42 (Sept. 1966): 71-76.

- - -. "Out of the Trap." *Midstream* 9.4 (1963): 88-89.

- - -. "Updike, Malamud and the Fire This Time." *Commentary* 54 (Oct. 1972): 68-74.

Balliett, Whitney. "Rub a Dub-Dub." Rev. of *The Fixer*, by Bernard Malamud. *New Yorker* 10 Dec. 1966: 234-35.

Baumbach, Jonathan. "The Economy of Love: The Novels of Bernard Malamud." *Kenyon Review* 25 (1963): 438-57.

- - -. "Malamud's Heroes: The Fate of Fixers." *Commonweal* 85.4 (18 Oct. 1966): 97-99.

Bell, Pearl. "Morality Tale Without Mercy." *New Leader* 18 Oct. 1971: 17-18.

Ben-Asher, Naomi. "Jewish Identity and Christological Symbolism in the Work of Three Authors." *Jewish Frontier* 39 (Nov. 1972): 9-15.

Benedict, Helen. "Bernard Malamud: Morals and Surprises." *Antioch Review* 41.1 (1983): 28-36.

Bishop, Morris. *Saint Francis of Assisi*. Boston: Little, Brown & Co., 1975.

Bradbury, Malcolm. Rev. of *The Fixer*, by Bernard Malamud. *Manchester Guardian Weekly* 96 (13 April 1967): 11.

Cohen, Sandy. *Bernard Malamud and the Trial by Love.* Melville Studies in American Literature, No. 1. Ed. Robert Brainsard Pearsall. Amsterdam: Rodopi N.V., 1974.

Desmond, John F. "Malamud's Fixer -- Jew, Christian, or Modern?" *Renascence* 27 (Winter 1975): 101-10.

Ducharme, Robert. *Art and Idea in the Novels of Bernard Malamud.* The Hague: Mouton & Co., n.v., 1974.

Edelman, Lily. Rev. of *Pictures of Fidelman,* by Bernard Malamud. *National Jewish Monthly* Jan. 1970: 48-49.

Epstein, Joseph. "Malamud in Decline." *Commentary* 74.4 (Oct. 1982): 28-36, 49-53.

Fanger, Donald. "*The Fixer* in Another Country." *The Nation* 203 (1966): 389-90.

Fiedler, Leslie. "Malamud's Travesty Western." *Novel* 10 (1977): 212-19.

Field, Leslie and Joyce Field. "An Interview with Bernard Malamud." *Bernard Malamud: A Collection of Critical Essays.* Twentieth Century Views. Englewood Cliffs, N.J.: Prentice-Hall, 1975. 8-17.

Finkelstein, Sidney. "The Anti-Hero of Updike, Bellow and Malamud." *American Dialog* 7.2 (1972): 12-14, 30.

Frankel, Haskel. Interview with Malamud. *Saturday Review* 10 Sept. 1966: 39-40.

Fuller, Edmond. "Malamud's Novel Aims High But Falls Short." Rev. of *The Fixer,* by Bernard Malamud. *Wall Street Journal* 9 Sept. 1966: 12.

Goldman, Mark. "Comic Vision and the Theme of Identity." *Critique* 7.2 (Winter 1964-65): 92-109. Rpt. in *Bernard Malamud and the Critics.* Ed. Leslie A. Field and Loyce W. Field. New York Univ. Press, 1970. 151-70.

Goodall, Jane. *In the Shadow of Man*. Boston: Houghton Mifflin Co., 1971.

Goodheart, Eugene. "Fantasy and Reality." *Midstream* 7 (Autumn 1961): 102-5.

Grebstein, Sheldon Norman. "Bernard Malamud and the Jewish Movement." *Contemporary American-Jewish Literature*. Ed. Irving Malin. Bloomington, Indiana: Indiana Univ. Press, 1973. 175-212. Rpt. in *Bernard Malamud: A Collection of Critical Essays*. 18-44.

Greenfield, Josh. "Innocence and Punishment." Rev. of *The Fixer*, by Bernard Malamud. *Wall Street Journal* 9 Sept. 1966: 12.

Gunn, Giles B. "Bernard Malamud and the High Cost of Living." *Adversity and Grace: Studies in Recent American Fiction*. Chicago: University of Chicago Press, 1968. 59-86.

Hardwick, Elizabeth. "*The Fixer*: Novel of Startling Importance." *Vogue* 1 Sept. 1966: 208.

Hardy, Thomas. "Hap" and "The Blinded Bird." *Collected Poems of Thomas Hardy*. New York: Macmillan Co., 1925. 7, 419.

Hassan, Ihab. "Bernard Malamud: 1976 Fictions Within Our Fictions." *The Fiction of Bernard Malamud*. Ed. Richard Astro and Jackson J. Benson, Corvaillis: Oregon State Univ. Press, 1977. 43-64.

- - -. "The Hopes of Man." Rev. of *Idiots First*, by Bernard Malamud. *New York Times Book Review* 13 Oct. 1963: 5.

- - -. "The Qualified Encounter." *Radical Innocence: Studies in the Contemporary American Novel*. Princeton Univ. Press, 1961. Rpt. in *Bernard Malamud and the Critics*. 199-206.

Hays, Peter. "The Complex Pattern of Redemption in *The Assistant*." *Centennial Review* 13.2 (Spring 1969): 200-14. Rpt. in *Bernard Malamud and the Critics*. 219-33.

Hentoff, Nat. "Bernard Malamud." Rev. of *Idiots First*, by Bernard Malamud. *Commonweal* 79 (1963): 328-29.

Hershinow, Sheldon. *Bernard Malamud*. New York: Frederick Ungar Publishing Co., Inc., 1980.

Hicks, Granville. "Hard Road to the Good Life." Rev. of *A New Life*, by Bernard Malamud. *Saturday Review* 7 Oct. 1961: 20.

- - -. "One Man to Stand for Six Million." Rev. of *The Fixer*, by Bernard Malamud. *Saturday Review* 14 Oct. 1966: 37-39.

Howe, Irving. "A Glossary of Yiddish Terms." *World of Our Fathers*. New York: Simon and Schuster, 1979. 683-84.

- - -. "The Stories of Bernard Malamud." *Celebrations and Attacks: Thirty Years of Literary and Cultural Comment*. New York: Horizon Press, 1979. 32-34.

Hoyt, Charles Alva. "The New Romanticism." *Contemporary American Novelists*. Ed. Harry T. Moore. Carbondale, Ill.: Illinois University Press, 1964, 171-84. Rpt. in *Bernard Malamud and the Critics*. 171-84.

Hyman, Stanley Edgar. "A New Life for a Good Man." *Standards: A Chronicle of Books for Our Time*. New York: Horizon, 1966. 33-37.

Jacobson, Dan. "Magic and Morality." Rev. of *The Magic Barrel*, by Bernard Malamud. *Commentary* 26 (Oct. 1958): 359-61.

- - -. "The Old Country." Rev. of *The Fixer*, by Bernard Malamud. *Partisan Review* 34 (1967): 307-9.

Kazin, Alfred. "The Alone Generation." *Writing in America*. Ed. John Tishner and Robert B. Silvers. New Brunswick, N.J.: Rutgers Univ. Press, 1960. 114-23.

- - -. *Bright Books of Life: American Novelists and Storytellers from Hemingway to Mailer*. Boston: Little, Brown & Co., 1971.

- - -. "Fantasist of the Ordinary." *Commentary* 24 (July 1957): 89-92.

Keats, John. "The Eve of St. Agnes." *Oxford Anthology of English Literature, II*. Ed. Frank Kermode and John Hollander. New York: Oxford Univ. Press, 1973. 524-35.

- - -. "To John Taylor." 27 Feb. 1818. Letter 10 in *English Romantic Poetry and Prose*. Ed. Russel Noyes. New York: Oxford UP, 1956.

Kegan, Robert. *The Sweeter Welcome: Voices for a Vision of Affirmation: Bellow, Malamud, and Martin Buber*. Needlam Heights, Mass.: Humanitas Press, 1976.

Kennedy, William. "The Frightening Beiliss Case in Fictional, Scholarly Perspective." *The National Observer* 5 Sept. 1966: 19.

- - -. "Malamud Finds Renewal in Fidelman Collage." *National Observer* 12 May 1969: 23.

Knopp, Josephine Zadovsky. "Jewish America: Bernard Malamud." *The Trial of Judaism in Contemporary Jewish Writing*. Urbana: Univ. of Illinois Press, 1975. 103-25.

- - -. "The Ways of Mentschlekhkayt: A Study of Morality in Some Fiction of Bernard Malamud and Philip Roth," *Tradition*, 13:3 (Winter 1973), 67-84.

Landis, Joseph C. "Reflections on Jewish American Writers." *Jewish Book Annual* 25 (1967-68): 140-47.

Lask, Thomas. "The Creative Itch." *New York Times* 3 May 1969:33.

Lasson, Robert. "The story of a professional giver." Rev. of *Pictures of Fidelman*, by Bernard Malamud. *Book World* 4 May 1969: 4.

Lawrence, D. H. "Why the Novel Matters." *D.H. Lawrence: Selected Literary Criticism*. Ed. Anthony Beal. New York: Viking Press, 1966.

Lefcowitz, Barbara. "The *Hybris* of Neurosis: Malamud's *Pictures of Fidelman*." *Literature and Psychology* 20.3 (1970): 115-20.

Lelchuk, Alan. "Malamud's Dark Fable." Rev. of *God's Grace* by Bernard Malamud. New York Times Book Review 29 Aug. 1982: 1, 14-15.

Leonard, John. "Cheever to Roth to Malamud." *Atlantic* (June 1973): 112-16.

Locke, Richard. "Malamud's Reach." Rev. of *Dubin's Lives*. *Saturday Review* 17 Mar. 1979: 67-69.

Maddocks, Melvin. "Life is Suffering But . . ." *Atlantic* (Nov. 1971): 132, 34, 36.

Malamud, Bernard. "Address from the Fiction Winner." John Fisher and Robert B. Silvers, ed. *Writing in America*. New Brunswick, N.J.: Rutgers University Press, 1960.

- - -. *Dubin's Lives*. New York: Farrar, Straus, and Giroux, 1979.

- - -. *The Fixer*. New York: Farrar, Straus, and Giroux, 1966.

- - -. *God's Grace*. New York: Farrar, Straus, and Giroux, 1982.

- - -. *Idiots First*. New York: Farrar, Straus and Co., 1963.

- - -. "Long Work, Short Life." *Michigan Quarterly Review* 26 (Fall 1987): 601-11.

- - -. *The Magic Barrel*. New York: Farrar, Straus, and Cudahy, 1958.

- - -. *The Natural*. New York: Farrar, Straus and Giroux, 1952.

- - -. *A New Life*. New York: Farrar, Straus and Cudahy, 1961.

- - -. *The People and Uncollected Stories*. Farrar, Straus and Giroux, 1989.

- - -. *Pictures of Fidelman: An Exhibition*. New York: Farrar, Straus, and Giroux, 1969.

- - -. *Rembrandt's Hat*. New York: Farrar, Straus and Giroux, 1973.

- - -. *The Stories of Bernard Malamud*. New York: Farrar, Straus, and Giroux, 1983.

- - -. *The Tenants*. New York: Farrar, Straus and Giroux, 1971.

Malcolm, Donald. "The Grooves of Academe." Rev. of *A New Life*, by Bernard Malamud. *New Yorker* 37 (27 Jan. 1962): 105-7.

Malin, Irving. Rev. of *Idiots First*, by Bernard Malamud. *The Reconstructionist* 29 (29 Nov. 1963): 25-28.

Maloff, Saul. "Loveliest Breakdown in Contemporary Fiction: Malamud's Lives." *Commonweal* 27 (Apr. 1979): 244-46.

Marcus, Mordecai. "The Unsuccessful Malamud." *Prairie Schooner* (Spring 1967): 88-89.

Marcus, Steven. "The Novel Again." *Partisan Review* 29 (Spring 1962): Adams, Phoebe. "The Burdens of the Past." *Atlantic* 212 (Nov. 1961): 184-85.

May, Charles E. "Bernard Malamud's 'A Summer's Reading.' " *Notes on Contemporary Literature* 2.4 (1972): 11-13.

- - -. "The Bread of Tears: Malamud's 'The Loan.' " *Studies in Short Fiction* 7 (1970): 652-54.

Mellard, James. "Malamud's Novels: Four Versions of the Pastoral." *Critique* 9.2 (1967): 5-19. Rpt. in *Bernard Malamud and the Critics*. 67-84.

Mesher, David. "Remembrance of Things Unknown: Malamud's 'The Last Mohican.' " *Studies in Short Fiction* 12 (Fall 1975): 397-404.

Miller, Theodore C. "The Minister and the Whore: An Examination of Bernard Malamud's 'The Magic Barrel.' " *Studies in Humanities* 3.1 (1972): 43-44.

Ozick, Cynthia. "Bernard Malamud." *Partisan Review* 53 (1986): 464-6.

Peden, William. "Dogged by a Sense of Injustice and Grief." Rev. of *The Magic Barrel*, by Bernard Malamud. *New York Times Book Review* 11 May 1958: 5.

Perrine, Laurence. "Malamud's 'Take Pity.' " *Studies in Short Fiction* 2 (Fall 1964): 84-86.

Pickrel, Paul. Rev. of *A New Life*, by Bernard Malamud. *Harper's* Nov. 1961: 120.

Pinsker, Sanford. "The Schlemiel as Moral Bungler: Bernard Malamud's Ironic Heroes." *The Schlemiel as Metaphor: Studies in the Yiddish and American Jewish Novel.* Carbondale: Southern Illinois Univ. Press, 1971. 82-124. Rpt. in *Bernard Malamud: A Collection of Critical Essays.* 45-71.

Podhoretz, Norman. "Achilles in Left Field." *Commentary* 15 (Mar. 1953): 321-26.

- - -. "The New Nihilism in the American Novel." *Partisan Review* 25 (Fall 1958): 176-78.

Popkin, Henry. "Jewish Stories." Rev. on *The Magic Barrel*, by Bernard Malamud. *Kenyon Review* 20 (Autumn 1958): 637-41.

Pritchett, V. S. "A Pariah." Rev. of *The Fixer*, by Bernard Malamud. *New York Review of Books* 22 Sept. 1966: 8,10.

Quart, Barbara Koenig. "Women in Bernard Malamud's Fiction." *Studies in American Jewish Literature* 3 (1983): 138-50.

Rahv, Philip. Introduction. *A Bernard Malamud Reader.* New York: Farrar, Straus, Giroux, 1967. vii-xiv.

Ratner, Mark L. "Style and Humanity in Malamud's Fiction." *Massachusetts Review* 5.4 (1964): 663-83.

Rev. of *Dubin's Lives*, by Bernard Malamud. *Atlantic* 243 (Mar. 1979): 132.

Rev. of *The Fixer*, by Bernard Malamud. *Times Literary Supplement* 6 April 67: 286.

Rev. of *Rembrandt's Hat*, by Bernard Malamud. "Poor in Spirit." *Times Literary Supplement* 5 Oct. 1973: 1158.

Reynolds, Richard. " 'The Magic Barrel': Pinye Salzman's Kaddish." *Studies in Short Fiction* 10 (1973): 100-102.

Richman, Sidney. *Bernard Malamud*. New York: Twayne Publishers, Inc., 1966.

Roth, Philip. "Imaging Jews." *Reading Myself and Others*. New York: Farrar, Straus and Giroux, Inc., 1975. 215-246.

- - -. "Pictures of Malamud." *New York Times Book Review* 20 (April 1986): 1, 40-41.

- - -. "Writing American Fiction." *The Novel Since World War I*. Ed. Marcus Klein. Greenwich, Conn.: Fawcett Publications, Inc., 1969. 142-58.

Rubin, Louis D. "Six Novels and S. Levin." *Sewanee Review* 70 (1962): 504-14.

Samuel, Maurice. *Blood Accusation: The Strange History of the Beiliss Case*. Philadelphia: The Jewish Publication Society of America, 1966.

Scholes, Robert. "Malamud's Latest Novel." Rev. of *The Fixer*. *Northwest Review* 8.2 (Fall/ Winter 1966-67): 106-8.

- - -. "Portrait of the Artist as Escape-Goat." *Saturday Review* 152 (10 May 1969): 32-34.

Shear, Walter. "Culture Conflict in *The Assistant*." *Midwest Quarterly* 7 (Spring 1966): 367-80. Rpt. in *Bernard Malamud and the Critics*. 207-18.

Shechner, Mark. "Jewish Writers." *Harvard Guide to Contemporary American Writing*. Ed. Daniel Hoffman. Cambridge, Mass.: The Belknap Press of Harvard Univ., 1979. 191-239.

- - -. "The Return of the Repressed." Rev. of *Dubin's Lives*. *Nation* 17 Mar. 1979: 277-79.

Siegel, Ben. "Through a Glass Darkly: Bernard Malamud's Painful Views of the Self." *The Fiction of Bernard Malamud*. 117-47.

- - -. "Victims in Motion: Bernard Malamud's Sad and Bitter Clowns." *Northwest Review* 4.2 (Spring 1962): 69-80. Rpt. in *Bernard Malamud and the Critics*. 123-34.

Sinclair, Clive. "The Falling-out in Paradise." Rev. of *God's Grace* by Bernard Malamud. *Times Literary Supplement* 29 Oct. 1982: 1188.

Solotaroff, Theodore. "Bernard Malamud's Fiction: The Old Life and the New." *Commentary* 33.3 (March 1962): 197-204. Rpt. in *Bernard Malamud and the Critics*. 235-48.

- - -. "Showing us 'what it means human.' " Rev. of *Idiots First*, by Bernard Malamud. *Book Week* 13 Oct. 1963: 5, 12.

Rev. of *The Fixer*, by Bernard Malamud. "Sons of Perdition." *Times Literary Supplement* 6 April 1967: 286.

Spiegel, Shalom. *The Last Trial*, trans. Judah Goldin. New York: Pantheon Books, 1967.

Stellar, Charles. Rev. of *Pictures of Fidelman*, by Bernard Malamud. *Studies in Short Fiction* (1971): 341-43.

Stern, Daniel. "The Art of Fiction: Bernard Malamud." Interview. *Paris Review* 61 (Spring 1975): 40-64.

Syrkin, Marie. "From Frank Alpine to Willie Spearmint. . ." *Midstream* (Nov. 1971): 64-68.

Tanner, Tony. "Bernard Malamud and the New Life." *Critical Quarterly* 10 (Summer 1968): 151-68.

- - -. *City of Words: American Fiction 1950-70*. London: Jonathon Cape, 1971.

Thurber, James. "The Ladies of Orlon. *Alarms and Diversions.*" New York: Harper Colophon Books, 1981. 1-5.

Towers, Robert. "A Biographical Novel." Rev. of *Dubin's Lives. New York Times Book Review* 18 Feb. 1979: 1, 31-32.

Turner, Frederick W., III. "Myth Inside and Out: Malamud's *The Natural." Novel* 1 (Winter 1968): 133-39. Rpt. in *Bernard Malamud and the Critics.* 109-19.

Tyler, Ralph. "A Talk with the Novelist." *New York Times Book Review* 18 Feb. 1979: 1, 31-34.

Waldman, Diane. *Mark Rothko, 1903-70, A Retrospective.* New York: Harry N. Abrams, Inc., 1978.

Wasserman, Earl R. "*The Natural*: Malamud's World Ceres." *Centennial Review of Arts and Sciences* 9.2 (1967): 438-60. Rpt. in *Bernard Malamud and The Critics* 45-65.

Wegelin, Christof. "The American Schlemiel Abroad: Malamud's Italian Stories and the End of American Innocence." *Twentieth Century Literature* 19.2 (April 1973): 77-88.

Weiss, Samuel. "Passion and Purgation in Bernard Malamud." *University of Windsor Review* 2.1 (1966): 93-99.

West, Jessamyn. Rev. of *A New Life,* by Bernard Malamud, *New York Herald Tribune Book Review* 8 Oct. 1961: 4.

Widmer, Kingsley. "Poetic Naturalism in the Contemporary Novel." *Partisan Review* 26 (1959): 467-72.

Winegarten, Renee. "Malamud's Head (*Rembrandt's Hat*)." Midstream 19:8 (Oct. 1973): 76-79. Rpt. in *Bernard Malamud: A Collection of Critical Essays.* 99-103.

Wisse, Ruth R. *The Schlemiel as Modern Hero*. Chicago: Univ. of Chicago
   Press, 1971. 110-18.

Updike, John. "Cohn's Doom." Rev. of *God's Grace* by Bernard Malamud.
   New Yorker 8 Nov. 1982: 167-70.

Zlotnick, Joan. "Malamud's *The Assistant*: Of Morris, Frank, and St. Francis."
   Studies in American Jewish Literature 1 (Winter 1975): 20-23.